WHITE STAR PUBLISHERS

GLOBAL 200

PLACES THAT MUST SURVIVE

AROUND THE WORLD WITH **WWF**
to save nature

Preface   Fulco Pratesi

Editorial coordination WWF-Italy   Simona Giordano

Texts   Simona Giordano, Fabrizio Bulgarini, Corrado Teofili, Stefano Petrella,

Fulvio Cerfolli, Myrta Mafai, Beatrice Frank, Marco Costantini

Editorial director Valeria Manferto De Fabianis

Graphic designer Patrizia Balocco Lovisetti

Collaborating editors Giorgio Ferrero, Marcello Libra, Giorgia Raineri

Coordination for WWF-Italia Ong - Onlus Barbara Franco, Advertising

and Multimedia Publishing Manager

A beautiful and diverse world

It is practically certain: among the billions of stars and planets of the Universe, there is bound to be one that resembles the Earth in some way. While I wish the best to the astrophysicists engaged in this extenuating search, I continue to maintain that the third planet of the Solar System is still – and will continue to be for centuries – the richest, most beautiful and diverse of the entire galaxy. Just think of the variety of its ecoregions, as portrayed by the authors of this book. They range from the sunny, arid landscapes of the African savannas to the somber fir and pine forests of the Siberian taiga, the endless grasslands of the Mongolian steppe, the infernal tangle of trees, shrubs, lianas and tree ferns of the Congo basin, the tracery of coral of the Great Barrier Reef and the ice cathedrals of Antarctica, to name but a few.

WWF's expert naturalists have identified thousands of ecoregions, hundreds of which are exceptionally important and symbolic, but those examined in this book are the most emblematic of all. Our admiration, however, must not be limited to viewing the landscapes and habitats. These places are above all monuments consecrated to the natural wonder that we call biodiversity. Indeed, every square foot of them represents a concentrate of animal life: from soil-dwelling mites and springtails, insects and spiders, beetles and butterflies, small rodents and reptiles, bats and birds, through to the large herbivores – the giraffes of Africa, the kangaroos of Australia, the bison of North America, the guanacos of Patagonia, the rhinoceros of India, the mountain gorillas, and so on. The top of the food chain is occupied by predators, such as condors, clouded leopards, tigers, sharks, lions and ki ler whales, forming an endless harmonious concert in which each instrument has its own unique place and role. Removing just one of them, even the smallest and most unimportant, can cause irreparable damage. Try, for example, removing a comma or a single consonant from a novel. You will see how everything changes, becoming a little more incomprehensible and losing its appeal and meaning.

It is the constant and widespread erosion that our increasingly arrogant and invasive species perpetrates on its own vital roots that WWF and the authors of this book are committed to fighting.

There is no better way of changing things than putting the reader – even the indifferent and uninterested reader – face to face with the last remaining paradises on Earth, where the inimitable symphony of natural biodiversity still survives in its full splendor (although it is uncertain for how much longer). Describing the problems and possible remedies (as this book does) may stimulate tangible and constant action aimed at defending it. Mother Earth certainly deserves it.

INTRODUCTION

Nature knows no boundaries. Words like "nation," "customs" or "passport" are meaningless to a forest, a lake or a coral reef. The indomitable will that drives a river to cross different countries, political barriers, economic systems, languages and cultures does not bend to the colonizing drive of humankind, who charts the landscape on a map, classifying it, naming it, organizing and ordering it, dividing it and separating it. However, while its principal manifestations resist these attempts, the nature that surrounds us is distressed and in some cases in its death throes. Although it is true, for example, that no frontier posts or customs barriers interrupt the course of a river, its waters are drained by dams and the increasingly frequent droughts caused by climate change. While the growth of a forest cannot be confined within the boundaries of a country, its area is drastically reduced by fire or unregulated felling to make room for farmland. Many animal species no longer freely roam their habitats, which may correspond to supranational territories, but are constrained within the remaining natural fragments or relegated to fenced parks and natural reserves belonging to individual countries.

"The earth has music for those who listen," Shakespeare wrote, but today it seems that this harmony, created by the interaction of different components in constant movement, like the strings of a guitar with infinite possibilities of variation, has become a faint background vibration to which we no longer wish to listen or have lost the sensibility to heed. Accustomed to increasingly familiar landscapes and urban locations where the land is planned, built and inserted in reassuring means of perception (like surfing the web), we no longer seem to realize Nature's physical presence and the values that she represents. This constitutes a serious problem if we consider today's extremely large human population, coupled with the Earth's limited surface area and consequently limited capacity to produce resources for everyone. At the beginning of the 20th century the world population was 1.6 billion, by the end of the century it had risen to over 6 billion, today it is already over 6.5 billion and, according to the United Nations World Population Prospect, it is expected to reach 9.2 billion by 2050. In such a crowded world it is essential that we carefully ponder our choices, actions and our very existence, which influences the delicate balance of our planet.

Although the evolution of life on Earth has always been closely and unfailingly accompanied by processes of extinction of species and reduction of natural habitats, today these phenomena appear greatly accelerated. John H. Lawton and Robert M. May, researchers at Oxford University, claim that 99 percent of the extinctions of the modern age can be attributed to human activities. These are many and varied, ranging from the direct exploitation of the natural resources produced by intensive farming and the expansion of industrial activities and communication infrastructures to those that

have indirectly influenced and continue to influence the environment, such as the emission of toxic substances and the increase in atmospheric carbon dioxide that is causing climate change. These factors are not only directly responsible for the loss of biodiversity, but also undermine the world's ecosystems, reducing their ability to resist and react, and threatening the ecological and evolutionary processes. The intentional or unintentional introduction of allochthonous species (non-native plants and animals) has an equally detrimental effect. In the majority of cases these introductions are made for purely commercial reasons and can seriously alter ecosystems. Indeed, the sudden arrival of new competitors, predators or parasites to which endemic species have not had the chance to adapt, often results in the drastic reduction of native species, the impoverishment of the food chains and a slow but inexorable loss of biodiversity. In the majority of cases this takes the form of an irrevocable sentence: extinction. And extinction is forever.

Another dangerous and increasingly frequent phenomenon is represented by the fragmentation of the habitats, and thus also the distribution areas, of animal and plant species. Consequently, the populations are gradually separated from each other, forming isolated and thus weaker subpopulations. One of the primary causes of this fragmentation and reduction of habitats is once again the uncontrolled growth of human settlements and infrastructures, with the increasing transformation of natural areas into zones managed by man for solely commercial purposes. The replacement of natural landscapes with metropolitan industrial scenarios also fragments human identity and conscience, depersonalizing the material life of "Modern Man" and creating increasingly irreversible divisions.

The Western model of consumer development no longer works. Currently, our economic and social systems subtract more resources than the natural systems are able to regenerate and introduce more pollutants than they are able to receive and metabolize. The human footprint on the Earth is staggering if we consider that we take and use for our own purposes over 20 percent of the energy generated by the world's ecosystems (although the figure rises to 70 percent in areas such as Western Europe, North America and Central and Southern Asia). The primary production of an ecosystem, i.e., the solar energy converted into organic material by photosynthesis, must be available to ensure the stability and integrity of its food chains (plants, herbivores, carnivores, saprophytes, detritivores, etc.) of which man is also a part. However, today we are witnessing the sorry sight of a large reservoir from which a single user – the dizzily growing human population (and almost exclusively its richer societies) – is drawing off up to 70 percent of its contents at a time. The remaining 30 percent is left for the rest of the world to use as it can to survive. Reversing this insane course of beha-

vior is the arduous task that the generations of the third millennium must humbly and determinedly accomplish.

The World Summit on Sustainable Development, held in Johannesburg in 2002, provided an opportunity for reflection during which the international community attempted to deal with the challenges posed by poverty and the growing shortage of resources. On this occasion the governments of the world approved a plan of action that attempts to reconcile the goals of environmental sustainability with economic and social objectives. It also clearly states the need for a significant reduction in the rate of destruction of the Earth's biodiversity and an improvement in living conditions in developing countries by 2010. The goal of the Johannesburg summit was the implementation of the Convention on Biological Diversity, signed at the Rio Earth Summit and approved in 1993, thus making it the main instrument for achieving the necessary concrete progress toward sustainable development.

On the basis of these aspects, and in consideration of the fact that both economic resources and the scope for biodiversity conservation action are limited, WWF International has launched an extensive and ambitious vision. It consists of the adoption of an Ecoregion-Based Conservation (ERBC) strategy to represent a "new mentality" – a new way of thinking and acting. Firstly, the scope of conservation efforts follows the spirit of nature, extending beyond the boundaries of a single country to encompass wider geographical, political and social contexts. This has given rise to the concept of the ecoregion, a new non-political territorial area that will be discussed in more detail in the following chapter. Secondly, the strategy is intended to be "pro-active" and not merely "reactive," which means intervening before the ecosystems have been damaged beyond repair. Finally, interest in the conservation of biodiversity must be extended to the material life of all categories of society. It can no longer be seen as merely "the business of environmentalists," but must feature on the agendas of political leaders, economists, the mass media, and the worlds of education and employment.

The participation of people belonging to very different and distant worlds requires considerable cultural efforts in terms of ideas and projects, particularly when it is not easy to glimpse the stages and goals of this ambitious course of action. An international scientific group coordinated by WWF has pinpointed the places (ecoregions) of the world with the greatest variety of life forms, where the evolutionary processes express the highest levels of biodiversity and adaptation, such as rainforests,

coral reefs, river deltas, estuaries and deserts. Within these areas 238 global priority ecoregions have been identified as requiring immediate protection and given the name of the Global 200. They are divided into terrestrial, marine and freshwater ecoregions and are home to 90 percent of the world's biodiversity.

Like in a game of Chinese boxes, we have chosen a group of the most representative ecoregions to present to the reader – a selection within a selection – in order to offer an introduction to the finest expressions of biodiversity. This is the intention behind this book, whose 28 chapters present 53 ecoregions. In some cases these are areas with an exceptionally high number of species, while others are deserts with few, scattered life forms, because biodiversity is not only expressed in terms of species density. Biodiversity is nature's capacity to give life to all of the Earth's habitats, exploiting their energy flows in the most efficient manner possible by means of evolution and adaptation. The number of different species is irrelevant; what should amaze us is the understanding that a ray of sun, a drop of water or a speck of organic substance is sufficient for life to express itself in the wondrous forms permitted by time and each individual situation.

This is what we have tried to convey in this book, some of whose chapters are dedicated to a single ecoregion, while others, such as Patagonia, comprise several. This depends on the size of the area or other factors, such as the appeal that the different areas may have for the reader, the number of exclusive species, the amount of information available, and so on. The latter factor is particularly worthy of reflection. Indeed, it is often difficult to describe certain areas, because our scientific knowledge of them is scant or fragmentary. We live in a society in which an overabundance of information and the ease of access to it lead us to believe that knowledge of anything can be obtained quickly and easily. However, this is not true in nature. Indeed, behind each photograph, organism and ecosystem lies an enormous amount of work by men and women who also have enthusiastically, patiently and skillfully gathered and interpreted the information necessary for this book.

The choice of these particular habitats and ecoregions is an attempt to take the first step toward an idea of variety that everyone should cultivate. It is an invitation to conserve and cherish diversity, understood as a value, but also as an authentic biological and aesthetic principle, the driving force of life and an antidote to cultural standardization. Above all, it is an attempt to avoid the future scenario of having to view nature only through the pages of a book.

A DIVERSE EARTH

ECOREGIONS AND BIODIVERSITY

The huge variety of animal and plant species on Earth, defined with the term biological diversity or biodiversity, is one of the necessary conditions for the continuous, incessant remodeling of life, and thus constitutes an essential resource for the survival of our species. This concept, or vision, of the totality of life systems is not particularly complex and is often a feature of traditional popular cultures and legends. Nonetheless, in modern societies the ancient wisdom that envisages man as part of and utterly dependent on natural systems seems to have been definitively lost. Forests, pastureland, tundra, deserts, steppe, mountains, perpetual snowfields, rivers, lakes and seas are increasingly threatened by environmental degradation, pollution and soil erosion. Throughout the world animal and plant species are dying out on a daily basis, but it is the rate at which this is happening and the certainty of man's responsibility for the process that give greatest cause for concern (it is no coincidence that the eminent paleontologist and naturalist Niles Eldredge has referred to our age as that of the "Sixth Mass Extinction").

Drastic action is necessary, but as humankind (and the political and economic world in particular) appears unable to summon up the will to change direction and assign sufficient resources to this decisive and epoch-making challenge, it is necessary to devise more appropriate strategies capable of optimizing the resources employed in the battles against the main environmental crises. At the beginning of the new millennium a new approach to the problem was developed. In order to achieve this, a new term (and concept) was coined: the ecoregion. An ecoregion is a relatively large unit of territory consisting of terrestrial, marine and/or freshwater habitats characterized by an assemblage of natural communities that share a large majority of plant and animal species, ecological dynamics and environmental conditions. Next, a method, known as Ecoregional Conservation (ERC), was developed in order to attempt to provide an answer to the problem of conservation. This is rapidly proving to be an effective and essential strategy for obtaining tangible and practical results. The aim is to preserve as many species, communities, habitats and ecological processes as possible of a particular ecoregion.

ERC has been officially adopted as a philosophy and method of intervention by WWF's international network and The Nature Conservancy (TNC), another important organization for the protection of nature. Following the mapping and classification of the most significant habitats – providing the first comparative analysis of the biodiversity of the entire planet – 1504 ecoregions (the most important areas for the protection of biodiversity) were identified worldwide, of which 825 are terrestrial,

450 marine and 229 freshwater. These areas are generally supranational, as large-scale ecological processes, e.g., the migration of birds, sea turtles or large mammals, are not subject to political boundaries. Consequently, the mapping of ecoregions not only generates a new environmental awareness, but also creates new geographical horizons and a new way of looking at and experiencing the world.

A key feature of Ecoregional Conservation, and also one of its objectives, is the biodiversity vision (i.e., desirable scenario). The biodiversity vision determines what the entire ecoregion should look like in the long term (10, 20 or 50 years). It also serves as a reference point to measure the success of the conservation action taken over the years.

The Ecoregion Conservation approach thus consists of a long-term vision, which indicates the high-priority areas in which biodiversity conservation activities and strategic objectives should be concentrated, and the definition of strategic objectives. An Ecoregional Plan of Action is drawn up to detail the objectives, resources, partners and timescale and means of intervention. In addition to the conservation goals, it is vitally important to consider other fundamental aspects, such as support policy, environmental education, the promotion of civil society and the monitoring of results and forecasting of the effects of conservation activities.

The ecoregional strategy comprises a series of very different activities that may be implemented on various levels (local, national, ecoregional) as long as they contribute to the success of the conservation of ecoregional biodiversity. A group of ecoregions has been chosen for each biogeographic realm, on the basis of a series of parameters, including species richness, the presence of endemic species (i.e., species that are not found elsewhere), and the level of habitat loss.

WWF has long been engaged in the battle to preserve biodiversity – the result of 3.5 billion years of evolution – and its constant ongoing efforts spanning several decades allow an ever-greater comprehension of the importance of nature conservation, which has become a central theme of policies regarding the sustainability of humankind's economic and social development. Leaving aside the scientific definition of the term and its importance from a purely practical viewpoint, the concept of "ecoregion" is actually based on a silently subversive notion. Indeed, it implies an overturning of our ideas of geography and the conventional view of the planet divided by political boundaries, because reconsidering the Earth in terms of ecoregions means reconsidering the primary role of Nature and her inhabitants.

15

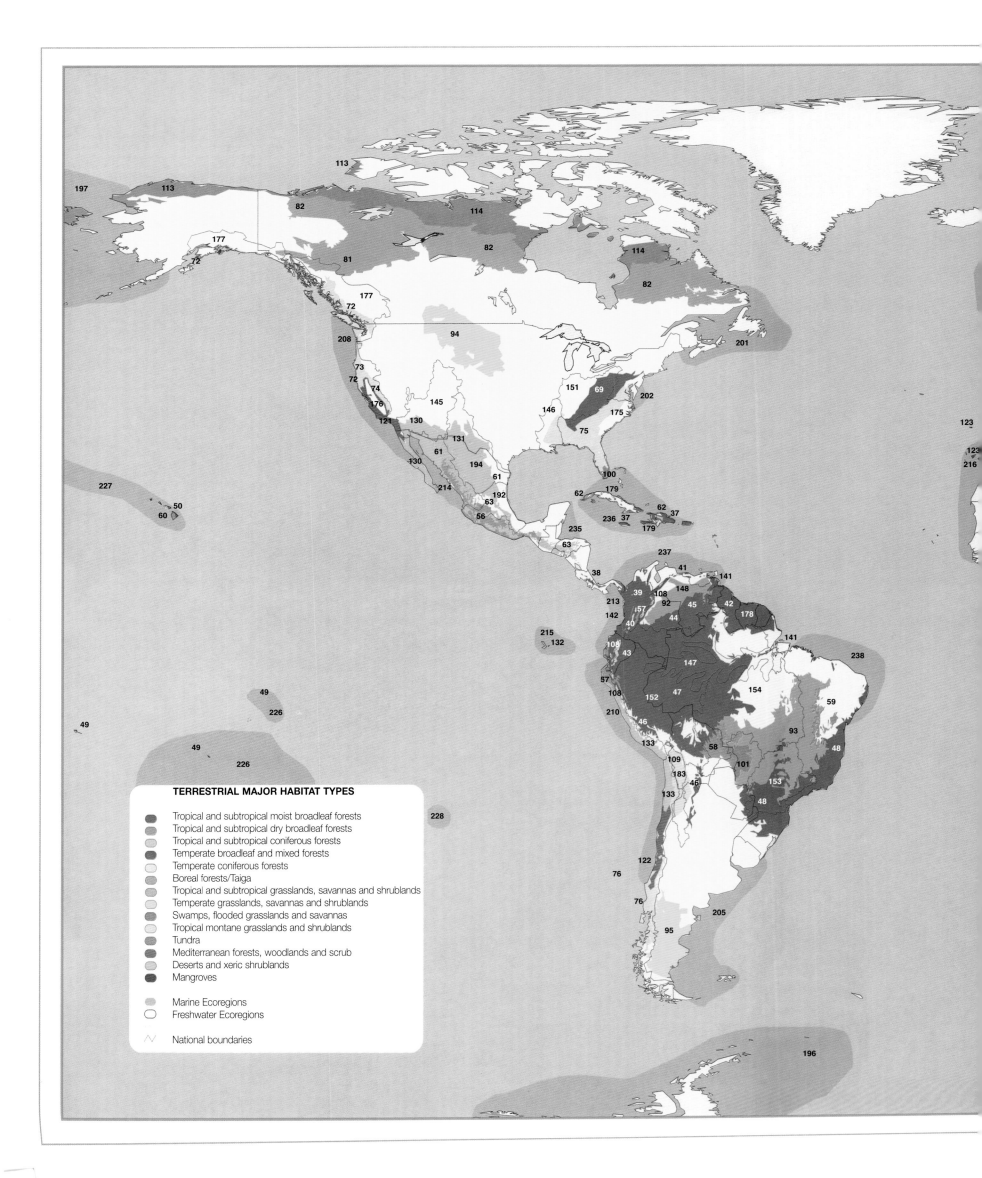

TERRESTRIAL MAJOR HABITAT TYPES

- Tropical and subtropical moist broadleaf forests
- Tropical and subtropical dry broadleaf forests
- Tropical and subtropical coniferous forests
- Temperate broadleaf and mixed forests
- Temperate coniferous forests
- Boreal forests/Taiga
- Tropical and subtropical grasslands, savannas and shrublands
- Temperate grasslands, savannas and shrublands
- Swamps, flooded grasslands and savannas
- Tropical montane grasslands and shrublands
- Tundra
- Mediterranean forests, woodlands and scrub
- Deserts and xeric shrublands
- Mangroves

- Marine Ecoregions
- Freshwater Ecoregions

- National boundaries

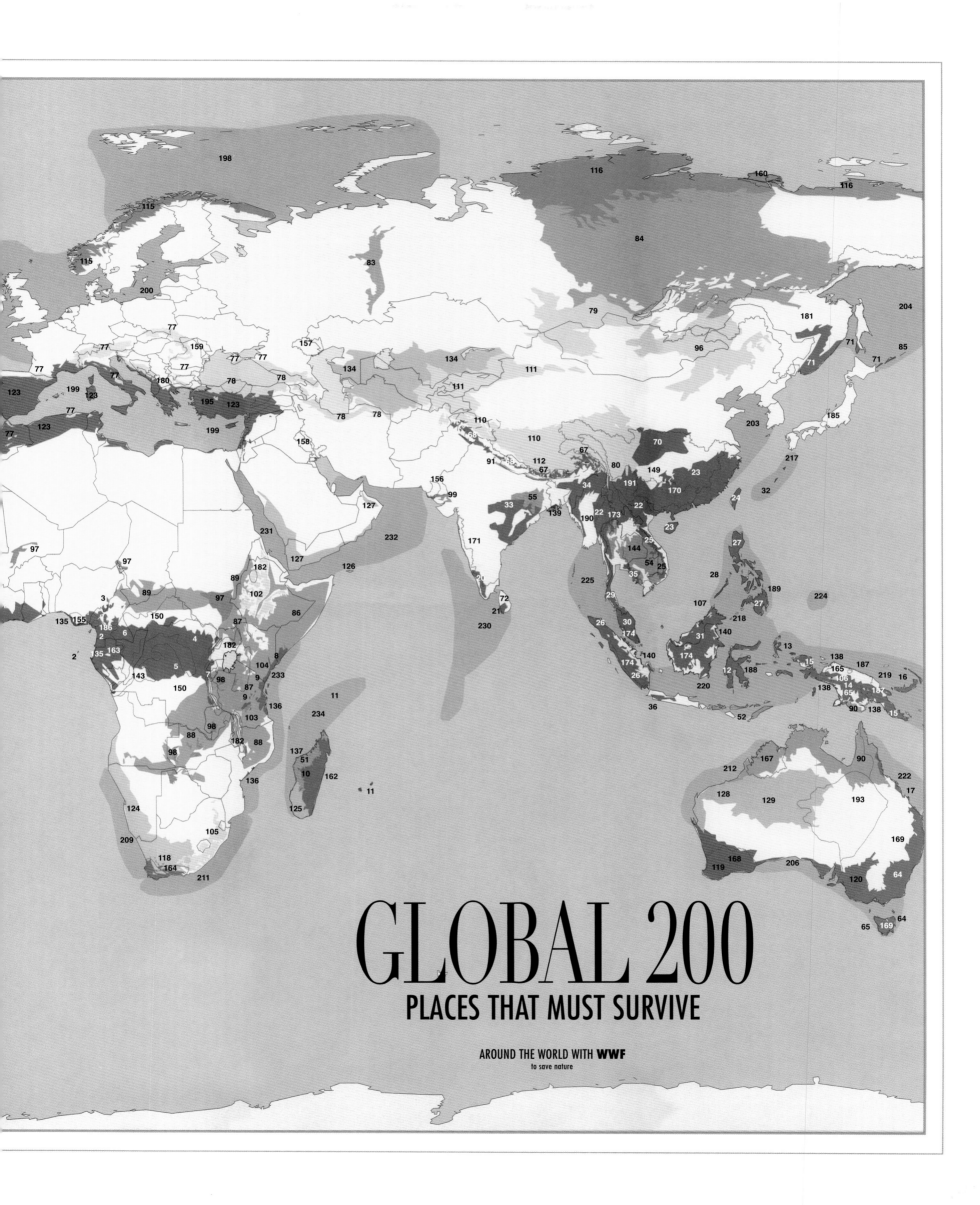

GLOBAL 200
PLACES THAT MUST SURVIVE

AROUND THE WORLD WITH **WWF**
to save nature

TERRESTRIAL ECOREGIONS

TROPICAL AND SUBTROPICAL MOIST BROADLEAF FORESTS

AFROTROPICAL
1 GUINEAN MOIST FORESTS - Benin, Côte d'Ivoire, Ghana, Guinea, Liberia, Sierra Leone, Togo
2 CONGOLIAN COASTAL FORESTS - Angola, Cameroon, Democratic Republic of Congo, Equatorial Guinea, Gabon, Nigeria, São Tomé & Principe, Republic of Congo
3 CAMEROON HIGHLANDS FORESTS - Cameroon, Equatorial Guinea, Nigeria
4 NORTHEASTERN CONGO BASIN MOIST FORESTS - Central African Republic, Democratic Republic of Congo
5 CENTRAL CONGO BASIN MOIST FORESTS - Democratic Republic of Congo
6 WESTERN CONGO BASIN MOIST FORESTS - Cameroon, Central African Republic, Democratic Republic of Congo, Gabon, Republic of Congo
7 ALBERTINE RIFT MONTANE FORESTS - Burundi, Democratic Republic of Congo, Rwanda, Tanzania, Uganda
8 EAST AFRICAN COASTAL FORESTS - Kenya, Somalia, Tanzania
9 EASTERN ARC MONTANE FORESTS - Kenya, Tanzania
10 MADAGASCAR FORESTS AND SHRUBLANDS - Madagascar
11 SEYCHELLES AND MASCARENES MOIST FORESTS - Mauritius, Reunion (France), Seychelles

AUSTRALASIA
12 SULAWESI MOIST FORESTS - Indonesia
13 MOLUCCAS MOIST FORESTS - Indonesia
14 SOUTHERN NEW GUINEA LOWLAND FORESTS - Indonesia, Papua New Guinea
15 NEW GUINEA MONTANE FORESTS - Indonesia, Papua New Guinea
16 SOLOMONS-VANUATU-BISMARCK MOIST FORESTS - Papua New Guinea, Solomon Islands, Vanuatu
17 QUEENSLAND TROPICAL FORESTS - Australia
18 NEW CALEDONIA MOIST FORESTS - New Caledonia (France)
19 LORD HOWE-NORFOLK ISLANDS FORESTS - Australia

INDO-MALAYAN
20 SOUTHWESTERN GHATS MOIST FORESTS - India
21 SRI LANKAN MOIST FORESTS - Sri Lanka
22 NORTHERN INDOCHINA SUBTROPICAL MOIST FORESTS - China, Laos, Myanmar, Thailand, Vietnam
23 SOUTHEAST CHINA-HAINAN MOIST FORESTS - China, Vietnam
24 TAIWAN MONTANE FORESTS - China
25 ANNAMITE RANGE MOIST FORESTS - Cambodia, Laos, Vietnam
26 SUMATRAN ISLANDS LOWLAND AND MONTANE FORESTS - Indonesia
27 PHILIPPINES MOIST FORESTS - Philippines
28 PALAWAN MOIST FORESTS - Philippines
29 KAYAH-KAREN / TENASSERIM MOIST FORESTS - Malaysia, Myanmar, Thailand
30 PENINSULAR MALAYSIAN LOWLAND AND MOUNTAIN FORESTS - Indonesia, Malaysia, Singapore, Thailand
31 BORNEO LOWLAND AND MONTANE FORESTS - Brunei, Indonesia, Malaysia
32 NANSEI SHOTO ARCHIPELAGO FORESTS - Japan
33 EASTERN DECCAN PLATEAU MOIST FORESTS - India
34 NAGA-MANIPURI-CHIN HILLS MOIST FORESTS - Bangladesh, India, Myanmar
35 CARDAMOM MOUNTAINS MOIST FORESTS - Cambodia, Thailand
36 WESTERN JAVA MOUNTAIN FORESTS - Indonesia

NEOTROPICAL
37 GREATER ANTILLEAN MOIST FORESTS - Cuba, Dominican Republic, Haiti, Jamaica, Puerto Rico (United States)
38 TALAMANCAN AND ISTHMIAN PACIFIC FORESTS - Costa Rica, Panama
39 CHOCÓ-DARIÉN MOIST FORESTS - Colombia, Ecuador, Panama
40 NORTHERN ANDEAN MONTANE FORESTS - Colombia, Ecuador, Venezuela, Peru
41 COASTAL VENEZUELA MONTANE FORESTS - Venezuela
42 GUIANAN MOIST FORESTS - Brazil, French Guiana (France), Guyana, Suriname, Venezuela
43 NAPO MOIST FORESTS - Colombia, Ecuador, Peru
44 RÍO NEGRO-JURUÁ MOIST FORESTS - Brazil, Colombia, Peru, Venezuela
45 GUAYANAN HIGHLANDS FORESTS - Brazil, Colombia, Guayana, Suriname, Venezuela
46 CENTRAL ANDEAN YUNGAS - Argentina, Bolivia, Peru
47 SOUTHWESTERN AMAZONIAN MOIST FORESTS - Bolivia, Brazil, Peru
48 ATLANTIC FORESTS - Argentina, Brazil, Paraguay

OCEANIA
49 SOUTH PACIFIC ISLANDS FORESTS - American Samoa (United States), Cook Islands (New Zealand), Fiji, French Polynesia (France), Niue (New Zealand), Samoa, Tonga, Wallis and Futuna Islands (France)
50 HAWAII MOIST FORESTS - Hawaii (United States)

TROPICAL AND SUBTROPICAL DRY BROADLEAF FORESTS

AFROTROPICAL
51 MADAGASCAR DRY FORESTS - Madagascar

AUSTRALASIA
52 NUSU TENGGARA DRY FORESTS - Indonesia
53 NEW CALEDONIA DRY FORESTS - New Caledonia (France)

INDO-MALAYAN
54 INDOCHINA DRY FORESTS - Cambodia, Laos, Thailand, Vietnam
55 CHHOTA-NAGPUR DRY FORESTS - India

NEOTROPICAL
56 MEXICAN DRY FORESTS - Guatemala, Mexico
57 TUMBESIAN-ANDEAN VALLEYS DRY FORESTS - Colombia, Ecuador, Peru
58 CHIQUITANO DRY FORESTS - Bolivia, Brazil
59 ATLANTIC DRY FORESTS - Brazil

OCEANIA
60 HAWAII'S DRY FORESTS - Hawaii (United States)

TROPICAL AND SUPTROPICAL CONIFEROUS FORESTS

NEARCTIC
61 SIERRA MADRE ORIENTAL AND OCCIDENTAL PINE-OAK FORESTS - Mexico, United States

NEOTROPICAL
62 GREATER ANTILLEAN PINE FORESTS - Cuba, Dominican Republic, Haiti
63 MESOAMERICAN PINE-OAK FORESTS - El Salvador, Guatemala, Honduras, Mexico, Nicaragua

TEMPERATE BROADLEAF AND MIXED FORESTS

AUSTRALASIA
64 EASTERN AUSTRALIA TEMPERATE FORESTS - Australia
65 TASMANIAN TEMPERATE RAIN FORESTS - Australia
66 NEW ZEALAND TEMPERATE FORESTS - New Zealand

INDO-MALAYAN
67 EASTERN HIMALAYAN BROADLEAF AND CONIFER FORESTS - Bhutan, China, India, Myanmar, Nepal
68 WESTERN HIMALAYAN TEMPERATE FORESTS - Afghanistan, India, Nepal, Pakistan

NEARCTIC
69 APPALACHIAN AND MIXED MESOPHYTIC FORESTS - United States

PALEARCTIC
70 SOUTHWEST CHINA TEMPERATE FORESTS - China
71 RUSSIAN FAR EAST TEMPERATE FORESTS - Russia

TEMPERATE CONIFEROUS FORESTS

NEARCTIC
72 PACIFIC TEMPERATE RAINFORESTS - Canada, United States
73 KLAMATH-SISKIYOU CONIFEROUS FORESTS - United States
74 SIERRA NEVADA CONIFEROUS FORESTS - United States
75 SOUTHEASTERN CONIFEROUS AND BROADLEAF FORESTS - United States

NEOTROPICAL
76 VALDIVIAN TEMPERATE RAINFORESTS / JUAN FERNANDEZ ISLANDS - Argentina, Chile

PALEARCTIC
77 EUROPEAN-MEDITERRANEAN MONTANE MIXED FORESTS - Albania, Algeria, Andorra, Austria, Bosnia and Herzegovina, Bulgaria, Croatia, Czech Republic, France, Germany, Greece, Italy, Liechtenstein, Macedonia, Morocco, Poland, Romania, Russia, Slovakia, Slovenia
78 CAUCASUS-ANATOLIAN-HYRCANIAN TEMPERATE FORESTS - Armenia, Azerbaijan, Bulgaria, Georgia, Iran, Russia, Turkey, Turkmenistan
79 ALTAI-SAYAN MONTANE FORESTS - China, Kazakstan, Mongolia, Russia
80 HENGDUAN SHAN CONIFEROUS FORESTS - China

BOREAL FORESTS / TAIGA

NEARCTIC
81 MUSKWA / SLAVE LAKE BOREAL FORESTS - Canada
82 CANADIAN BOREAL FORESTS - Canada

PALEARCTIC
83 URAL MOUNTAINS TAIGA - Russia
84 EASTERN SIBERIAN TAIGA - Russia
85 KAMCHATKA TAIGA AND GRASSLANDS - Russia

TROPICAL AND SUBTROPICAL GRASSLANDS, SAVANNAS AND SHRUBLANDS

AFROTROPICAL
86 HORN OF AFRICA ACACIA SAVANNAS - Eritrea, Ethiopia, Kenya, Somalia, Sudan
87 EAST AFRICAN ACACIA SAVANNAS - Ethiopia, Kenya, Sudan, Tanzania, Uganda
88 CENTRAL AND EASTERN MIOMBO WOODLANDS - Angola, Botswana, Burundi, Democratic Republic of Congo, Malawi, Mozambique, Namibia, Tanzania, Zambia, Zimbabwe
89 SUDANIAN SAVANNAS - Cameroon, Central African Republic, Chad, Nigeria, Democratic Republic of Congo, Eritrea, Ethiopia, Kenya, Sudan, Uganda

AUSTRALASIA
90 NORTHERN AUSTRALIA AND TRANS-FLY SAVANNAS - Australia, Indonesia, Papua New Guinea

INDO-MALAYAN
91 TERAI-DUAR SAVANNAS AND GRASSLANDS - Bangladesh, Bhutan, India, Nepal

NEOTROPICAL
92 LLANOS SAVANNAS - Colombia, Venezuela
93 CERRADO WOODLANDS AND SAVANNAS - Bolivia, Brazil, Paraguay

TEMPERATE GRASSLANDS, SAVANNAS AND SHRUBLANDS

NEARCTIC
94 NORTHERN PRAIRIE - Canada, United States

NEOTROPICAL
95 PATAGONIAN STEPPE - Argentina, Chile

PALEARCTIC
96 DAURIAN STEPPE - China, Mongolia, Russia

FLOODED GRASSLANDS AND SAVANNAS

AFROTROPICAL
97 SUDD-SAHELIAN FLOODED GRASSLANDS AND SAVANNAS - Cameroon, Chad, Ethiopia, Mali, Niger, Nigeria, Sudan, Uganda
98 ZAMBEZIAN FLOODED SAVANNAS - Angola, Botswana, Democratic Republic of Congo, Malawi, Mozambique, Namibia, Tanzania, Zambia

INDO-MALAYAN
99 RANN OF KUTCH FLOODED GRASSLANDS - India, Pakistan

NEOTROPICAL
100 EVERGLADES FLOODED GRASSLANDS - United States
101 PANTANAL FLOODED SAVANNAS - Bolivia, Brazil, Paraguay

MONTANE GRASSLANDS AND SHRUBLANDS

AFROTROPICAL
102 ETHIOPIAN HIGHLANDS - Eritrea, Ethiopia, Sudan
103 SOUTHERN RIFT MONTANE WOODLANDS - Malawi, Mozambique, Tanzania, Zambia
104 EAST AFRICAN MOORLANDS - Democratic Republic of Congo, Kenya, Rwanda, Tanzania, Uganda
105 DRAKENSBERG MONTANE SHRUBLANDS AND WOODLANDS - Lesotho, South Africa, Swaziland

AUSTRALASIA
106 CENTRAL RANGE SUBALPINE GRASSLANDS - Indonesia, Papua New Guinea

INDO-MALAYAN
107 KINABALU MONTANE SCRUB - Malaysia

NEOTROPICAL
108 NORTHERN ANDEAN PARAMO - Colombia, Ecuador, Peru, Venezuela
109 CENTRAL ANDEAN DRY PUNA - Argentina, Bolivia, Chile, Peru

PALEARCTIC
110 TIBETAN PLATEAU STEPPE - Afghanistan, China, India, Pakistan, Tajikistan
111 MIDDLE ASIAN MONTANE STEPPE AND WOODLANDS - Afghanistan, China, Kazakstan, Kyrgyzstan, Tajikistan, Turkmenistan, Uzbekistan
112 EASTERN HIMALAYAN ALPINE MEADOWS - Bhutan, China, India, Myanmar, Nepal

TUNDRA

NEARCTIC
113 ALASKAN NORTH SLOPE COASTAL TUNDRA - Canada, United States
114 CANADIAN LOW ARCTIC TUNDRA - Canada

PALEARCTIC
115 FENNO-SCANDIA ALPINE TUNDRA AND TAIGA - Finland, Norway, Russia, Sweden
116 TAIMYR AND SIBERIAN COASTAL TUNDRA - Russia
117 CHUKOTE COASTAL TUNDRA - Russia

18

MEDITERRANEAN FORESTS, WOODLANDS AND SCRUB

AFROTROPICAL
118 FYNBOS - South Africa

AUSTRALASIA
119 SOUTHWESTERN AUSTRALIA FORESTS AND SCRUB - Australia
120 SOUTHERN AUSTRALIA MALLEE AND WOODLANDS - Australia

NEARCTIC
121 CALIFORNIA CHAPARRAL AND WOODLANDS - Mexico, United States

NEOTROPICAL
122 CHILEAN MATORRAL - Chile

PALEARCTIC
123 MEDITERRANEAN FORESTS, WOODLANDS AND SCRUB - Albania, Algeria, Bosnia and Herzegovina, Bulgaria, Canary Islands (Spain), Croatia, Cyprus, Egypt, France, Gibraltar (United Kingdom), Greece, Iraq, Israel, Italy, Jordan, Lebanon, Libya, Macedonia, Madeira Islands (Portugal), Malta, Monaco, Morocco, Portugal, San Marino, Slovenia, Spain, Syria, Tunisia, Turkey, Western Sahara (Morocco), Yugoslavia

DESERTS AND XERIC SHRUBLANDS

AFROTROPICAL
124 NAMIB-KAROO-KAOKEVELD DESERTS - Angola, Namibia, South Africa
125 MADAGASCAR SPINY THICKET - Madagascar
126 SOCOTRA ISLAND DESERT - Yemen
127 ARABIAN HIGHLAND WOODLANDS AND SHRUBLANDS - Oman, Saudi Arabia, United Arab Emirates, Yemen

AUSTRALASIA
128 CARNAVON XERIC SCRUB - Australia
129 GREAT SANDY-TANAMI DESERTS - Australia

NEARCTIC
130 SONORAN-BAJA DESERTS - Mexico, United States
131 CHIHUAHUAN-TEHUACÁN DESERTS - Mexico, United States

NEOTROPICAL
132 GALÁPAGOS ISLANDS SCRUB - Ecuador
133 ATACAMA-SECHURA DESERTS - Chile, Peru

PALEARCTIC
134 CENTRAL ASIAN DESERTS - Kazakstan, Kyrgyzstan, Uzbekistan, Turkmenistan

MANGROVES

AFROTROPICAL
135 GULF OF GUINEA MANGROVES - Angola, Cameroon, Democratic Republic of Congo, Equatorial Guinea, Gabon, Ghana, Nigeria
136 EAST AFRICAN MANGROVES - Kenya, Mozambique, Somalia, Tanzania
137 MADAGASCAR MANGROVES - Madagascar

AUSTRALASIA
138 NEW GUINEA MANGROVES - Indonesia, Papua New Guinea

INDO-MALAYAN
139 SUNDARBANS MANGROVES - Bangladesh, India
140 GREATER SUNDAS MANGROVES - Brunei, Indonesia, Malaysia

NEOTROPICAL
141 GUIANAN-AMAZON MANGROVES - Brazil, French Guiana (France), Suriname, Trinidad and Tobago, Venezuela
142 PANAMA BIGHT MANGROVES - Colombia, Ecuador, Panama, Peru

FRESHWATER ECOREGIONS

LARGE RIVERS

AFROTROPICAL
143 CONGO RIVER AND FLOODED FORESTS - Angola, Democratic Republic of Congo, Republic of Congo

INDO-MALAYAN
144 MEKONG RIVER - Cambodia, China, Laos, Myanmar, Thailand, Vietnam

NEARCTIC
145 COLORADO RIVER - Mexico, United States
146 LOWER MISSISSIPPI RIVER - United States

NEOTROPICAL
147 AMAZON RIVER AND FLOODED FORESTS - Brazil, Colombia, Peru
148 ORINOCO RIVER AND FLOODED FORESTS - Brazil, Colombia, Venezuela

PALEARCTIC
149 YANGTZE RIVER AND LAKES - China

LARGE RIVER HEADWATERS

AFROTROPICAL
150 CONGO BASIN PIEDMONT RIVERS AND STREAMS - Angola, Cameroon, Central African Republic, Democratic Republic of Congo, Gabon, Republic of Congo, Sudan

NEARCTIC
151 MISSISSIPPI PIEDMONT RIVERS AND STREAMS - United States

NEOTROPICAL
152 UPPER AMAZON RIVERS AND STREAMS - Bolivia, Brazil, Colombia, Ecuador, French Guiana (France), Guyana, Peru, Suriname, Venezuela
153 UPPER PARANÁ RIVERS AND STREAMS - Argentina, Brazil, Paraguay
154 BRAZILIAN SHIELD AMAZONIAN RIVERS AND STREAMS - Bolivia, Brazil, Paraguay

LARGE RIVER DELTAS

AFROTROPICAL
155 NIGER RIVER DELTA - Nigeria

INDO-MALAYAN
156 INDUS RIVER DELTA - India, Pakistan

PALEARCTIC
157 VOLGA RIVER DELTA - Kazakhstan, Russia
158 MESOPOTAMIAN DELTA AND MARSHES - Iran, Iraq, Kuwait
159 DANUBE RIVER DELTA - Bulgaria, Moldova, Romania, Ukraine, Yugoslavia
160 LENA RIVER DELTA - Russia

SMALL RIVERS

AFROTROPICAL
161 UPPER GUINEA RIVERS AND STREAMS - Côte D'Ivoire, Guinea, Liberia, Sierra Leone
162 MADAGASCAR FRESHWATER - Madagascar
163 GULF OF GUINEA RIVERS AND STREAMS - Angola, Cameroon, Democratic Republic of Congo, Equatorial Guinea, Gabon, Nigeria, Republic of Congo
164 CAPE RIVERS AND STREAMS - South Africa

AUSTRALASIA
165 NEW GUINEA RIVERS AND STREAMS - Indonesia, Papua New Guinea
166 NEW CALEDONIA RIVERS AND STREAMS - New Caledonia (France)
167 KIMBERLEY RIVERS AND STREAMS - Australia
168 SOUTHWEST AUSTRALIA RIVERS AND STREAMS - Australia
169 EASTERN AUSTRALIA RIVERS AND STREAMS - Australia

INDO-MALAYAN
170 XI JIANG RIVERS AND STREAMS - China, Vietnam
171 WESTERN GHATS RIVERS AND STREAMS - India
172 SOUTHWESTERN SRI LANKA RIVERS AND STREAMS - Sri Lanka
173 SALWEEN RIVER - China, Myanmar, Thailand
174 SUNDALAND RIVERS AND SWAMPS - Brunei, Malaysia, Indonesia, Singapore

NEARCTIC
175 SOUTHEASTERN RIVERS AND STREAMS - United States
176 PACIFIC NORTHWEST COASTAL RIVERS AND STREAMS - United States
177 GULF OF ALASKA COASTAL RIVERS AND STREAMS - Canada, United States

NEOTROPICAL
178 GUIANAN FRESHWATER - Brazil, French Guiana (France), Guyana, Suriname, Venezuela
179 GREATER ANTILLEAN FRESHWATER - Cuba, Dominican Republic, Haiti, Puerto Rico (United States)

PALEARCTIC
180 BALKAN RIVERS AND STREAMS - Albania, Bosnia and Herzogovina, Bulgaria, Croatia, Greece, Macedonia, Turkey, Yugoslavia
181 RUSSIAN FAR EAST RIVERS AND WETLANDS - China, Mongolia, Russia

LARGE LAKES

AFROTROPICAL
182 RIFT VALLEY LAKES - Burundi, Democratic Republic of Congo, Ethiopia, Kenya, Malawi, Mozambique, Rwanda, Tanzania, Uganda, Zambia

NEOTROPICAL
183 HIGH ANDEAN LAKES - Argentina, Bolivia, Chile, Peru

PALEARCTIC
184 LAKE BAIKAL - Russia
185 LAKE BIWA - Japan

SMALL LAKES

AFROTROPICAL
186 CAMEROON CRATER LAKES - Cameroon

AUSTRALASIA
187 LAKES KUTUBU AND SENTANI - Indonesia, Papua New Guinea
188 CENTRAL SULAWESI LAKES - Indonesia

INDO-MALAYAN
189 PHILIPPINES FRESHWATER - Philippines
190 LAKE INLE - Myanmar
191 YUNNAN LAKES AND STREAMS - China

NEOTROPICAL
192 MEXICAN HIGHLAND LAKES - Mexico

XERIC BASINS

AUSTRALASIA
193 CENTRAL AUSTRALIAN FRESHWATER - Australia

NEARCTIC
194 CHIHUAHUAN FRESHWATER - Mexico, United States

PALEARCTIC
195 ANATOLIAN FRESHWATER - Syria, Turkey

MARINE ECOREGIONS

POLAR SEAS

ANTARCTIC
196 ANTARCTIC PENINSULA & WEDDELL SEA - Antarctic Peninsula & Weddell Sea

ARCTIC
197 BERING SEA - Canada, Russia, United States
198 BARENTS-KARA SEA - Norway, Russia

TEMPERATE SHELFS AND SEAS

MEDITERRANEAN
199 MEDITERRANEAN SEA - Albania, Algeria, Bosnia and Herzegovina, Croatia, Cyprus, Egypt, France, Gibraltar (United Kingdom), Greece, Israel, Italy, Lebanon, Libya, Malta, Monaco, Morocco, Slovenia, Spain, Syria, Tunisia, Turkey, Yugoslavia

NORTH TEMPERATE ATLANTIC
200 NORTHEAST ATLANTIC SHELF MARINE - Belgium, Denmark, Estonia, Finland, France, Germany, Ireland, Latvia, Lithuania, Netherlands, Norway, Poland, Russia, Sweden, United Kingdom
201 GRAND BANKS - Canada, St. Pierre and Miquelon (France), United States
202 CHESAPEAKE BAY - United States

NORTH TEMPERATE INDO-PACIFIC
203 YELLOW SEA - China, North Korea, South Korea
204 OKHOTSK SEA - Japan, Russia

SOUTHERN OCEAN
205 PATAGONIAN SOUTHWEST ATLANTIC - Argentina, Brazil, Chile, Uruguay
206 SOUTHERN AUSTRALIAN MARINE - Australia
207 NEW ZEALAND MARINE - New Zealand

TEMPERATE UPWELLING

NORTH TEMPERATE INDO-PACIFIC
208 CALIFORNIAN CURRENT - Canada, Mexico, United States

SOUTH TEMPERATE ATLANTIC
209 BENGUELA CURRENT - Namibia, South Africa

SOUTH TEMPERATE INDO-PACIFIC
210 HUMBOLDT CURRENT - Chile, Ecuador, Peru
211 AGULHAS CURRENT - Mozambique, South Africa

TROPICAL UPWELLING

CENTRAL INDO-PACIFIC
212 WESTERN AUSTRALIAN MARINE - Australia

EASTERN INDO-PACIFIC
213 PANAMA BIGHT - Colombia, Ecuador, Panama
214 GULF OF CALIFORNIA - Mexico
215 GALÁPAGOS MARINE - Ecuador

EASTERN TROPICAL ATLANTIC
216 CANARY CURRENT - Canary Islands (Spain), Gambia, Guinea-Bissau, Mauritania, Morocco, Senegal, Western Sahara (Morocco)

TROPICAL CORAL

CENTRAL INDO-PACIFIC
217 NANSEI SHOTO - Japan
218 SULU-SULAWESI SEAS - Indonesia, Malaysia, Philippines
219 BISMARCK-SOLOMON SEAS - Indonesia, Papua New Guinea, Solomon Islands
220 BANDA-FLORES SEA - Indonesia
221 NEW CALEDONIA BARRIER REEF - New Caledonia (France)
222 GREAT BARRIER REEF - Australia
223 LORD HOWE-NORFOLK ISLANDS MARINE - Australia
224 PALAU MARINE - Palau
225 ANDAMAN SEA - Andaman and Nicobar Islands (India), Indonesia, Malaysia, Myanmar, Thailand

EASTERN INDO-PACIFIC
226 TAHITIAN MARINE - Cook Islands (New Zealand), French Polynesia (France)
227 HAWAIIAN MARINE - Hawaii (United States)
228 RAPA NUI - Chile
229 FIJI BARRIER REEF - Fiji

WESTERN INDO-PACIFIC
230 MALDIVES, CHAGOS, LAKSHADWEEP ATOLLS - Chagos Archipelago (United Kingdom), India, Maldives, Sri Lanka
231 RED SEA - Djibouti, Egypt, Eritrea, Israel, Jordan, Saudi Arabia, Sudan, Yemen
232 ARABIAN SEA - Djibouti, Iran, Oman, Pakistan, Qatar, Saudi Arabia, Somalia, United Arab Emirates, Yemen
233 EAST AFRICAN MARINE - Kenya, Mozambique, Somalia, Tanzania

WESTERN TROPICAL ATLANTIC
235 MESOAMERICAN REEF - Belize, Guatemala, Honduras, Mexico
236 GREATER ANTILLEAN MARINE - Bahamas, Cayman Islands (United Kingdom), Cuba, Dominican Republic, Haiti, Jamaica, Puerto Rico (United States), Turks and Caicos Islands (United Kingdom), United States
237 SOUTHERN CARIBBEAN SEA - Aruba (Netherlands), Columbia, Netherlands Antilles (Netherlands), Panama, Trinidad and Tobago, Venezuela
238 NORTHEAST BRAZIL SHELF MARINE - Brazil

8-9 Tigers are solitary animals that are generally unwilling to share their hunting territory with others of their kind.

20-21 The dense plumage and thick layer of subcutaneous fat of the emperor penguin provide excellent insulation against the cold, allowing it to survive the icy Antarctic temperatures.

THE FENNO-SCANDIA ALPINE TUNDRA and TAIGA

"Taavetti Rytkönen sized up the landscape.
He gloomily noted that, had he been younger,
he would have loved to chart the territory:
the view encompassed a land of hills,
lakes dotted with bays, thick woods and peasant villages.
There was everything necessary for a fine map."
Arto Paasilinna.

This ecoregion extends for over 117,000 sq. miles (303,000 sq. km) in Finland, Norway, Sweden and Russia. The Scandinavian Mountains form an important range that crosses the entire peninsula, with a maximum elevation of just over 8000 ft (2438 ft). In the west the mountains drop toward the North Sea and the Norwegian Sea, forming characteristic deep fjords, while some of the glaciers reach the sea, where they present spectacular ice falls.

The Fenno-Scandia alpine tundra and taiga ecoregion has an unusually rich flora and fauna for mountainous parts of the Arctic. Many of the species are unique and can be found only in certain areas. This is partly due to the presence of the tail end of the Gulf Stream and the Atlantic Ocean in general, which make an otherwise cold climate more moderate, although very wet, with snowstorms in the winter and heavy rains in the summer. The high precipitation feeds a dense network of lakes, pools and watercourses. The phenomenon of permafrost, whereby the deepest layers of the soil remain frozen all year round, causes the stagnation of water and the flooding of many forests.

The ecoregion is characterized by extensive conifer woods with firs and pines (*Abies* spp. and *Pinus* spp.). Approximately a third is made up of Alpine tundra, with rocky terrain and sparse herbaceous vegetation, while another third is represented by low-lying shrubland with dwarf birch (*Betula nana*), willow (*Salix* spp.) and numerous pools and lakes.

Many animal species inhabit these cold lands all year round. They include the Arctic fox (*Alopex lagopus*), which has two color phases: an all-white one and a blue one. Other species include the wolverine (*Gulo gulo*), a large member of the weasel family; the brown bear (*Ursus arctos*); the wolf (*Canis lupus*) and the reindeer (*Rangifer tarandus*), which is also widespread in North America, where it is known as the caribou. In Scandinavia almost the entire reindeer population is domesticated.

The Dovrefjell-Sunndalsfjella National Park, in southern Norway, is home to around 150 musk oxen (*Ovibos moschatus*), which were reintroduced from Greenland after having become extinct in the region in the 1950s.

There are also several non-migratory birds that remain in the area all year round, bravely bearing the severe winters, such as grouse, typical of the Scandinavian forests and moors. They include the capercaillie (*Tetrao urogallus*), the black grouse (*Tetrao tetrix*) and the hazel grouse (*Bonasa bonasia*), as well as the willow ptarmigan (*Lagopus lagopus*). Birds of prey, both diurnal and nocturnal, occupy all the niches offered by this extraordinary ecosystem. They include the golden eagle (*Aquila chrysaetos*), the white-tailed sea eagle (*Haliaeetus albicilla*), the osprey (*Pandion haliaetus*) the rough-legged hawk (*Buteo lagopus*), the eagle owl (*Bubo bubo*), the short-eared owl (*Asio flammeus*), the northern hawk owl (*Surnia ulula*), the Eurasian pygmy owl (*Glaucidium passerinum*) and the boreal owl (*Aegolius funereus*).

During the short Arctic summer numerous insects complete their life cycles and plants bloom, setting the meadows ablaze with a thousand colors. Migrant birds from Africa and southern Europe flock to the region to take advantage of this explosion of life. They are insectivorous passerines and waterfowl, such as geese, ducks and waders. The forests, silent and covered with a thick blanket of snow throughout the long winter, now come to life and are filled with melodious birdsong. The brambling (*Fringilla montifringilla*) calls from the treetops and the male common snipe (*Gallinago gallinago*), lures females using a distinctive technique called "drumming," produced by air passing through the outer feathers of its tail. Ruffs (*Philomachus pugnax*) assemble in small groups called leks for competitive mating displays, while red-necked phalaropes (*Phalaropus lobatus*) start to dance in the little pools of water.

However, for some species the breeding season commences while the snow is still on the ground. This is the case of the woodpeckers, which start to make holes for their nests very early in the year, filling the forests with an incessant drumming noise. The main problems in this region are caused by climate change, which melts the permafrost, eroding the soil, and human activity, which slows the regrowth of the vegetation. However, radioactive fallout from Chernobyl is still found in lichens and fungi and continues to harm wildlife and people, while deforestation and overgrazing by domesticated reindeer cause the impoverishment of the topsoil.

This is also the land of the Sami, considered the oldest Northern European people. A star map, which also proposes names for stars and constellations, has been discovered carved into a rock and dates from to 4000-4100 years ago, not long after the first historical definition of the constellations 4600-4700 years ago.

WWF has national offices in all three Scandinavian countries and WWF International has implemented a specific Arctic Program. Numerous projects are currently underway, many of which are the result of international collaboration, such as the conservation project for the gray seal (*Halichoerus grypus*), jointly conducted by Finland and Sweden. Another important project is aimed at studying one of the rarest geese of the Palearctic region, the lesser white-fronted goose (*Anser erythropus*), using radio collars. The Arctic Program has also enabled WWF to address the problems of climate change, the effects of toxic substances, and overfishing, which afflict the Northeast Atlantic Shelf Marine ecoregion and its fauna, in particular the millions of seabirds that live along the Scandinavian coasts: cormorants and shags (*Phalacrocorax* spp.), auks, Atlantic puffins (*Fratercula artica*), eiders (*Somateria* spp), pochards (*Aythya* spp.) and kittiwakes (*Larus tridactylus*).

24 top left and right and center left Ivalo is a village in Finnish Lapland with just 4000 inhabitants, surrounded by forests and lakes. The largest of these is Lake Inari, which covers an area of over 400,000 square miles dotted with more than 3000 islands. It freezes over completely between November and June.

24 center right The taiga is a typical forest habitat of Scandinavia. The unbroken woodland also covers the slopes of the mountains and the shores of the fjords.

24 bottom The musk ox is a large member of the Bovidae family, which was reintroduced to Scandinavia during the 1950s, following its extinction in the region. It now inhabits the Dovrefjell-Sunndalsfjella National Park, in Norway.

24-25 Lapland is characterized by permafrost, a phenomenon whereby the deepest layers of the soil remain frozen all year round. When the ice thaws at the beginning of summer, it causes the formation of bogs and watercourses on top of the impermeable underlayer.

26 top The Tannforsen waterfall is one of the largest falls in Sweden. The water plummets directly into the sea from the glaciers, dropping over 130 ft (40 m) at a rate of over 14,000 cu. ft (400 cu. m) per second.

26 bottom In spring the conifer and beech forests of southern Lapland are covered with bright green foliage that contrasts with the vivid red of the undergrowth.

27 The brown bear is distributed throughout Scandinavia, but particularly in Finland, where many bears from Russia can also be found. It is easy to come across tracks left by this species on the bark of the trees while walking in the forest.

28-29 In winter everything is covered with a thick blanket of snow. The trees appear as soft, dazzling white shapes rising from the ground, like clouds resting on the earth.

THE EUROPEAN
MOUNTAINS

"The mountains are speechless masters
and make silent disciples."
Johann Wolfgang von Goethe

Three great mountain ranges cross Europe, albeit interruptedly, from east to west: the Carpathians, stretching from Romania to the border between Slovakia and Poland; the Pyrenees, running from the Bay of Biscay to the Gulf of Lions and forming a visible boundary between France and Spain; and the Alps, a natural barrier on the northern frontier of Italy, extending for about 750 miles (1200 km) from Slovenia and Austria to France and Liguria.

Like all places of great natural presence, which dominate the collective imagination, the mountains are a somewhat contradictory and unknown world, except to mountaineers and geologists. On the one hand, there is the tangle of emotions that they trigger. Their rugged and inhospitable nature is intimidating, while the power of their towering heights instills a sense of challenge. Their isolation, silence and clear air heighten emotions. On the other hand, there is a tendency to succumb to the clichés of picture-postcard representations: sunny snow-capped peaks, herds of lazy cows dotted over picturesque meadows, snapshots of a simple life far removed from the frenetic urban reality. The outcome is that mountains often become the tangible projection of the thoroughly human yearning for a paradise: a pure and uncontaminated place in which to seek refuge.

However, these emotional and symbolic approaches are misleading, for they oversimplify the mountain environment that is actually is one of the most complex ecosystems. Who could imagine, for example, that those humps that give the landscape its distinctive "ridged" appearance are really moraine deposited and abandoned thousands of years earlier by a glacier, which has now perhaps retreated to a higher altitude? And who could guess that this landscape is actually a treasure trove of information about the past? Walking in the entire region it is possible to find the traces of previous ice ages, in their most varied forms – cirques, hanging valleys, moraine, lakes – and, at lower altitudes, enclosures that the vegetation has created around glacial structures, protecting them from erosion and preserving the form of ancient features that would not otherwise have survived, allowing us to reconstruct the original landscape.

The mountains constitute a precious ecosystem, with numerous distinctive features, where it is possible to encounter very different environments just a few dozen miles apart, due to the variations in altitude.

The piedmont zone is characterized by broad-leaved forests that gradually give way to more open woods, while above 6000-6500 ft (1828-1980 m) – depending on the conditions and the exposure of the slopes – the woods are replaced by a band of contorted shrubs and high-altitude pastures.

Higher still is a zone with scree and bare rocks, where the pioneer vegetation is well adapted to the particular climatic conditions. The final zone is covered with perpetual snow and ice.

In order to comprehend the incredible diversity of flora and fauna, it is sufficient to realize that it would be necessary to cover a distance of at least 2500 miles (4025 km) on flat land in order to find a similar natural variety.

Of course, this alternation of plant life is accompanied by an equally rich array of animal species. The Alps, Pyrenees and Carpathians constitute authentic "islands" separated by plains and hills, and above all by human settlements. These conditions have favored the evolution of species or endemic forms that are found in only one of the three mountainous areas. The Pyrenees are home to the Pyrenean chamois, which differs from those found in the Alps and Carpathians. The species of large raptors are very similar, despite the fact that humankind has caused the extinction of some of them in certain areas. However, there have been recent reports of returns. Species include the great vultures, such as the bearded vulture (*Gypaetus barbatus*) and the griffon vulture (*Gyps fulvus*), in the Alps and the golden eagle (*Aquila chrysaetos*) and Eastern imperial eagle (*Aquila heliaca*) in the Carpathians.

The European mountains are also inhabited by a group of birds typical of the great northern forests: the grouse. Three species of this family can be found in these mountainous regions, namely the capercaillie (*Tetrao urogallus*), the black grouse (*Tetrao tetrix*) and the hazel grouse (*Bonasa bonasia*), as well as the rock ptarmigan (*Lagopus mutus*) on the highest peaks. The woodpeckers are another family of birds found in the forests of these three mountainous areas. Species include the black woodpecker (*Dryocopus martius*) and the Eurasian three-toed woodpecker (*Picoides tridactylus*).

The three great European predators were once widespread throughout the continent, but today the largest populations of brown bear (*Ursus arctos*), wolf (*Canis lupus*) and lynx (*Lynx lynx*) are the eastern ones that inhabit the Carpathians. However, all three species are currently returning to both the Alps and Pyrenees, both of their own accord and through reintroduction programs.

The flora of the Alps, Carpathians and Pyrenees boasts a rich variety of species and endemisms – species enedemic to the area. Rhododendrons, for example, form characteristic groups beyond the tree line, with two species in the Alps and one in the Carpathians. The snow-white flower of the edelweiss has become the symbol of the Alps, but it is also found in the Carpathians and Pyrenees. Other species that color the Alpine meadows in late spring include gentians, aconites and saxifrages.

31

32 A male capercaillie fans his tail feathers in a courting display. This bird is widespread in alpine forest regions.

33 Lakes are one of the distinctive features of the Alps, where glaciers have eroded the rock, leaving large depressions. Following the thawing of the ice, these areas were freed and filled with the melt water.

All three of these mountainous regions are characterized by extensive forests, composed chiefly of conifers, firs and pines, although the lower altitudes are also home to woods of broad-leaved trees. They have abundant water supplies, and their springs, streams and rivers are also a precious resource for man.

Although the influence of humankind has been mainly concentrated on the plains over the centuries, the European mountains have also suffered to some degree. While in the past traditional human activities were eco-compatible, today intensive forest exploitation, the regimentation of watercourses and the development of tourism pose serious threats to these habitats. The idea of the mountains as a refuge has become obsolete, as pollution – environmental, "ideological" and visual – is everywhere. In recent decades the natural complexity of the mountain landscapes has been defaced by the vapid architecture of ski resorts, whose rash of hotels, swimming pools, recreational areas, restaurants and discos are transforming these ecosystems into urban appendages. These places present themselves as an alter ego of the metropolis, while remaining wild at heart, a pulsating center of energy yet to be explored, which fascinates and draws hordes of tourists each year.

WWF has promoted ecoregional conservation in both the Alps and the Carpathians, building a future scenario for biodiversity and involving all the neighboring countries. For the first time a combined effort is being made for the conservation of biodiversity without frontiers in these regions. The main guidelines include the conservation of the great predators (bear, wolf and lynx), the protection of watercourses and the control of endangering factors, including winter tourism.

34 left Lake Carezza, at the foot of the Latemar range in the Dolomites, is one of the most picturesque alpine lakes. According to legend, a sorcerer put a spell on it, making its waters reflect all the colors of the rainbow.

34 right In autumn, when the leaves turn red and yellow, the water of the alpine torrents dwindles, before drying up completely during winter.

34-35 The Aletsch Glacier extends for 15 miles in the Jungfrau-Aletsch-Bietschhorn region of Switzerland and is a UNESCO World Heritage Site.

35 bottom The European mouflon, native to Corsica and Sardinia, has been introduced to the Alps for the purpose of hunting.

36-37 The Dent du Géant is one of the most imposing peaks of the Western Alps, rising over 13,000 ft (3962 m). It is part of the Mont Blanc massif and was first climbed in July 1882.

37 top The Brenta Group is part of the Rhaetian Alps and is bounded by the Sole Valley to the north. It is part of the Dolomites, which owe their name to the French geologist Déodat de Dolomieu.

37 center left The golden eagle is a very widespread predator in the Alps. Its favorite prey consists of marmots, although it will also take foxes and black grouse.

37 center right The chamois is both a grazer and a browser. In summer it can be found in the mountain zone between 5000 and 8000 ft (1525 and 2438 m), while in winter it frequents wooded areas at lower altitudes.

THE EUROPEAN MOUNTAINS

37 bottom In winter everything is covered with a snowy blanket and life seems to be suspended. The animals appear to have disappeared: some migrate to other regions or to lower elevations and others hibernate, while only a few continue to seek food in the harsh winter climate.

38-39 The Ordesa and Monte Perdido National Park in the Spanish Pyrenees is one of the largest and most important protected areas of the range that forms the border between France and Spain. It is home to bearded and griffon vultures and chamois. The area is characterized by imposing rock faces hundreds of feet high, such as that of Monte Arruebo.

38 bottom The horns of the Spanish ibex are less curved than those of the Alpine one. In spring the males engage in incredible fights, and the noise of their horns clanging together rings through the valleys.

39 The griffon vulture is still widespread in the Pyrenees and is slowly returning to the Alps as well, following a series of reintroduction programs. Quarrels with other predators attracted by carrion, such as foxes, are a common sight.

40 top Hunted almost to extinction, the lynx is slowly returning to the mountains of Europe. Several groups breed in captivity, such as that of the Bavarian Forest National Park.

40 bottom The wolf became extinct in the Alps, but is now slowly regaining the territories from which it was driven. Italian wolves have spread from the Northern Apennines to the Maritime Alps, France and Switzerland.

41 Very few brown bears are left in the Pyrenees and Alps. A recent project introduced several individuals from Slovenia, but others cross the eastern boundaries of the Alps of their own accord.

THE MEDITERRANEAN BASIN

"The only sound was the murmur of the sea,
whispering its old refrain among the cliffs,
because the sea is homeless too,
and can be listened to by anyone anywhere in the world…."
Giovanni Verga.

The Mediterranean Sea is "enclosed" by three continents: Europe to the north, Asia to the east and Africa to the south. It has a total area of over 1 million sq. miles (2.6 million sq. km) and an average depth of approximately 4600 ft (1372 m). However, it reaches its maximum depth of over 16,800 ft (5120 m) in the Matapan Trench of the Ionian Basin. The total length of the coastline (excluding the islands) is 7900 miles (12,715 km), while the maximum width (from Gibraltar to the Lebanese coast) is approximately 2250 miles (3620 km). The Mediterranean connects with the Atlantic Ocean via the Strait of Gibraltar, which is just 8 miles (12.8 km) wide.

Travel in the Mediterranean is an extraordinary experience, in some ways comparable to a miniature round-the-world trip. Indeed, the Mediterranean Basin is a "cradle of civilization" and a veritable crossroads of peoples, which offers an unrivaled variety of landscapes, cultures and traditions. Leaving aside the aspects closely connected with its great biodiversity, which we will discuss later, suffice it to say that if we could transform ourselves into tiny human satellites, the astonishing richness of this ecoregion would be apparent at a glance. The Mediterranean coasts are home to well-preserved historical remains, including the Greek temples of Greece and Sicily, the Egyptian pyramids and even traces of entire cities, such as Carthage and Pompeii, while the traveler can stumble across prehistoric vestiges in Sardinia, Turkish Islam in the former Yugoslavia, and the Roman world in Lebanon. The Mediterranean is characterized by waters dotted with tuna-fishing nets and old fishing boats, and countryside covered with vineyards and olive groves, but also by apparently unchanging and decadent landscapes like Venice, or the bustling, chaotic ports of Genoa, Naples and Marseilles, the Moorish architecture of Granada, or the miles of hot coasts of the Maghreb.

Today the countries bordering the Mediterranean Sea are home to between 380 and 400 million people and constitute two distinct and contrasting worlds that coexist within the basin, each with its own distinctive history. In the northwestern area five nations (with a total population of 165 million inhabitants) belonging to the European Union represent the wealthy, developed and westernized part. By contrast, the standard of living of at least 235 million people who inhabit the eastern and southern coasts of the Mediterranean (with the exception of Israel) – including the new Balkan states that are slowly recovering from the recent ethnic wars – is about four times lower.

Population density also varies greatly in the Mediterranean Basin, from 2,842 inhabitants per sq. mile (1,080 per sq. km) in Malta, the country with the highest population density in the world after Monaco and Singapore, to just 74 inhabitants per sq. mile (28 per sq. km) in Corsica. The demographic trends also represent two diametrically opposite situations: while the population of the northwestern area is stabilizing, that of the other regions of the Mediterranean is constantly increasing. The latter trend is in line with the situation in other poor and underdeveloped countries constantly struggling with the problems associated with high rates of demographic growth in areas unable to sustain them either socially or economically.

The Mediterranean is one of the most important areas in the world for biodiversity. Although it accounts for only 0.3 percent of the Earth's water, it is home to approximately 6 percent of its marine species, and the figure increases to 18 percent for certain groups. Around a quarter of these species are endemic, i.e., they are not found in any other part of the world. There are several reasons for this high level of endemism, which is greater than that of any other European region. Firstly, the Mediterranean is a relatively "closed" and circumscribed basin. Secondly, local differentiation has given rise to endemic taxa. Thirdly, the area is subdivided into various districts by numerous islands, peninsulas and mountain ranges. Our knowledge of the distribution of the species is relatively good, especially in the case of vascular plants and vertebrates. Even so, scientific field research never stops adding new species to the national lists. This is particularly true for invertebrates and flora, but sometimes also for far more visible species, such as superior vertebrates. In 1975 a new bird species was discovered in the remnants of Algerian fir (*Abies numidica*) forests in Algeria: the Algerian nuthatch (*Sitta ledanti*), which inhabits just four areas with a total population of a few hundred individuals. More recently, the use of new DNA testing technologies has made it possible to determine the existence of new vertebrate species even in Italy, including the Apennine hare (*Lepus corsicanus*), the Sardinian long-eared bat (*Plecotus sardus*) and the Sicilian pond turtle (*Emys trinacris*).

The high degree of endemism is also testified by the recognition of the Mediterranean Basin as one of the world's top 24 biodiversity hotspots. Various reasons account for this richness. First of all, the region's wide variety of environments and climates makes it possible for species accustomed to temperate zones to live alongside species accustomed to subtropical climates. This mingling commenced with the reopening of the Strait of Gibraltar, when the succession of ice ages and warm periods triggered a series of invasions of pop-

43

ulations from cold and subtropical regions of the Atlantic, which joined the species typical of more temperate-waters. There has also been a massive influx of animals from the Red Sea, via the Suez Canal, which continued throughout the 1970s and '80s. Finally, the greenhouse effect and the consequent rise in temperature have aided the emigration and settlement of species accustomed to warmer waters.

The Mediterranean has been estimated to contain at least 8500 species, excluding the thousands of microorganisms. For over 10,000 years this community has lived in close contact with man, who has modified it. Indeed, human activities have influenced the development of the landscape and the biodiversity of the Mediterranean Basin, in conjunction with natural phenomena such as the processes of immigration, extinction and regional differentiation that have occurred over the geological eras. However, the voyages, forays and trade of the region's navigator and merchant populations have also left indelible traces on the formation of its flora and fauna. For example, the thorny squat plants that we call prickly pears come from America, while the oranges, lemons and mandarins that nestle among the dark green foliage of the citrus trees that we consider so typical of the Mediterranean, actually originated in the Far East and were brought to the region by the Arabs. The examples are endless, from tomatoes, native to Peru, to maize, endemic to Mexico. The Mediterranean is thus a stratification of elements and colors, a rich collage of living organisms and a laboratory in which a constant, skilled process of naturalization is underway.

The extraordinary importance of the Mediterranean Basin requires equally significant commitment on the part of WWF. Indeed, a special WWF International office for the Mediterranean has been active in the area for over ten years, with the aim of launching projects for the conservation of biodiversity in those countries that do not yet have national offices. This activity is flanked by the work of the national organizations, which conduct independent but coordinated programs focusing on conservation and the promotion of sustainable activities. Thus WWF is not only active in France, Greece, Italy, Spain and Turkey through its national organizations, but also in the countries of the Maghreb and the Balkans.

The area is the focus of ecoregional conservation, a new approach that aims to identify the priorities for action targeted at the conservation of the biodiversity of the entire ecoregion. However, it is also at the center of specific projects aimed at saving the most threatened species and habitats, such as the sea turtle and cetaceans, the silver fir forests, the sandy coasts, the cork forests, the Marsican brown bear, the otter, etc. Unfortunately, the threats with which the Mediterranean region is faced are increasingly imminent and evident, ranging from the uncontrolled exploitation of its resources to the leakage (and often also direct discharge) of pollutants into the sea and the pressure exerted by constantly expanding tourism and the plethora of related facilities that suffocates the coasts and natural resources. In the years to come it is hoped that the creation of an increasing number of protected areas and sanctuaries for endangered species will manage to re-establish the natural equilibrium and that the Mediterranean Sea, with its rich legacy of history and tradition, may be restored to life.

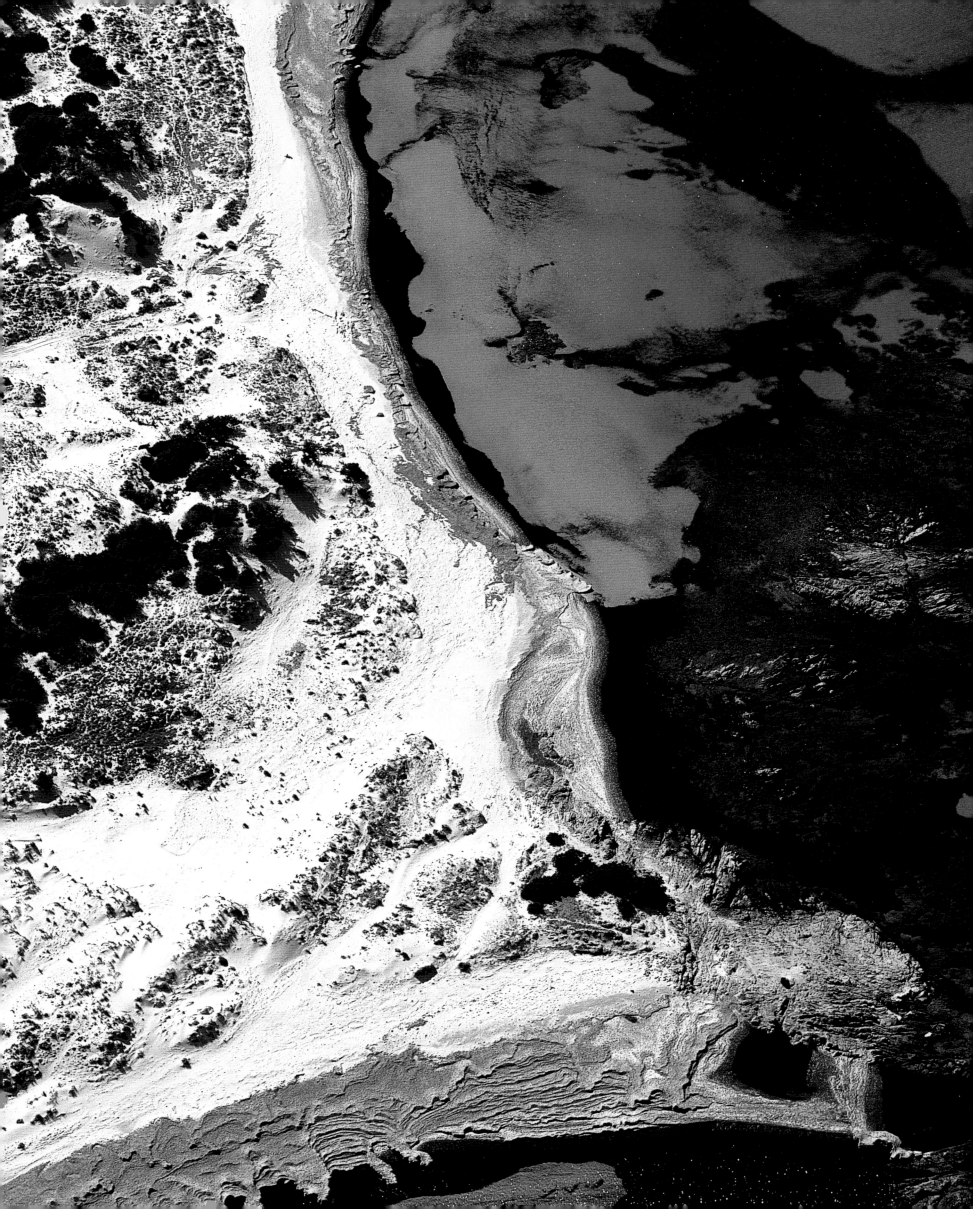

46 top left The northernmost tip of Majorca in the Balearic Islands is known as Cap de Formentor. The highest point rises 1260 ft (384 m) above sea level.

46 top right and center The Balearic Islands are situated in the western Mediterranean. The archipelago comprises four main islands: Majorca, Minorca, Ibiza and Formentera, as well as several minor islands, including Cabrera.

46 bottom The southern coast of Corsica is formed of limestone, as revealed by the towering white cliffs of Bonifacio that fall sheer into the blue sea. The area is part of an International Marine Park.

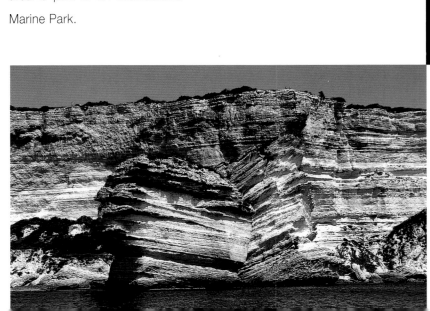

46-47 The southern coast of France is typically Mediterranean. One of the most spectacular areas is the Côte des Calanques in Provence, between Marseilles and Cassis.

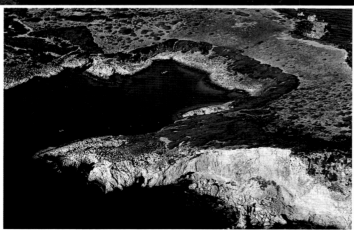

48

48-49 The island of Pianosa, which covers an area of just 4 sq. miles (10 sq. km), was home to a prison until 1998. It is now part of the Tuscan Archipelago National Park.

48 bottom The Tremiti Islands are an archipelago of four islands in the Adriatic: San Domino, the largest, San Nicola, Capraia and Pianosa.

49 top The Amalfi coast overlooks the Gulf of Salerno and comprises the Sorrentine Peninsula. In 1997 it was inscribed on UNESCO's list of World Heritage Sites.

49 center left Cala Rossa, on the southern coast of the island of Capraia, bears witness to the volcanic origins of the third largest island of the Tuscan Archipelago.

49 center right The island of Palmarola is situated in the Pontine Islands in the Tyrrhenian Sea, off the coast of the Italian region of Lazio. It is inhabited only during the summer season.

THE MEDITERRANEAN BASIN

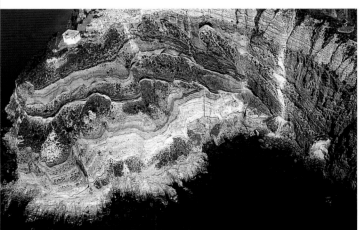

49 bottom The island of Ischia, at the northern end of the Bay of Naples, has an area of around 18 sq. miles (47 sq. km). It is a volcanic island; the volcano was active until the 14th century.

50 top and 50-51 The island of Lampedusa is 5.5 miles (8.8 km) long and just a mile across. Although it is the southernmost point in Italy, geologically the island belongs to the African plate and is situated farther south than both Tunis and Algiers.

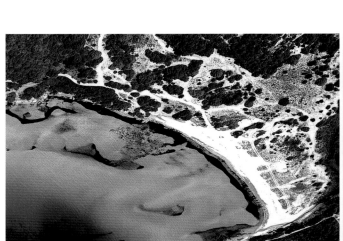

50 left and top center The coast of the Gallura region is renowned for the luxurious hotels and villas of the Costa Smeralda frequented by the jet set. However, it remains one of the most beautiful stretches of Sardinia's coast, with little coves and sandy beaches of incredible colors.

50 bottom center The Scalata dei Turchi ("Turks' Climb") in the province of Agrigento is a limestone cliff that owes its name to a legend that tells of Saracen raids on the villages.

50 bottom Alicudi is the westernmost of the Aeolian Islands. It is a huge extinct volcano whose foot is 5000 ft (1524 m) below sea level, and whose peak rises about 2000 ft (61 m) above the surface of the sea.

52-53 The island of Budelli in the Maddalena Arcipelago National Park is famous for its pink beach, but the crystal-clear waters of the other little coves of the tiny island are equally breathtaking.

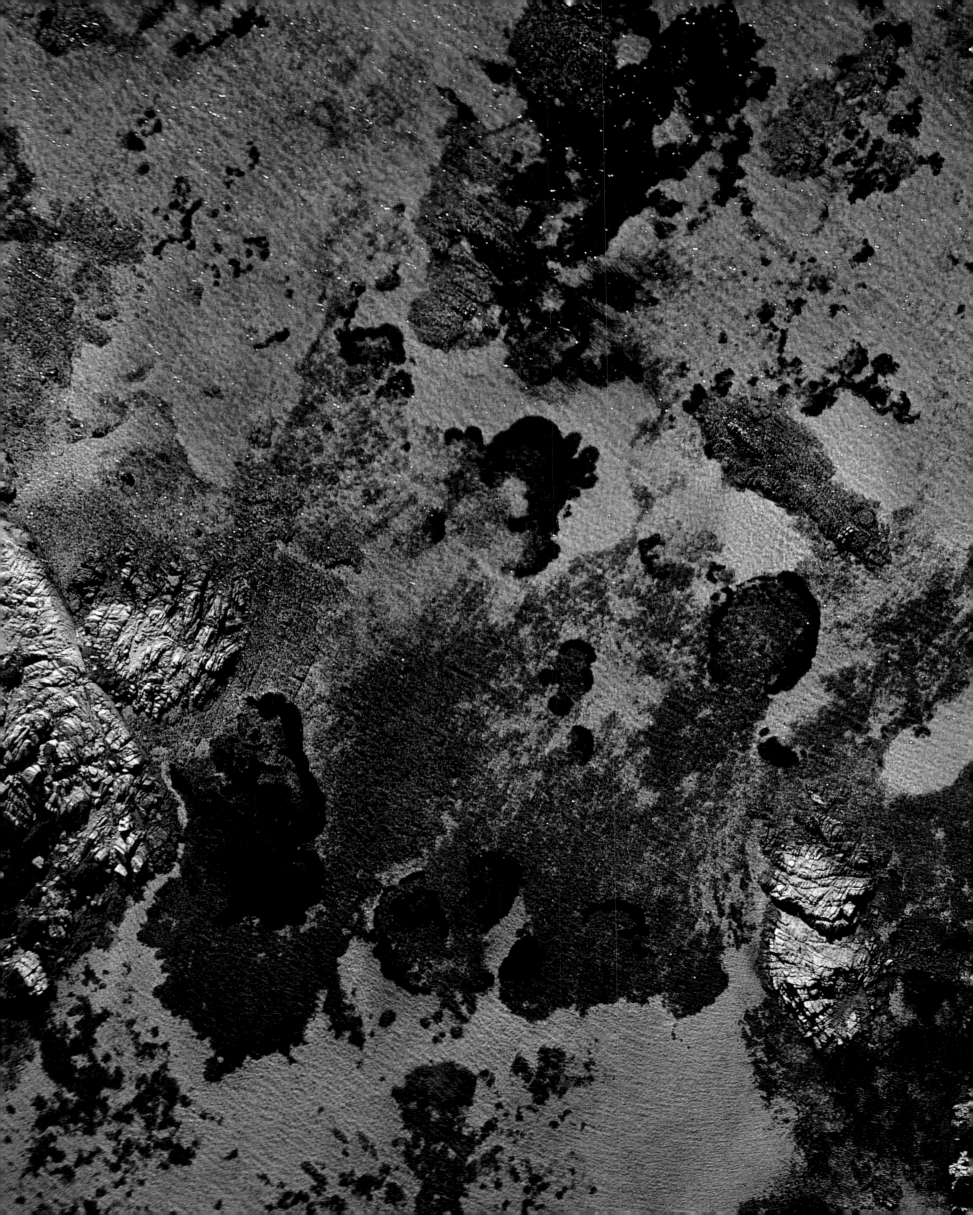

54-55 and 55 bottom The Maddalena Archipelago, in the Straits of Bonifacio, is famous for its clear waters. In addition to the main island it comprises the famous islands of Budelli, Caprera, Spargi and Santa Maria, and a myriad of islets and rocks.

54 bottom The pink of Budelli's famous pink beach is due to its particular sedimentary composition. In order to conserve it, the number of tourists permitted to visit the beach is now limited.

55 top Brightly colored wildflowers adorn the sand dunes of the coast north of Palau, near Porto Pollo. Sardinia's scenic northeastern coast is one of the best-known and most loved Mediterranean tourist destinations.

GLOBAL 200
THE MEDITERRANEAN BASIN

56 top Milos, in the Cyclades, is a volcanic island. Its beautiful beaches and rock formations, such as those at Sarakiniko, are world famous.

56 center The coast around Elinda on the island of Chios has many bays and inlets. The mild climate allows the growth of lush Mediterranean scrub vegetation.

56 bottom Patmos is a little island of the Dodecanese group in the Aegean Sea. The historic centre of Chorá, with the Monastery of Saint John the Theologian and the Cave of the Apocalypse, has been declared a UNESCO World Heritage Site.

56-57 Zakynthos is one of the many Greek islands of the Eastern Mediterranean. Lying west of the Peloponnesus, it is famous for its beautiful bays.

57 bottom Lindos on the island of Rhodes is not only famous for its crystal-clear sea, but also for its acropolis, mentioned by Homer.

GLOBAL 200

59 top Cala en Turqueta, on the southern coast of the island of Minorca, owes its name to the deep turquoise color of the sea and is famous for its beautiful beach.

59 center left The Croatia's Kornati Archipelago is located south of Zadar and is one of the wildest and most beautiful areas of Dalmatia's four national parks.

59 center right Malta not only comprises the main island of the same name, but also Gozo, Comino, Filfa and Cominotto, which has an area of just 0.1 square miles.

59 bottom The breathtaking Turkish coast in the area around Kafl is rugged and rocky and is lapped by the Eastern Mediterranean with its many hues of blue.

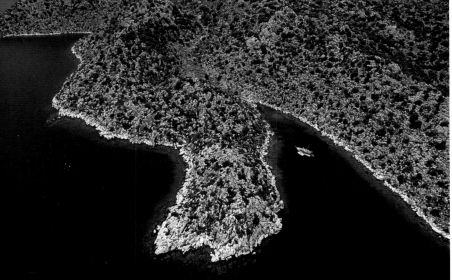

GLOBAL 200
THE MEDITERRANEAN BASIN

60-61, 61 top and center right The southern coast of the Mediterranean is often sandy, especially in Egypt, where it is strongly influenced by the Sahara desert that lies behind it and by the transportation of debris by the Nile.

61 center left The Mediterranean coast of Morocco in the mountainous Rif region is characterized by bare slopes that descend to the sea.

61 bottom The Libyan coast is still one of the most unspoiled of the entire Mediterranean, due to both the absence of tourist resorts and the low exploitation of fishery resources.

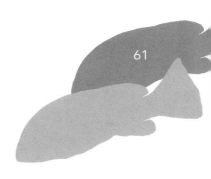

62 and 63 bottom left The Mediterranean has an incredibly rich variety of life forms, comparable in certain respects to those of the tropical seas, with red gorgonians, corals and thousands of invertebrates.

63 top left The rich fisheries of the Mediterranean are probably one of the reasons why many civilizations were able to thrive on its shores. Today this wealth is severely endangered due to overexploitation.

63 top right The dusky grouper lives throughout the Mediterranean, especially on rocky seafloors. It is brown with lighter markings and its diet consists principally of mollusks, crustaceans and other fish.

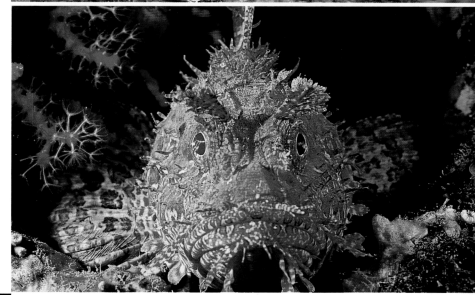

63 bottom right The bigscale scorpionfish is a typical Mediterranean species and can reach a length of 20 inches. It has three highly poisonous spines on its back that are capable of inflicting severe pain on predators or unwary fishermen.

THE RIFT VALLEY LAKES

"Unknowable, unimaginable, unbelievable.
And completely unforgettable."
Ernest Hemingway

The Rift Valley is a deep fracture, or rift, in the Earth's crust, which extends for around 4000 miles (6437 km) from Mozambique to Syria. It commences near Lake Malawi before forming two branches: the western rift, which includes Lakes Tanganyika and Albert, among others, and the eastern rift, with Lakes Magadi, Naivasha and Baringo. It continues with Lakes Turkana and Abaya before splitting into two further branches: the eastern one is marked by the Gulf of Aden, while the western one corresponds to the Red Sea. This deep rift, which crosses ten countries of East Africa, is characterized by intense volcanic phenomena, with rising magma, which has created impressive volcanic edifices, including Mount Kenya and Kilimanjaro.

The formation of the Rift Valley commenced 40 million years ago, between the Mesozoic and Cenozoic eras. As it did so, it caused volcanic events that created depressions and barriers, which gave rise to a series of very diverse lakes. Intense seismic and geothermal activity widened the rift and caused the lithosphere to thin dramatically, from its typical continental thickness of 62 miles (100 km) to a mere 12.5 miles (20 km). The lithosphere will probably rupture again in several million years' time, dividing East Africa from the rest of the continent and creating a new ocean (according to the theory of continental drift, the Atlantic Ocean formed in the same way when Africa and South America split apart). The width of the valley varies from 18.5 to 62 miles (30 to 100 km) , while its depth ranges from a few hundred to several thousand feet.

Lake Tana, on the northwest plateau of Ethiopia, forms the main reservoir for the Blue Nile, whose legendary sources were discovered by the Jesuit Pedro Páez in 1617, and subsequently explored by James Bruce, who visited the country in 1765. This ecoregion holds a series of records: Lake Tanganyika is the second deepest freshwater lake in the world (over 5200 ft/1585 m); Lake Victoria is the second largest in surface area; and Lake Malawi is also very deep (about 2600 ft./792 m) and is the third largest lake in Africa.

Sadly, Lake Victoria is the scene of one of the most serious ecological disasters of recent years. The introduction of an allochthonous species, the Nile perch (*Lates niloticus*), for commercial purposes has decimated the lake's fish population, constituted by around 500 species of cichlids (a family of freshwater fish), including many endemic ones, in the space of just a few years

In the eastern rift, volcanic soils and high rates of evaporation have allowed the creation of a group of soda lakes, such as Lake Natron in Tanzania. As already noted for Lake Victoria, The Rift Valley Lakes are renowned for their incredible diversity of cichlids which have lived in their waters for millions of years, evolving in complete isolation, in a sort of limbo or special niche that has allowed them to reproduce undisturbed. About 800 species of cichlids live in the lakes, but many more are still waiting to be discovered. One researcher recently caught 7000 fish representing 38 families in one 4300 sq. ft (400 sq. m) sampling area in Lake Tanganyika. Cichlids are also renowned for the care that they lavish on their young, which swim into their parent's mouth for protection in the face of danger. Copepods, ostracods, shrimps, crabs, and mollusks are represented by high numbers of endemic species.

Another characteristic inhabitant of these lakes is the flamingo, represented by two species: the greater flamingo (*Phoenicopterus roseus*) and the lesser flamingo (*Phoenicopterus minor*). They form colonies of millions of individuals on Lakes Natron, Nakuru and Bogoria, which offer ideal conditions for these species. The numerous birds that frequent the lakes throughout the year are joined by many European migratory species during the winter and include pelicans (*Pelecanus* spp.), the African skimmer (*Rynchops flavirostris*), the African jacana (*Actophilornis africana*), cormorants (*Phalacrocorax* spp.) and the Oriental darter (*Anhinga rufa*).

Many of these lake habitats are also home to large populations of hippopotamus (*Hippopotamus amphibius*) and Nile crocodile (*Crocodylus niloticus*), while the vegetation around the shores offers refuge to many typical African species. Lake Nakuru National Park, for example, is home to the waterbuck (*Kobus ellipsiprymnus*), Rothschild's giraffe (*Giraffa camelopardalis rothschildi*) and the white rhinoceros (*Ceratotherium simum*), which was introduced here in order to save it from extinction.

The Rift Valley is also very important from an anthropological point of view, for it is believed to be the cradle of the human species. Numerous bones of the hominid ancestors of modern man have been found in the region, including "Lucy," an australopithecine skeleton discovered by anthropologist Donald Johanson, and Laetoli footprints discovered by Richard and Mary Leakey. Indeed the sediment deposited in the Rift Valley, caused by the rapid erosion of the plateaus, is ideal for preserving fossil remains.

The introduction of exotic species, increased sedimentation from the deforestation of the slopes surrounding the lakes, water pollution from urban areas, and overfishing are the greatest threats to this ecoregion. The strain on the delicate ecosystems is compounded, often irreversibly, by demographic growth and the development of human settlements, which require ever more land and resources. However, a encouraging development in recent years is an international agreement aimed to prevent the introduction of invasive species to Lake Victorian and to encourage forms of development allowing the conservation of the aquatic resources and biodiversity of the lakes (Partnership Agreement on the Promotion of Sustainable Development in the Lake Victoria Basin).

WWF has been involved in nature conservation in East Africa since 1962, when it started to purchase the land that subsequently became Lake Nakuru National Park in Kenya. In 1986 the WWF Eastern Africa Regional Programme Office (WWF EARPO) was founded in Nairobi, with the task of developing conservation projects in Kenya, Tanzania, Uganda, Ethiopia, Rwanda and Burundi. Emblematic species of its conservation campaigns include the black rhinoceros and the mountain gorilla.

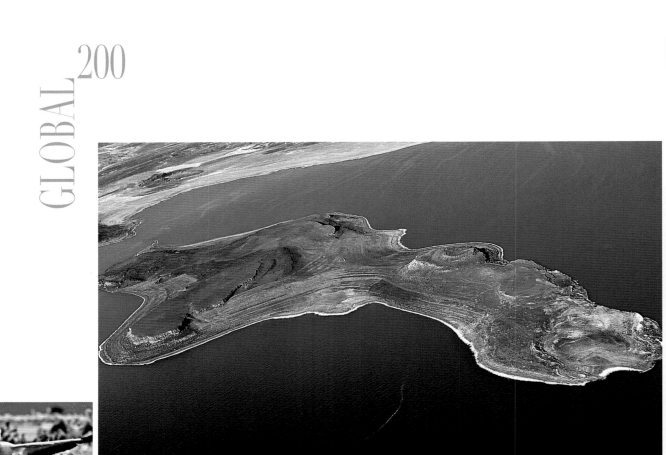

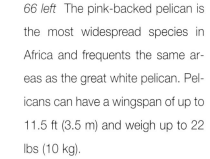

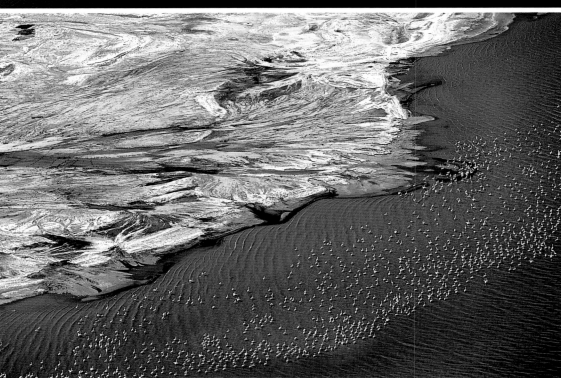

66 left The pink-backed pelican is the most widespread species in Africa and frequents the same areas as the great white pelican. Pelicans can have a wingspan of up to 11.5 ft (3.5 m) and weigh up to 22 lbs (10 kg).

66 top right Lake Turkana is home to large populations of crocodile and hippopotamus and numerous species of fish. The paleontologist Richard Leakey found many hominid fossils dating back 3 million years in this area.

66 bottom right Lake Bogoria, in Kenya, is one of the most northernmost Rift Valley lakes. Its origins are volcanic and it is characterized by geysers and hot-water springs.

66-67 The Rift Valley lakes are famous for being having one of the largest flamingo populations in the world. The lesser flamingo is the most numerous species and gathers in groups of thousands of birds.

67 bottom The Murchison, or Kabalega, Falls are situated in Uganda, about 20 miles (32 km) east of Lake Albert. The water forms a series of 3 cascades, each about 130 ft high (40 m), with a total drop of around 400 ft (122 m).

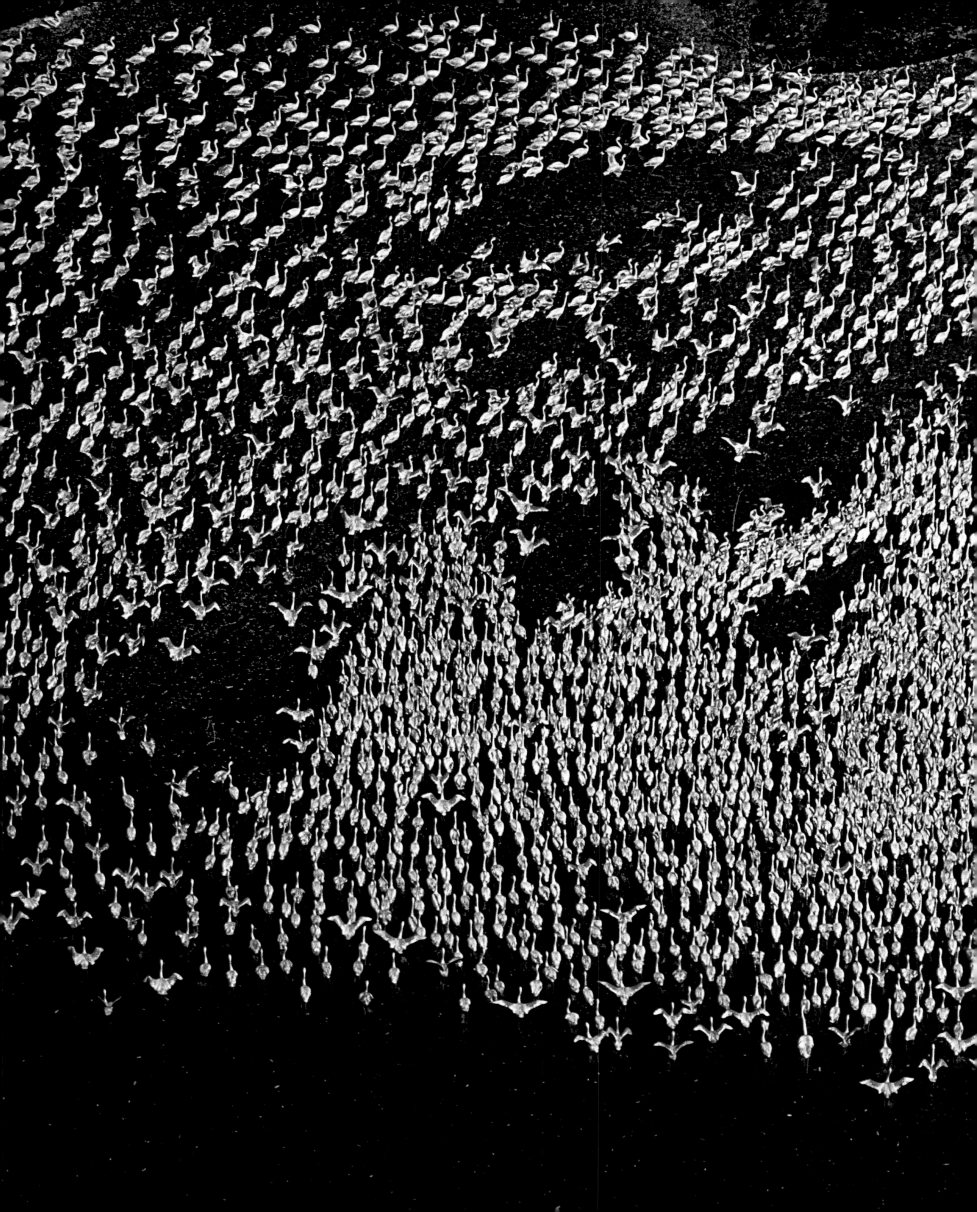

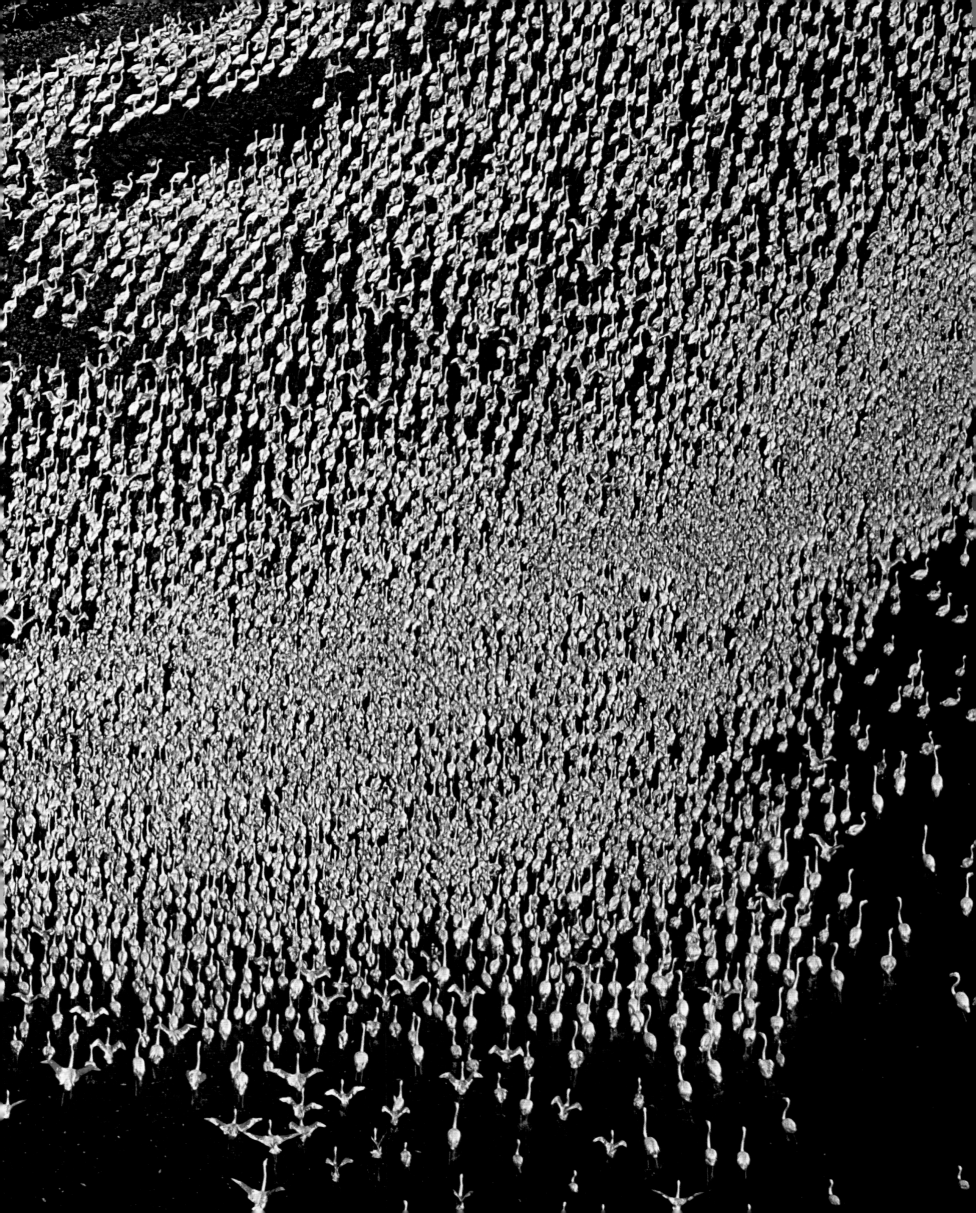

68-69 Millions of flamingoes choose Lake Natron in Tanzania as a safe refuge and nesting ground. Temperatures in the region often rise to over 120° F (48.8° C) in the dry season and the area is so remote and inhospitable to make the shores of this salt lake virtually free of predators.

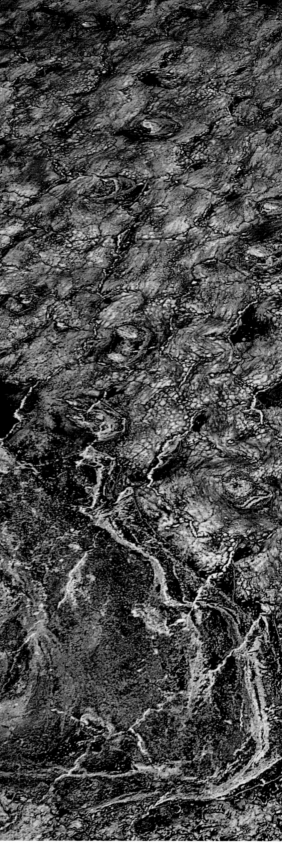

GLOBAL 200

70

70 and 71 High evaporation causes the water level of Lake Natron
to vary according to the season,
but the variation not generally exceed 10 ft (3 m).

72-73 The reddish-orange color of
Lake Natron is due to the pigment of
the extremophile bacteria that are one
of the few life forms other than flamingoes able to thrive in these waters.

74 top Unlike Lake Bogoria or Lake Natron, the lakes of the westernmost part of the Rift Valley, shared by several Central African countries, are important freshwater areas.

74 center The white rhinoceros was introduced to the Lake Nakuru National Park to save it from extinction in South Africa. Over the past few years the population has slowly grown, and there are now many projects for the reintroduction of the species to its original range.

74 bottom During courtship male zebras become very aggressive and competitive, biting rivals to defend their harems and according the same rough treatment to females during mating.

74-75 Hippopotamuses spend the entire day in the water to protect their sensitive skin from the sun, emerging at night to graze along the banks of the rivers and lakes.

75 bottom Nile crocodiles lie in wait for their prey to approach the water. These reptiles can reach over 16 ft (4.8 m) in length and weigh up to 1100 lbs (500 kg).

THE EAST AFRICAN ACACIA SAVANNAS

"There is a difference between wild animals living a natural life and famous buildings. Palaces can be rebuilt if they are destroyed in wartime, but once the wild animals of the Serengeti are exterminated no power on earth can bring them back."
Bernhard Grzimek, Serengeti Shall Not Die

The savanna ecosystem covers a huge area in Africa, stretching from the southern boundaries of the Sahara to the equatorial region. It extends for over 220,000 sq. miles (570,000 sq. km) in Ethiopia, Kenya, Sudan, Tanzania, and Uganda.

In this ecoregion Nature still rules supreme, with her fascinating rhythms and relentless lifecycles. Here we can see a fallen gazelle and a lion bounding away from it after feeding, or the motionless carcass of a zebra and a vulture vibrating with life. Here we can be immersed in a silence that shouts and whispers, in a sleeping world that gasps, and feel the ferment of a life that is still unfettered.

The East Africa acacia savannas ecoregion is a huge, evocative area characterized by typical savanna vegetation. The savanna is a type of grassland with fast-growing grasses and shrubs and scattered trees, particularly acacias (*Acacia* spp.). The savannas separate the tropical forest region from the arid and desert areas and constitute one of the ecosystems with the highest biodiversity on Earth, where biological processes, such as the migration of large mammals, have been continuing since time immemorial.

The varying levels of precipitation in the region have led to the development of different types of savanna: wet savanna in areas with an average rainfall exceeding 47 inches (120 cm); dry savanna with an average rainfall of 20-43 inches (50-110 cm), and thorny savanna with less than 20 inches (50 cm). The first two types share an important characteristic: precipitation is concentrated in just a few months each year, known as the rainy season.

The climate is characterized by the alternation of periods of drought and wet monsoon months. The amount and periodic frequency of rainfall regulate the lifecycles of thousands of species. Temperatures are fairly mild throughout the year.

The savanna is perhaps one of the world's best-known landscapes. We are familiar with mammals such as lions, elephants and giraffes from our earliest years, and these animals often become the focus of our games and stories. The sight of great herds that migrate hundreds of miles in the search for green pastures, or big cats silently and regally prowling their territory fire our imagination and fuel our curiosity, possibly because this is also the land in which the origins of our own species lie. Around two million years ago Australopithecus left the forests, which were thinning due to climate change, and took to the savannas, where an upright stance, and consequent greater height, were an advantage for sighting potential predators. This marked the start of the long evolutionary journey that culminated in the emergence of modern man (*Homo sapiens sapiens*).

One of the most representative areas of the African savanna is the huge upland expanse that extends between Tanzania and Kenya and includes the Masai Mara and Serengeti ("Great Plain" in Swahili) reserves, which cover an area of almost 10,000 sq. miles (25,900 sq. km).

Visitors are immediately struck by the unique smells, sounds and colors of these places: over a million plains zebra (*Equus quagga*) and blue wildebeest (*Connochaetes taurinus*) move across the savanna, while Grant's and Thomson's gazelles (*Gazella granti* and *Gazella thomsonii*) leap high among the tall grass, trying to elude predators such as lions, cheetahs and hyenas. However, the stars of the show are the great carnivores. The lion (*Panthera leo*) is probably the most famous of the big cats and the Serengeti has a current estimated population of 2500-3000 individuals. This species is also one of the most extensively studied, commencing with the research commenced in the 1960s by George Schaller.

The most numerous predator, however, is the spotted hyena (*Crocuta crocuta*), with a population of around 7000. The other large carnivores are the leopard (*Panthera pardus*), the cheetah (*Acinonyx jubatus*) and the seriously endangered African wild dog (*Lycaon pictus*), which is a symbol of these rolling plains dotted here and there with small granite outcrops known as kopjes.

The northernmost areas in particular are home to large herds of African elephant (*Loxodonta africana*), which are unfortunately still persecuted by poachers for their ivory tusks. The black rhinoceros (*Diceros bicornis*) often suffers the same fate, as it is systematically slaughtered for its horn. There are many species of antelopes, from the little dik-dik (*Madoqua* spp.) to the large eland (*Taurotragus oryx*).

Visitors to the savanna cannot fail to be enchanted by the elegant and solemn movements of the giraffe (*Giraffa camelopardalis*) and the "moving clouds" formed by the large herds of African buffalo (*Syncerus caffer*).

78 The leopard stalks its prey at dawn or dusk, following habitual paths that allow it to patrol its territory and keep other leopards at bay.

79 The Serengeti is home to over 2500 lions. Although they are deadly predators, these animals are very attentive parents, particularly the females, who often need to defend their cubs from the attacks of adult males.

Although many large areas of the East African Acacia Savannas are protected, the region nonetheless suffers from a series of problems associated with the increase in local population and tourism. Poaching still continues in many protected areas, seriously endangering species such as the black rhinoceros, the African elephant and many antelopes. The increase in human population is unfortunately accompanied by land use conflicts generated by grazing, agriculture and the expansion of settlements. These changes are reflected in increasingly frequent attacks on the local people by lions, due to the increase in the population of both species, compounded by the fact that much of the lions' wild prey has now disappeared. These are everyday problems for the native populations, the Maasai, divided into many tribes with a shared language and customs.

Assuring the conservation of such a complex ecosystem is no easy task, and indeed over 40 years ago the father-and-son team of naturalists Bernhard and Michael Grzimek launched an appeal in their book entitled *Serengeti Shall Not Die*.

While the East African savanna is one of the most extensively studied ecosystems in the world and the subject of continuous research since the early 1950s, paradoxically many of the problems associated with the dwindling of its animal species still remain unsolved. The more we learn about ecosystems, the more we realize how little we are able to intervene once certain balances have been upset. Decades of study in the Serengeti have revealed the complex and synergetic relationships between predators and prey, between the migratory herbivores and the renewal of the grasslands, and between the growth of the grass and the rain, all of which are maintained by a dynamic but ever-changing equilibrium.

WWF's East Africa Regional Program Office (EARPO) develops projects for the conservation of the species and habitats and has contributed to the establishment and management of many national parks, and to the direct protection of numerous charismatic species, including the black rhinoceros and the African elephant.

80-81 Giraffes live mainly in the tree savanna, feeding on acacia leaves. However, they can often be seen on the open grass-lands, moving in pairs or small groups.

80 bottom Young leopards scan the savanna in search of prey: a Thomson's gazelle, a zebra, a warthog or an impala. The cubs re-main with their mother until the age of 13-20 months.

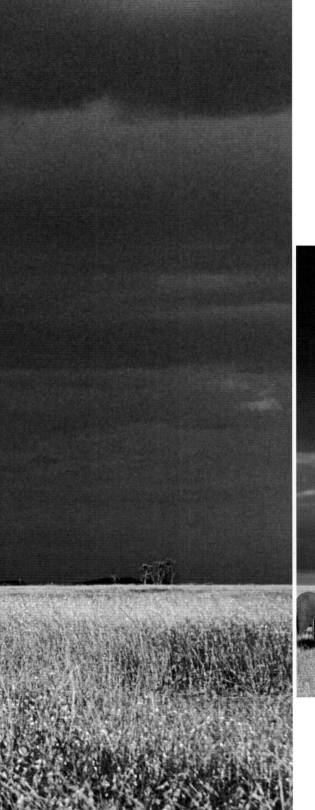

THE EAST AFRICAN ACACIA SAVANNAS

81 top The acacia scrub is undoubtedly the most characteristic and ubiquitous landscape of the African savanna. The acacia is a very old genus and one of the main foods of the great African herbivores.

81 bottom Elephants form family groups composed of females, young males and calves. They have no natural predators, for the calves are the only vulnerable members of the herd and are effectively protected by the older animals.

82-83 The leopard is a solitary animal. It spends the day resting between the branches of a tree to avoid the heat and other predators, becoming active at night, when it stalks its prey.

83 top left The African plains are crossed by great rivers, such as the Mara and the Grumeti. These are precious areas, as water is essential for life, and their banks are lined with splendid riparian forests.

83 center left According to a legend, the baobab was planted upside down, with its roots in the air! The tree is a symbol of Africa, and its intertwining branches offer refuge to a number of animal species.

83 bottom left Following the rainy season, the African savanna is covered with a luxuriant carpet of grass, which attracts millions of wildebeest, zebras and gazelles.

83 top right The impala is the favorite prey of the leopard, but its agility seems to flaunt the fact that a healthy individual is very difficult to capture!

83 bottom right The black rhinoceros has a prehensile upper lip that it uses to grasp leaves and twigs when feeding.

83

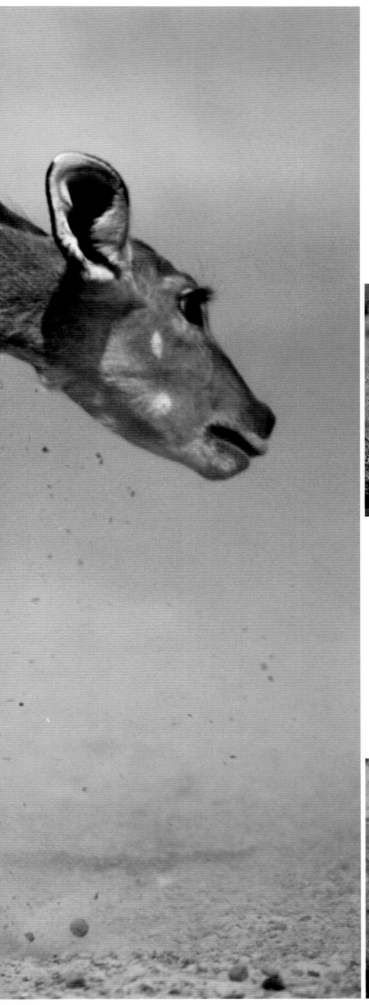

84 and 85 Once the lioness has isolated her prey, she tries to fell it by biting it on the back and neck with her sharp canines. A lioness hunting alone will generally kill a zebra or a kudu, although a group may fell a buffalo. Lions and lionesses develop genuine hunting strategies, which are not based merely on instinct. Indeed, the methods used for this essential but arduous activity vary substantially from region to region, from pride to pride and according to type of prey.

GLOBAL 200

86 and 87 The great African plains are the scene of the annual migration of the wildebeest, one of the wonders of nature, in which hundreds of thousands of these animals move eastwards from the Serengeti, crossing the Mara and Grumeti rivers. They are awaited by enormous Nile crocodiles, which attack those that linger too long near the water or during the crossing. At the end of the wet season, when the plains are impoverished, the wildebeests head west and north, to the transitional areas where they breed.

88-89 Are zebras white with black stripes or black with white stripes? The optical effect depends on the width of the stripes. The extraordinary thing is that no two zebras are exactly alike, for their striped patterns vary from one individual to another.

THE CONGO BASIN

"We simply need that wild country available to us....
For it can be a means of reassuring ourselves
of our sanity as creatures, a part
of the geography of hope."
Wallace Stegner

The rainforests of the Congo River in Central Africa extend uninterruptedly as far as the eye can see across the boundaries of five nations: Cameroon, Gabon, the Republic of Congo, the Democratic Republic of Congo and the Central African Republic. This ecoregion covers an area of about 600,000 sq. miles (1.55 million sq. km), making it second in size only to that the Amazon. A third of the entire area is a wilderness still waiting to be explored, much of it at an altitude of 1000-2500 ft (305-762 m), with an average annual rainfall of 55-80 inches (140-200 cm).

Imagine a moist shady habitat, with muffled, dull, elusive sounds, lush vegetation and silently throbbing life. And men who move rapidly through these contorted and claustrophobic spaces, illuminated by the dappled sunlight that penetrates the dense foliage. You are imagining the forest of the Congo basin and its inhabitants, the BaAka, BaKa and BaKola pygmies. These people are a unique presence in an area in which the human population density is e and consider the forest a source of shelter, food and medicine as well as culture and spiritual life.

Rainforest, concentrated in the northern part of the country in particular, accounts for most of this ecosystem and covers such a vast area as to make it the second largest forest in the world, following the Amazonian rainforest. Considering the fact that it is home to 35 percent of the world's biodiversity and that the entire country has been defined as a "geological scandal" due to its extraordinary wealth of mineral and natural resources, it comes as a rude shock to learn that the gross domestic product of the Democratic Republic of Congo is among the lowest in the world, that 20 percent of children do not reach the age of five and that 16 percent of those who do risk dying of hunger. It is as though there has been a short circuit between nature and the country's inhabitants, a sort of irreversible power failure that has interrupted all connections.

Congo is an incandescent land, which knows no peace. Its rich gold and diamond mines and the presence of many other minerals, such as copper, zinc, tin, cobalt, uranium and, most recently, coltan (used by the aerospace, telecommunications and IT industries), have long constituted a double-edged weapon that has attracted not only marauders and adventurers to the region, but also the colonial powers in the past. Today the same resources are at the center of bloody civil wars characterized by ethnic hostilities for the control and exploitation of the area. In addition to the predictable and tragic consequences in terms of human lives, these conflicts have also had a negative impact on the ecosystem, further aggravating the living conditions of the population.

Felling of the rainforest by poachers constitutes a great threat to the entire ecosystem, because the presence of vegetation is the most important factor to ensure the return of the rains. Indeed, 77 percent of rainfall in the Congo Basin is generated by the transpiration of the plants of the region, while just 23 percent reaches the region from the distant oceans, transported by the winds. If deforestation continues, the loss of surface water will increasingly outstrip its replacement by condensation and infiltration. The soil will thus be subject to greater erosion, gradually becoming sterile. Without the transpiration of the plants, the heavy tropical rainfall will disappear. The destruction of the forests marks the beginning of the end and the first step in the process of transformation from moist area to arid area.

There are two types of rainforest in this region: tropical and subtropical, with palms, lianas and luxuriant creepers. The area is recognized as one of the regions of greatest biodiversity in the world, despite remaining substantially unknown. The inhabitants of the Congo rainforest include 1000 species of birds and 400 species of mammals (many of which are endemic), these two figures are the highest for the whole of Africa. The region is home to populations of gorillas, chimpanzees, bonobos and mandrills, a wide array of ruminants and rodents, and forest elephants (*Loxodonta africana cyclotis*). It is also the habitat of the okapi (*Okapia johnstoni*), a distant relative of the giraffe, which has adapted to life in the thick forest vegetation rather than on the savanna. The okapi is an unusual animal, with nocturnal, shy and solitary habits, which perfectly symbolizes the spirit of this ecosystem. It resembles a cross between a giraffe and a zebra, with a dark body and striped legs. Despite its nocturnal habits, it is also active during the day in the quietest areas of the forest. It marks the area in which it lives with urine and a liquid secreted by scent glands on each foot. This behavior is typical of territorial animals, which mark and constantly defend their domain.

The region also boasts an extraordinary variety of birds and the Odzala National Park alone, which covers an area of 1100 sq. miles (2850 sq. km), is home to 442 different species. However, this number is destined to rise, as new species, such as the forest robin (*Stiphornis sanghensis*), continue to be discovered. Multicolored frogs, gray and crested chameleons and poisonous snakes are easily spotted, but the Odzala National Park conceals a throbbing and mysterious "dark heart" of unspoiled and not yet completely explored nature. Forest elephants, imposing lowland gorillas, small herds of sitatungas, buffaloes, red river hogs, cattle egrets, yellow-billed oxpeckers and gray parrots: a teeming multitude of wildlife that we cannot afford to risk losing.

The forest is threatened by the opening of new roads, poaching, illegal deforestation and timber concessions, all of which contribute to reducing its biodiversity. Many forest animals, such as the leopard, the golden cat and the crowned hawk-eagle are hunted because they compete for food with the local popu-

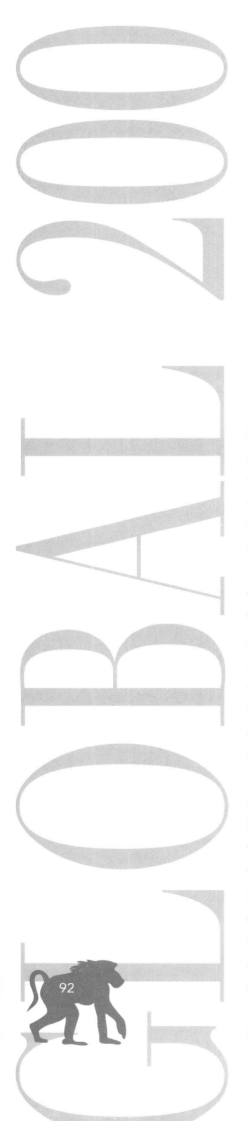

93 The Odzala National Park in the Democratic Republic of Congo was founded in 1940 and has an area of 425 sq. miles (1100 sq. km). It is largely covered by rainforest and is home to a great variety of plant and animal species.

lations. Other species, such as gorillas, elephants, crocodiles, lizards and gray parrots are killed as trophies, fetishes and goods for bartering. This is compounded by the damage caused by the civil war. Minerals, timber and wild game have been the main focus of interest of the warring factions and the area has often been exploited to the detriment of the local populations. Furthermore, the mass movements of refugees and their presence in refugee camps and even in parks and reserves have had a negative impact on the natural resources.

Despite this dramatic backdrop, WWF has been active in North Kivu since 1988, where it has launched the Virunga Environmental Programme (PEVi) with the support of the Istitut Congolais pour la Conservation de la Nature (ICCN), which has played a vital role in reducing the damage caused by the presence of refugees in the area. This is exemplified by the Virunga National Park, which is exceptionally important, due not only to its size (3100 sq. miles/8030 sq. km) and the extraordinary number of animal and plant species that it protects, but also because it is the only natural habitat of the mountain gorilla. During the Congo's recent conflicts, the fleeing population invaded the park. Consequently, a buffer area was created around its perimeter, whose resources were made available for sustainable use in order to prevent the refugees from drawing on those of the actual park, thereby endangering the lives of many animals.

WWF is also actively engaged in forestry conservation. Each year in the Congo Basin 5800 sq. miles (15,000 sq. km) of rainforest are destroyed – an area a third of the size of Switzerland. WWF launched the battle against illegal deforestation with the implementation of a highly successful reforestation scheme within the Virunga Environmental Programme. Over 5 million trees have been planted since the scheme was started. Furthermore, three of Cameroon's leading logging companies have committed themselves to responsible forest management, following the strict directives of the Forest Stewardship Council (FSC) that ensure sustainable use. One of the main objectives of the Virunga Environmental Programme is to establish strong bonds with the local communities. In order to achieve this goal programs of agricultural development and environmental education have been drawn up and material aid has been given for the reconstruction of basic social infrastructures.

Today the country is slowly returning to conditions of peace, making it the ideal time to ensure that its huge wealth finally manages to benefit its people.

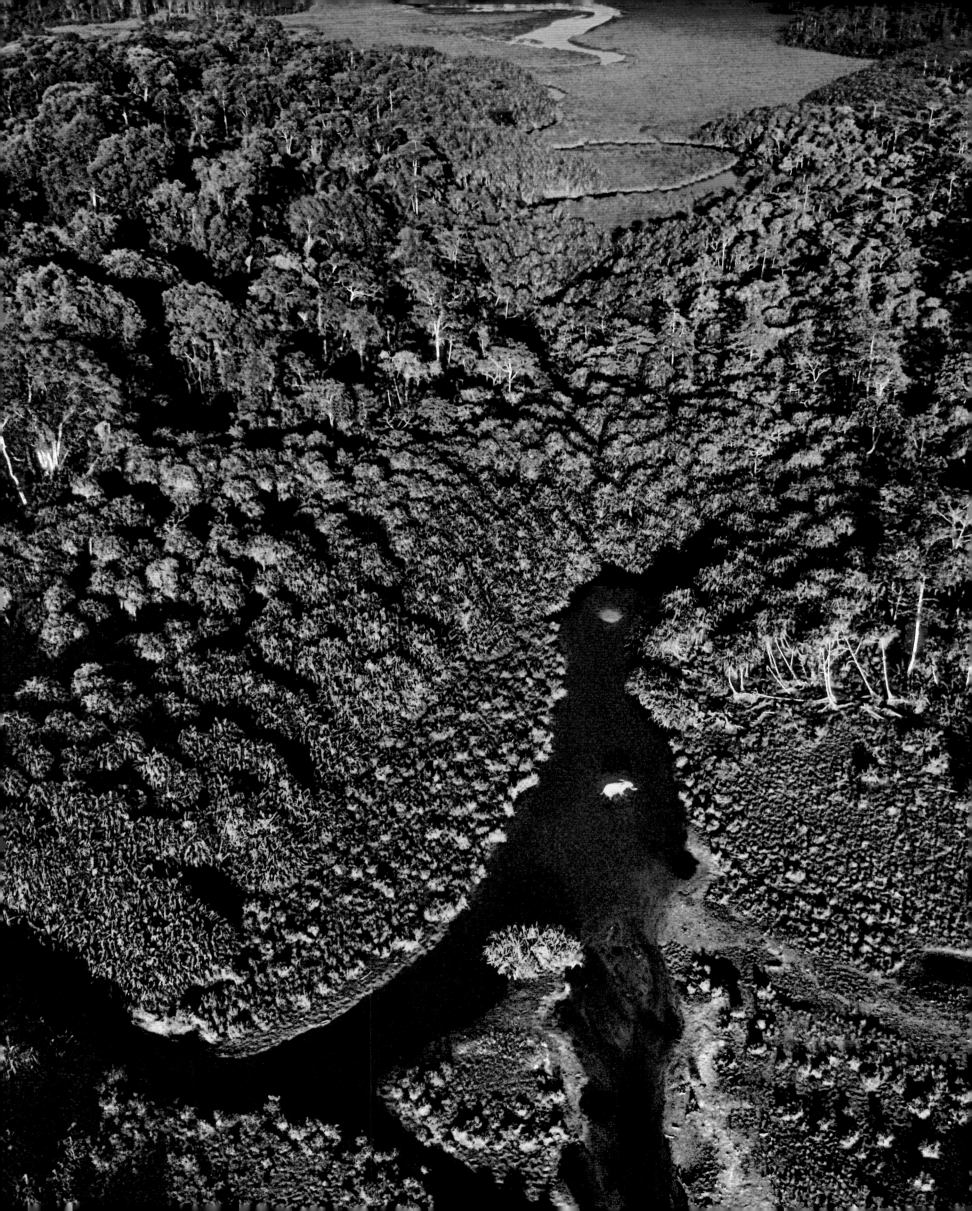

94 top The eyes, ears and nostrils of crocodiles (in this case a dwarf crocodile) are located on top of their heads, allowing them to lie in wait below the surface of the water to ambush their prey.

94 center left The okapi was not discovered until the early 20th century and is the closest relative of the giraffe. It has a very flexible blue tongue, which it uses to grasp leaves and shoots.

94 center right The hippopotamus is widespread throughout sub-Saharan Africa as far as South Africa. Despite its lazy appearance, it is very aggressive and territorial, and undoubtedly the most dangerous African wild animal.

94 bottom and 95 bottom Where the tropical forest is crossed by rivers, the dense vegetation is broken and many species gather in these areas that offer the necessary resources for life. The rivers are also often the only routes of access to the forest for man.

94-95 African forest elephants live in small family groups of 3-6 individuals and are typical animals of the dense woodlands, where they move with ease. The elephant is the largest terrestrial mammal and can consume up to 650 lbs (295 kg) of food and 20 gallons of water a day.

96-97 Much of the Congo basin, one of the Earth's green lungs, was once impenetrable. Today this habitat has been greatly reduced by logging, farming and oil drilling.

98 top   The mandrill lives in the forests of the Congo basin. Males do not acquire their distinctive coloring until reaching sexual maturity, at the age of 5-6 years. They are very long-lived, and have been known to survive up to 46 years in captivity.

98 top center   The Odzala National Park is one of the protected areas in which the lowland gorilla breeds. Role-playing is of utmost importance among these primates for learning.

98 bottom center   Young chimpanzees are dependent on their parents for many years. The relationship established with their mother will subsequently allow them to move surely in the forest.

98 *bottom* Baboons are certainly not among the leopard's easiest prey, especially when in troops. However, even isolated individuals are capable of defending themselves fiercely with their well-developed canines.

98-99 The lowland gorilla inhabits the rainforests of the Congo River ecoregion. The little that remains of the natural habitat necessary for the survival of the species is now threatened by deforestation.

100 top and 100-101 Adult male gorillas spend much time playing with the young members of the group. The behavior and gestures of these primates during play closely resemble those of humans.

100 bottom The Congo basin is home to the Western lowland gorilla and the Cross River gorilla, while farther east the mountain gorilla and Eastern lowland gorilla can be found. Male gorillas are the largest primates and have a distinctive patch of silver hair on their back, which forms with age.

THE CAPE REGION

"I have walked that long road to freedom.
I have tried not to falter; I have made missteps along the way.
But I have discovered the secret that after climbing a great hill,
one only finds that there are many more hills to climb."
Nelson Mandela

South Africa is bordered by Namibia, Botswana and Zimbabwe to the north and Mozambique and Swaziland to the northeast, while Lesotho is an independent enclave. Its coasts are lapped by the Atlantic and Indian Oceans. The Cape region occupies the southern tip of Africa, extending for about 125 miles (200 km) north of Cape Town. The climate of the region is extremely variable, with annual rainfall ranging from 8 to over 120 inches (from 20 to over 305 cm). Average temperatures are between 54 and 66° F (12 and 19° C), but snow is not unusual on the mountains in the winter. The flora of this area is extremely rich and varied, constituting one of the world's "floral kingdoms," despite occupying an area of just 35,000 sq. miles (90,650 sq. km).

This southern tip of Africa is a unique corner of land, whose flora and fauna is completely different from that of the rest of the area, and which shares with California, a stretch of the Chilean coast and southwestern Australia climatic and natural characteristics very similar to those of the Mediterranean region. However, the Cape Region is an unpredictable area that is difficult to classify. The fine sandy cove extending between the granite rocks of Boulders Beach, on the east coast of the Cape Peninsula, offers the evocative spectacle of penguins on the beach, mingling with the tourists and diving off rocks into the icy water. In areas such as the Cape Peninsula Park visitors may find themselves "attacked" by monkeys that jump onto moving cars, and crossing landscapes characterized by low scrubland with a distinctly Mediterranean feel. Finally, after having rounded a rocky spur, they will find themselves high above the sea, buffeted by a chill, roaring wind, while two oceans – a warm, tranquil one and a cold, raging one – meet beneath their feet, creating surges and foam as they hurl themselves against the rocks. Plants of familiar forms and colors inhabit a thoroughly African land, where wealth and beauty have an older and bitterer flavor, and where not only privileges but also fundamental human rights have been attained at an exceptionally high price, following violent clashes and social tensions.

Consisting predominantly of a plateau, the territory is characterized by sudden drops and slopes that make it incline irregularly toward the sea. The flora is highly varied because it is closely associated with the rainfall, which differs from area to area and constitutes one of South Africa's principal resources. The rains feed underground springs and rivers, which supply water for domestic, agricultural and industrial use. They regenerate the soil, allowing the growth of trees and plants and creating ponds and lakes, which in turn offer vital resources. In many areas of the country the beginning of the rainy season is hailed as the most important event of the year.

The flora is more homogeneous in character. The shrubland vegetation of the entire coastal area of Western Cape Province, known as the Cape floral kingdom, is constituted by Mediterranean scrub, dominated by evergreen sclerophyll species, known locally as *fynbos*. The word *fynbos* (Afrikaans for "fine bush") refers to the fine, needle-like leaves of many of the plants of the region. The flowering of the *fynbos*, which reaches the height of its splendor during the austral spring, is an exceptional sight. This ecosystem boasts a very rich flora with a high degree of plant endemism: 68 percent of the 8600 species are autochthonous. They belong to many families, including the Asteraceae, Ericaceae, Leguminosae, Iridaceae and Restionaceae with several dominant genera, such as Protea, Erica, Senecio, Leucospermum and Restio.

There are also numerous species of proteas. As suggested by their name – derived from Proteus, the Greek sea god who could change his shape at will – they are chameleonic plants whose original artichoke-like appearance is transformed into an explosion of breathtaking beauty when in flower. Once they have reached maturity their huge colorful blooms are irresistible magnets for pollinating birds. One of the most important members of the family is the king protea, which is the national flower of South Africa. Heaths are generally smaller, with many tubular flowers and needlelike leaves, while, restios, almost all of which are endemic, are similar to grass and grow in wetter areas.

However, this highly varied flora is not matched by an equally rich array of fauna, due to the low level of nutrients contained in the plants and also because many of them contain toxic, indigestible or unappetizing substances for herbivores, such as tannins. The *fynbos* community is nonetheless home to a wide variety – albeit with a low density – of endemic vertebrates, including 9 species of mammals, 6 species of birds, 19 species of freshwater fish, 9 species of frogs and toads and about 20 species of reptiles.

The sunbirds, which resemble the American hummingbirds in appearance, but belong to a different family, are a typical species of the region. They play a vital role in the ecosystem as pollinators. They hover above the flowers and suck their nectar, dusting their bodies with pollen in the process, which they then transport to other flowers, involuntarily pollinating them. Their role is so important that several plants have "lengthened" their corollas, changing their shape in order to make them accessible to the beaks of these birds alone, and not to insects. This preference is due to the fact that birds are safer emissaries as they can cover considerable distances even in bad weather conditions, increasing the plant's chances of fertilization.

105 At 16-23 ft (4.8 to 7 m) long, the white shark is the largest known predator. It rarely approaches the coast and, as it is not a specialized hunter, its diet and prey vary according to the area in which it lives.

106-107 The humpback whale may reach a length of over 50 ft (15.2 m) and weigh up to 45 tons. This species is a seasonal migrant, moving from its summer feeding grounds around the poles to its warm tropical breeding grounds in winter.

Endemic mammals include two species of mole rat (*Cryptomys* spp.) – a strange burrowing rodent that digs extensive tunnel systems – and many other small rodents, such as the Cape spiny mouse (*Acomys subspinosus*) and the African marsh rat (*Dasymys incomtus*). The large herbivores that still inhabit the area include the rare Cape mountain zebra (*Equus zebra zebra*), an endemic subspecies; the elusive klipspringer (*Oreotragus oreotragus*); a large antelope known as the bontebok (*Damaliscus pygargus pygargus*); and the Cape grysbok (*Raphicerus melanotis*), a small scrubland antelope.

As in all Mediterranean-type habitats, fire plays an important role in controlling the evolutionary processes. For example, many seeds of the plants of the *fynbos* germinate only after exposure to the intense heat caused by a fire. Every four to six years a large amount of organic plant material accumulates, which acts as a "fuel tank" for natural fires. This results in spontaneous combustion with cycles of 6 to 30 years.

This was one of the first ecoregions to have been targeted by conservation projects. WWF has already launched and is currently implementing a Conservation Plan with the participation of the most important authorities and organizations of the area. The involvement of the parks and nature reserves of the area is fundamental. They include the Bontebok National Park, founded to save the last remaining bonteboks; the West Coast National Park, with its important colonies of penguins and other seabirds; the spectacular Cape of Good Hope Nature Reserve; and the Pilanesberg National Park, one of the most important reserves, which covers an area of 214 sq. miles (554 sq. km). The area facing the greatest threat is the fertile Springbok Flats plain, where it is estimated that 60 percent of land has been converted to agricultural use, while only 1 prcent has been preserved in the Nylsvlei Nature Reserve.

South Africa also belongs to a group of African countries in which WWF and the TRAFFIC (Trade Records Analysis of Flora and Fauna in Commerce) project monitor trade in order to prevent the illegal commerce of animal and plant species, and has also been the focus of a program of economic reform to promote sustainable development.

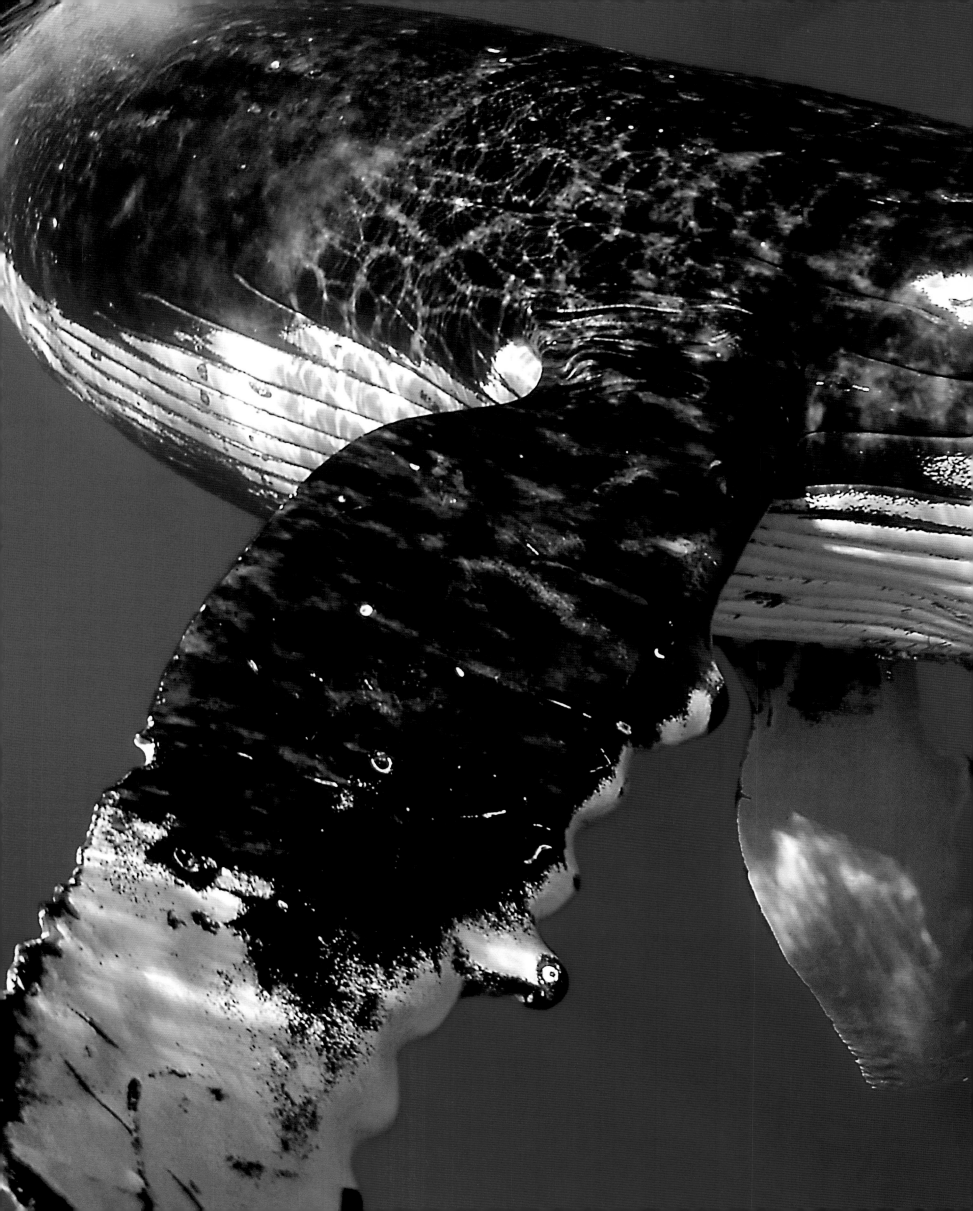

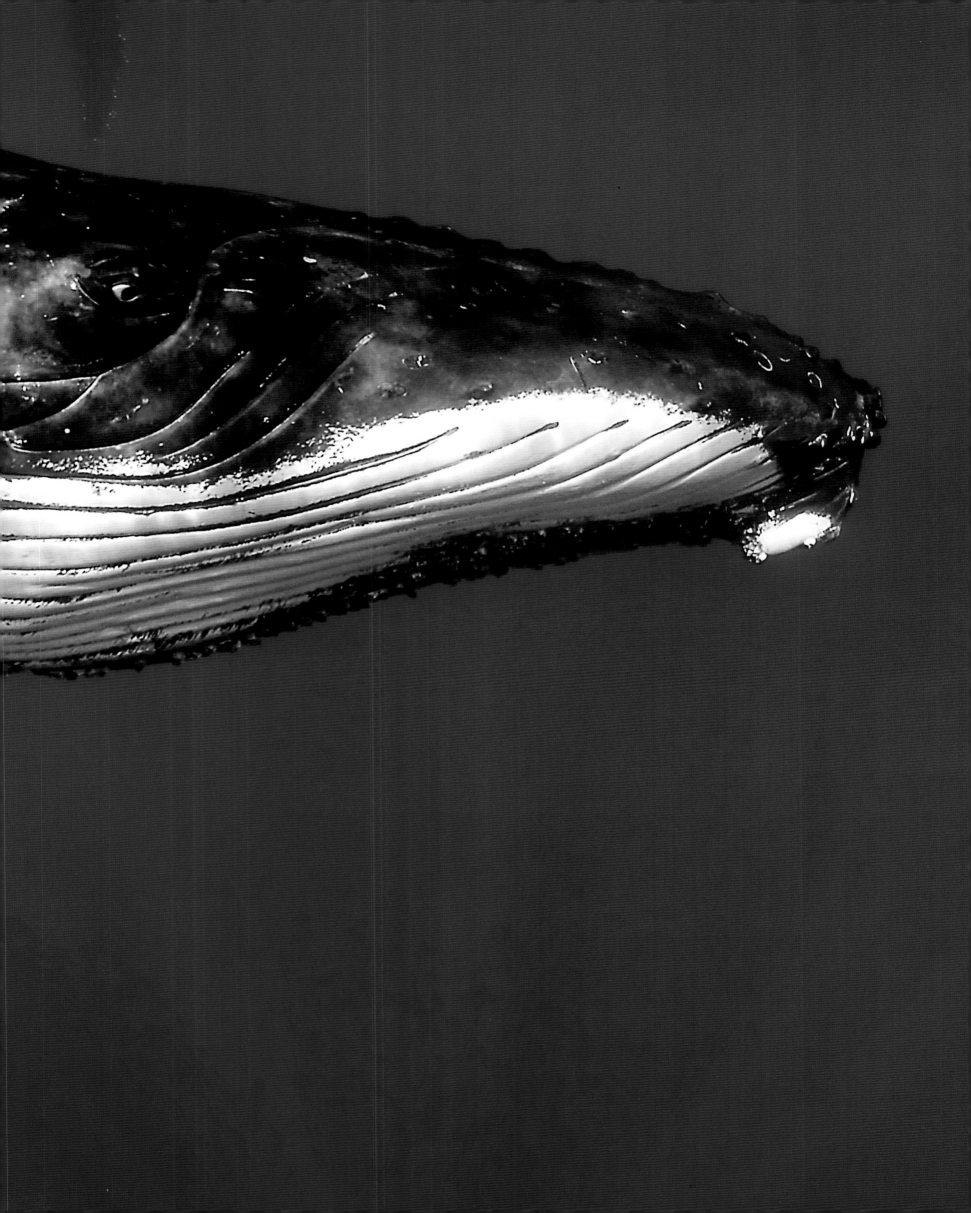

109 top and center The Cape Peninsula, in Western Cape Province, extends from Cape Town to the Cape of Good Hope. Its coasts are pummeled by the powerful ocean breakers to the west and lapped by the calmer waters of False Bay to the east.

109 bottom South Africa's beaches often offer the evocative sight of groups of penguins waddling over the sand or swimming in the sea. The African penguin is the only species of penguin found on the continent. Its distribution coincides with the beaches suitable for nesting and the cold and fish-rich Benguela current of the South Atlantic.

108-109 The scrub vegetation of the coastal strip of the Western Cape is known as *fynbos* ("fine bush"). The particular climate of the area has given rise to this form of vegetation that is very similar to the Mediterranean scrub, despite being constituted largely by endemic South African species.

110-111 The quiver tree or Kokerboom (*Aloe dichotoma*) is a solitary tree with a thick trunk and repeatedly forked branches that grows in the dry, stony regions of Namibia and the Northern Cape Province of South Africa.

111 top left The Garden Route is a stretch of the southern coast of South Africa with a Mediterranean climate, where the *fynbos* and the temperate forest form an exceptionally beautiful landscape.

111 bottom left An expanse of *Aster-aceae* tinges the grassland as far as the eye can see. The richness of the flora of the Cape Province is famous through-out the world, with hundreds of species for each genus.

111 top right The blesbok (*Damaliscus pygargus phillipsi*) can be recognized by its curved horns, brown body and white stripe on its face. Although the species is seriously endangered, the population is currently increasing slightly, due to con-siderable conservation efforts.

111 bottom right Two female leopards fighting in the Mala Mala Game Re-serve, adjoining the Kruger National Park.

THE MADAGASCAR FORESTS and SHRUBLANDS

"Le vent du soir se lève;
la lune commence à briller au travers
des arbres de la montagne.
Allez, et préparez le repas."
Evariste De Parny

Madagascar is an island nation in the Indian Ocean, off the southeast coast of Africa, 250 miles (400 km) from Mozambique. It is 1000 miles (1610 km) long and 350 miles (563 km) wide.

Imagine being immersed in a red landscape and walking on iron-rich laterite soil the color of blood. Imagine spits of white land that slope gently into the sea, crystal-clear waters and a young and friendly population, composed of 18 different ethnic groups, half of whom are under 14 years old. We are imagining Madagascar, the fourth largest island in the world.

Madagascar is an autonomous microcosm that remained a world unto itself, completed isolated from the rest of the Earth's landmasses, for around 165 million years. This allowed evolution to follow paths that it did not explore elsewhere, to the extent that almost all (90 percent) of the island's plant and animal species, including 12,000 species of flowers and almost all the species of palms, are not found anywhere else in the world.

The island has been defined as a "living laboratory" or "the seventh continent," not just for its high rate of endemism, but also because it has a wide variety of landscapes and climates that result from its large dimensions. Indeed, the general predominance of red earth contrasts with an extensive array of forest landscapes, ranging from impenetrable rainforests to temperate baobab woods and spiny thickets. The central plateau is characterized by hills and mountains with fertile valleys, which have allowed the development of agriculture and are covered with countless rice paddies. Fishing and hunting are practiced along the thickly forested eastern coast, while the south is home to areas of savanna and grassland, dotted with prickly pears (known as raketa in Malagasy), and livestock farming is concentrated in the western part of the island.

An equally varied fauna populates these varied landscapes. The forest mammals include all the world's lemur species, two-thirds of its chameleon species and numerous species of tortoises and geckos. They are flanked by many endemic species of rodents, including the Malagasy giant rat (*Hypogeomys antimena*), which lives in the Kirindy forests; six endemic genera of carnivores, including the fossa (*Cryptoprocta ferox*) and the Malagasy civet (*Fossa fossana*); as well as numerous species of bats and mongooses, including the famous ring-tailed mongoose (*Galidia elegans*). The eastern forests are inhabited by 15 species of lemurs, such as the aye-aye (*Daubentonia madagascariensis*), the hairy-eared dwarf lemur (*Allocebus trichotis*) the indri (*Indri indri*), the eastern woolly lemur (*Avahi laniger*), diademed sifaka (*Propithecus diadema*), the Milne-Edwards' sifaka (*Propithecus diadema edwardsi*) and the golden bamboo lemur (*Hapalemur aureus*).

Of the 165 birds species recorded in the eastern forests, 42 are endemic and many are not represented in other parts of the world. These forests are home to several very rare species, including the Madagascar serpent eagle (*Eutriorchis astur*) and the Madagascar red owl (*Tyto soumagnei*).

The rainforest is home to numerous reptiles, such as chameleons, geckos and non-venomous snakes, including three different species of boas, crocodiles and turtles. It is also the habitat of an incredible range of amphibians, with many species still awaiting scientific classification. It is a world that is both very ancient – as exemplified by the lemurs, the ancestors of the monkeys and man – and incredibly contemporary and capable of renewal, for new species continue to be discovered, hinting at the incompleteness of our knowledge of the biodiversity of this ecoregion.

Despite the richness and still virgin potential of Madagascar's resources, this ecosystem is threatened by deforestation. The forest is felled and burned to make way for crops such as rice, cassava and maize.

After two or three years of cultivation the soil becomes almost sterile and is abandoned and used for grazing. Then new spaces are sought and cleared for farming, felling more areas of forest.

This problem had already become apparent by 1927, when Madagascar's French colonists started to establish a network of national parks and reserves to protect the country's natural heritage and its endangered species, and the tradition continued over the following decades. WWF has been present in Africa for 40 years, with 128 projects staffed by 518 people in its offices and in the field. In Madagascar WWF has promoted the Marojejy and Andringitra National Parks and sponsors four Environmental Education Centers, where people of all ages can participate in courses. WWF's magazine Vintsy is distributed free of charge in all 1500 of the island's secondary schools. In 1998 the schools planted approximately 300,000 trees during a forest campaign. With the support of WWF 13 local communities in the Manambolo Valley of southeastern Madagascar have started to manage their forests independently, drawing up a series of policies defining the territories destined for sustainable use.

The Manambolo Forest in the southeastern part of the island is part of the corridor that connects the Ranomafana and Andringitra National Parks.

These forests are home to a wide variety of animal species – including several very rare ones such as the ring-tailed lemur (*Lemur catta*) – but up until a few years ago their area was rapidly diminishing, since the Malagasy forests were state-owned and could be felled at will. However, since the government transferred the exploitation rights to the people, the local communities have also assumed the responsibility for the protection of the forests.

The excellent results of this project have led WWF to extend the strategy to other villages, in the hope that, in time, the scourge of deforestation will recede, replaced by lush vegetation that will rise, phoenixlike, from its ashes.

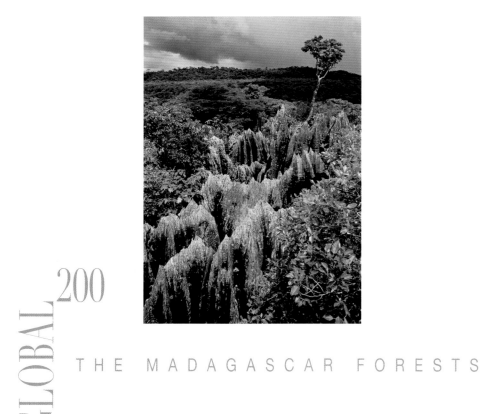

114 top The Ankarana Special Reserve is home to ancient limestone karst pinnacles called *tsingy* and an extensive system of caves and canyons. It also has underground rivers, some of which are home to crocodiles.

114 bottom The mangroves covering the tidal coastal strip protect the coastline, filter the sediments heading for the sea and act as a nursery for countless species of fish.

114-115 The fertile volcanic region of Itasy, in the highlands around the capital Antananarivo, is renowned for its farmland producing rice, cassava, maize, vegetables, papaya and pineapple and for the lake of the same name.

115 bottom Lemurs are endemic to
Madagascar and the Comoro Islands
and are considered the evolutionary
predecessors of monkeys. The thick-
furred sifaka gets its name from the
cry that it emits when in danger.

116 top Around half of the world's existing chameleon species live in Madagascar. They include Parson's chameleon, one of the largest known species, which can grow up to 24 in. (64 cm) long, including its tail. In addition to their turquoise and yellow color, the males are easily recognizable because they appear to be wearing a sort of helmet!

116 center This nocturnal treefrog is endemic to Madagascar and belongs to the Mantellidae family. It has a wide range, covering the tropical forests from Masola to Kalambatrita, where it can be found mainly in pools of water.

116 bottom The ring-tailed lemur is fairly widespread in southwest Madagascar. It is a diurnal species that spends much time on the ground, despite being a tree dweller. It forms troops with a very rigid hierarchy, headed by a female.

116-117 Six of the seven species of baobab found in Madagascar are endemic. The ability of these trees to store water in their swollen trunks allows them to survive the dry season, before bursting into flower and producing great quantities of nectar, a favorite food of lemurs.

MALDIVES-LAKSHADWEEP-CHAGOS ARCHIPELAGO TROPICAL MOIST FORESTS

"[T]hat same image, we ourselves see in all rivers and oceans.
It is the image of the ungraspable phantom of life…."
Herman Melville

These three archipelagos, whose ecoregion covers an area of about 115 sq. miles (330 sq. km) constitute the largest atoll system in the world. Lakshadweep is the closest group to the Asian mainland, lying about 185 miles (300 km) off the southern coast of India. Lakshadweep's land area of 12.5 sq. miles (32 sq. km) is divided between 36 tiny islands. A few of these islands are little more than sandbanks scattered in the sea, and only ten are inhabited. Maldives, to the south of Lakshadweep, is the largest group of islands in the Indian Ocean. There are approximately 1190 of them, but the number fluctuates as the islands come and go with changes in climate and sea level. The Maldives cover a total area of 115 sq. miles (330 sq. km). Lying about 300 miles (482 km) south of the Maldives, the Chagos Islands are uninhabited, apart from Diego Garcia, which is used as a US military base. The archipelago comprises more than 50 islands, with a total area of 30 sq. miles (78 sq. km).

Flying over the Maldives, Lakshadweep and Chagos Archipelago one is presented with the image of a "ringed sea," formed by soft white circles set in the crystal-clear, silent waters. This unique spectacle was patiently constructed by nature until achieving the delicate and geometric perfection of small atolls. Many of the islands rise just 16 ft (4.8 m) above sea level, seeming to dissolve like powder beneath a thin layer of water when viewed from the sky.

This group was formed over millions of years by volcanic activity and coral growing on the crest of the submarine Chagos-Laccadive Ridge. The Chagos Archipelago has the largest expanse of coral reefs in the Indian Ocean. In addition to its five atolls, considered the largest in the world, it also boasts two areas of raised reef and several large submerged reefs Although some of the islands have small lakes and rainwater reservoirs, fresh water is a scarce resource that limits the possibilities for life. Annual rainfall varies from 63 inches (160 cm) in the Lakshadweep Islands to 150 inches (381 cm) in the Maldives.

When we think of the natural wealth of these islands, the multicolored life of the coral reefs immediately comes to mind, and we largely ignore the biodiversity of terrestrial life. However, where the soil is substantial enough, the islands are covered with spectacular rainforest, which is replaced by drought-resistant bushes in areas with poorer soil. Lakshadweep is still home to shrubland dominated by *Scaevola* and *Argusia*. Chagos, the least disturbed group, has woodland of *Ficus*, *Morinda* and *Terminalia*, coconut woodland, Scaevola scrub, and salt marshes. The native mangroves (*Bruguiera parviflora*) are still relatively intact on Mincoy Island, covering an area of 27,000 sq. ft (2500 sq. m).

The flora of these islands does not have any significant endemism. The plants present are of pantropical or cosmopolitan distribution, chiefly from Sri Lanka (44 percent), Africa (28 percent) and Malaysia (25 percent). Terrestrial animals are limited on these islands, and most species are widely distributed throughout other Indo-Pacific atolls. The only native mammals on the islands are two species of fruit bat: the Indian flying fox (*Pteropus giganteus ariel*) and the variable flying fox (*Pteropus hypomelanus maris*), both of which are endangered.

The islands are particularly important for breeding birds, including an endemic subspecies known as the Maldivian pond heron (*Ardeola grayii phillipsi*), the white tern (*Gygis alba monte*), the lesser frigate (*Fregata ariel iredalei*), the black-naped tern (*Sterna sumatrana*), the brown-winged tern (*S. anaethetus*), and the large-crested tern (*S. bergi*). An important colony of red-footed boobies (*Sula sula*) inhabits Chagos.

The atolls are also home to two geckoes (*Hemidactylus* spp.), two agamids including the changeable lizard (*Calotes versicolor*), two snakes (*Lycodon aulicus* and *Typhlos braminus*), the snake skink (*Riopa albopunctata*), the short-headed frog, (*Rana breviceps*), and a large toad (*Bufo melanostictus*). Many invertebrates are present on the islands, including two endemic butterflies (*Hypolimnas bolina euphorioides* and *Junonia villida chagoensis*).

Most native vegetation was cleared during the 19th century and replaced by coconut plantations and other crops, including bananas, sweet potatoes, mangoes, watermelons, citrus fruits and pineapples. The introduction of domestic animals such as cats, chickens, goats, rabbits, house mice and donkeys has severely affected the native fauna. The collection of birds and eggs as a source of food for islanders, though now illegal, is still widespread. The two endemic fruit bats of the ecoregion are also severely threatened by culling, as local farmers believe that they cause damage to crops such as almonds and mangoes.

Other threats to the islands' biodiversity include pollution from factories, increased shipping traffic with the risk of oil spills, depletion of freshwater reserves, inadequate waste disposal, and the overuse of water pumps and fertilizers for agriculture. The only protected areas on these island groups are several atolls of the Chagos Islands, which were designated as nature reserves following the establishment of the military base on Diego Garcia.

Another serious problem is constituted by the unchecked growth of the tourist industry, banned only on the few protected islands, in the name of which natural vegetation is often cleared to make the islands "more attractive." On several islands the organic litter is burned, with serious effects on the atmosphere.

Overfishing is having negative effects on the health of the coral reefs and on the biodiversity of the islands. Changes in the lifestyles of the islanders such as the production of plastic and aluminum refuse have brought with them serious conservation concerns, owing to the high cost of disposal. The situation is compounded by global climate change, which is causing a rise in both the level and the temperature of the oceans. Severe coral bleaching occurred during 1998, with mortality rates as high as 90 percent in some parts of the Maldives.

Many of the projects for this area thus focus on the sea and its inhabitants. One of these, promoted by WWF's Global Marine Programme, is aimed at achieving sustainable fishing over a period of one generation. WWF is also working towards the creation of a network of well-managed and ecologically representative Marine Protected Areas, covering at least 10 percent of the world's seas, including offshore areas.

119

120 top Following an explosive eruption that destroys the volcanic cone, corals colonize the remains. The reef that forms over the course of thousands of years encloses what is known as a tropical lagoon.

120 center Atolu is the name given by the inhabitants of the Maldives to the ring-like formations constituted by islands, coral reefs and tropical lagoons. The coral reef extends both inside and outside the atolls, in the lagoon area and on the outer walls surrounded by the open sea. The islands are covered in lush tropical vegetation.

120 bottom A solitary gray heron, perching on the edge of a lagoon encircled by coral reefs, waits for small fish and invertebrates to surface in order to catch them with lightning fast movements.

121 The "living rock" of corals, which are actually animals with a tree-like appearance and a calcareous skeleton, creates imposing underwater formations. The reef is a unique and colorful habitat with an exceptionally high level of biodiversity.

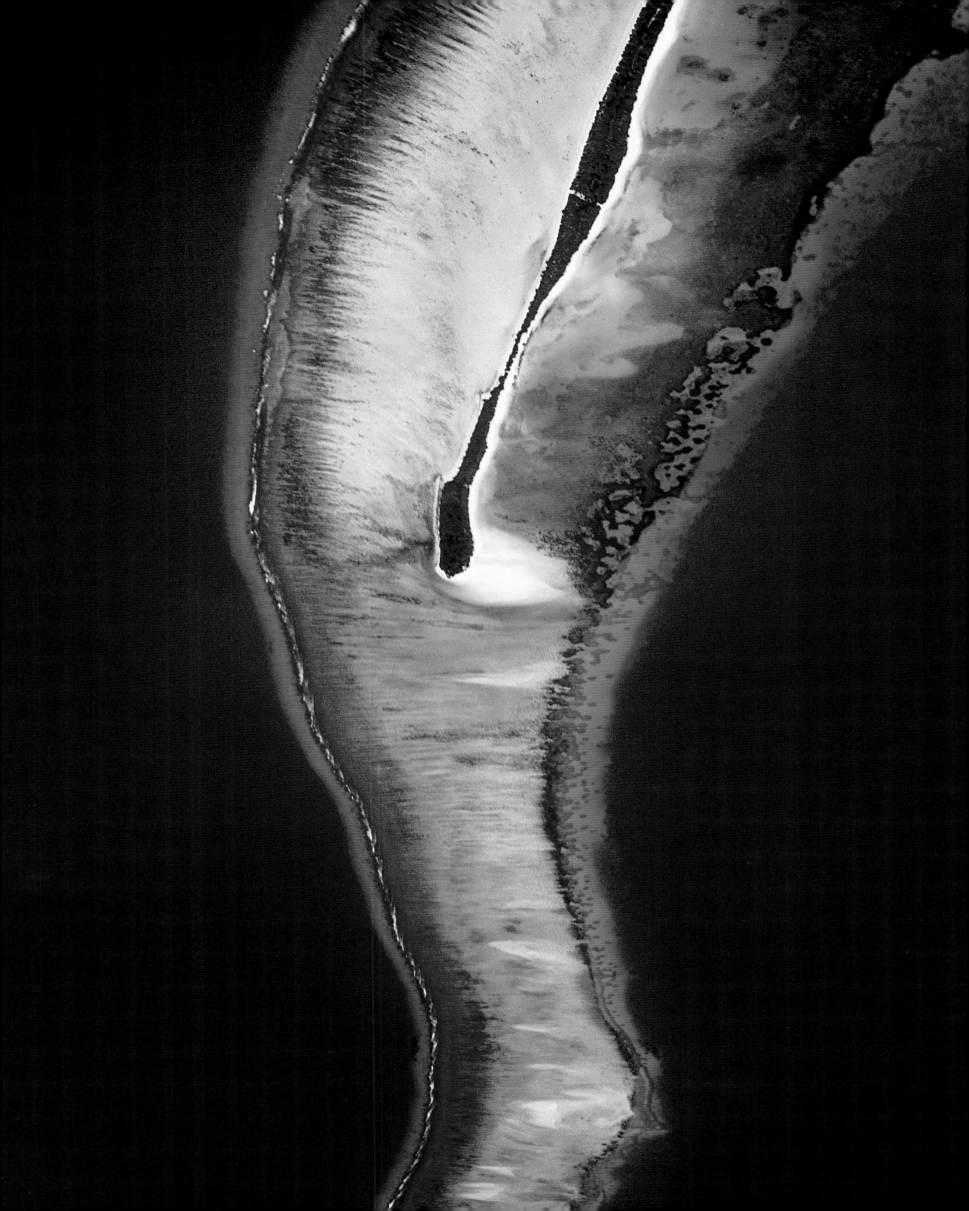

122 top White terns nest in the Maldives, laying their eggs on slender forked branches or among the rocks on the beach. During courtship the male presents the female with little fish captured in the coral lagoon.

122 center With a wingspan of up to 7.5 ft (2.2 m), the frigatebird is an expert flier, which specializes in stealing food from other seabirds. During courtship the males inflate their red throat pouches.

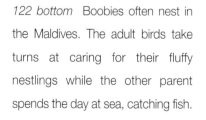

122 bottom Boobies often nest in the Maldives. The adult birds take turns at caring for their fluffy nestlings while the other parent spends the day at sea, catching fish.

122-123 The lush islands of the Maldives offer a splendid contrast to the beauty of the coral reefs. Many seabirds nest among the vegetation, exploiting the fish-rich seas to feed their young.

GLOBAL 200

MALDIVES-LAKSHADWEEP-CHAGOS ARCHIPELAGO
TROPICAL MOST FORESTS

124 top While the moray eel vaguely resembles a snake, it does not have venomous fangs or form coils. During the day it captures its prey by lurking out of sight, while at night it glides over the bottom of the reef to feed on fish and mollusks.

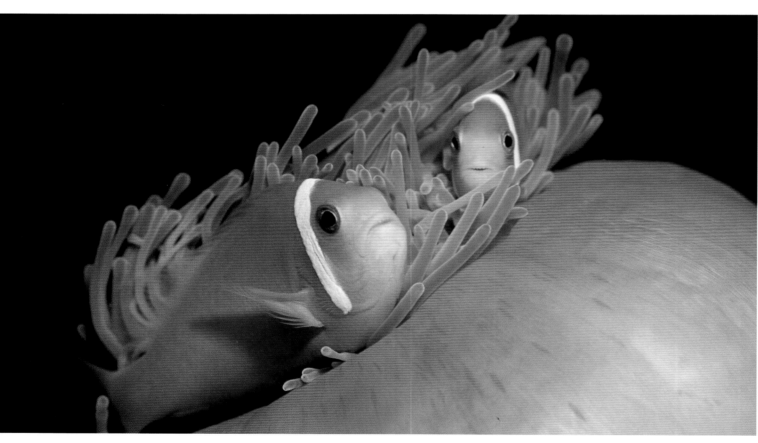

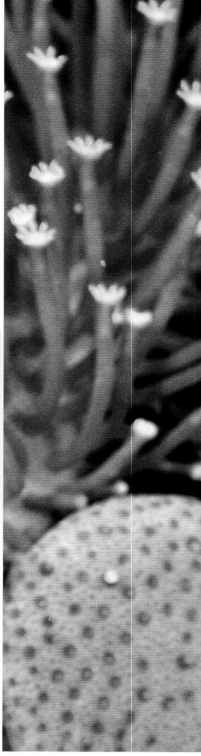

124 bottom Clownfish spend their whole lives among the tentacles of sea anemones. They even lay their eggs there, which the male fans and defends until they hatch.

124-125 This tropical grouper finds refuge from predators among the reef, but also camouflage from its own prey, which mistakes it for a harmless coral formation.

125 bottom A shoal of curious *Plectorhinchus* approaches the photographer. These colorful fish, commonly known as sweetlips, form large groups to reduce the risk of predation.

126-127 Bannerfish live in pairs or form large gregarious groups. When young, they act as cleaners, feeding on parasites on the bodies of other fish.

126 bottom Like many other reef species, the powder blue tang usually moves in large shoals, in order to reduce the risk of predation.

127 top The manta ray is a cartilaginous fish with winglike pectoral fins (measuring up to 23 ft (7 m) across), which swims as though flying, taking in water through its mouth and filtering out the plankton on which it feeds.

127 bottom Young reef sharks live in the tropical lagoons where they were born, venturing into the deeper waters outside the atolls only when fully grown.

127

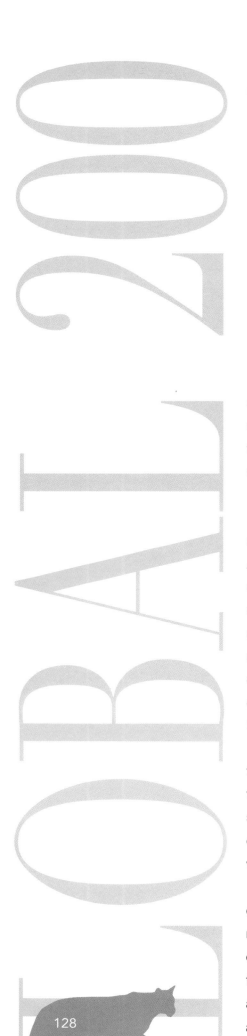

THE TERAI-DUAR SAVANNAS and GRASSLANDS

At the beginning of time all mountains had wings and could fly hither and thither.
One day the god Indra clipped their wings and they continued,
as they still do today, to flutter around the highest peaks in the form of clouds.
Ancient Himalayan legend

Situated at the foot of the Himalayas, this huge ecoregion covers an area of about 13,400 sq. miles/34,700 sq. km (about twice the size of Hawaii) and is a continuation of the Gangetic floodplain. It extends north to Nepal, from the Bhabar and the Dun Valleys, east to Banke and along the Rapti River, taking in the Dang and Deokhuri Valleys. A small part reaches into Bhutan and the ends of the region cross the border into the Indian states of Uttar Pradesh and Bihar.

Defining a geographic region that is home to the highest concentration of some of the world's largest and most striking animal species (which are also among the most seriously endangered in the whole of Asia) is an arduous task. Should the Terai-Duar savannas and grasslands be considered a very fortunate or a very unfortunate region? Is it an area where nature has been particularly lavish and where the ancient game of natural selection has gradually painted a picture of extraordinary biodiversity? Or is it instead the scene of an absurd game of Russian roulette that, shot after shot, is eliminating the ancient and venerable examples of this intricate mosaic of life – one that has made this strip of land at the foot of the world's highest mountains a unique reservoir of biodiversity? Whichever way we see it, and whatever answer we manage to give this question (assuming that there is an answer), welcome to the Terai-Duar savannas and grasslands.

This ecoregion covers an area of over 13,000 sq. miles (33,700 sq. km) between northeast India and the mountainous spurs of Nepal, in one of the most geologically dynamic areas of the Earth's crust. Here the plate of the Indian subcontinent, which broke away during the fragmentation of the large southern supercontinent of Gondwana, collided with Asia and became part of it. The immense tectonic pressure on the two continental rims caused them to deform and overlap, before raising them to form what is the world's youngest, highest and most rugged mountain range: the Himalayas.

This region is also very interesting from a biogeographical point of view, as it constitutes the point of encounter and overlap for the tropical fauna typical of the Oriental region and the temperate or cold fauna of the Palearctic region. Indeed, up to an altitude of 8200 ft (2500 m) the Terai-Duar and the southern slopes of the Himalayas are dominated by tropical species of Indo-Malayan or Indian origin, while farther north the 1850-mile (2980 km) mountainous barrier that stretches from the Hindu Kush to the Pamirs and the Himalayas is home to the cold fauna that developed during the Tertiary Period in the two distinct areas of Turkistan and Tibet.

The Ganges and numerous other watercourses that rise in the Himalayas strongly influence both the physical characteristics of the Terai-Duar and its habitats (Terai actually means "wetland").

Indeed, the region is home to a huge variety of habitats that have adapted to the different humidity levels of the environment: from grasslands and savannas to tropical monsoon forests and steppes. The climate is particularly hot and humid in summer, when the temperature often reaches 105° F (40.5° C). The annual monsoon floods regularly cause the rivers to overflow, fertilizing the soil with their rich silt.

The grasslands of this ecoregion have the highest species richness in the world. They are particularly important because they are tall grasslands, which are much more rare and endangered than the familiar low, open ones, typified by the prairies of North America. This characteristic indicates the presence of a nutrient-rich soil and has led to the conversion of almost three quarters of the fertile land to agricultural use, which in turn has resulted in its rapid deterioration and erosion. The areas not yet converted to farmland are home to some of the tallest species of the Poaceae family: *Saccharum spontaneum*, *Saccharum benghalesis*, *Phragmites kharka*, *Arundo donax*, *Narenga porphyrocoma*, *Themeda villosa*, *Themeda arundinacea*, and *Erianthus ravennae*. Other shorter herbaceous species include *Imperata ylindrical*, *Andropogon* spp. And *Aristida ascensionis*. All of these plants have developed great hardiness and resistance to both fire and long flooded periods, and are able to grow back rapidly as soon as favorable environmental conditions are reestablished.

However, the Terai-Duar is not completely dominated by grasslands. The region is home to an alternating succession of habitats that form a layered or terraced landscape, with savannas followed by evergreen and deciduous forests, arid forests or steppes, depending on the level of humidity. Wild sugarcane (*Saccharum spontaneum*), is the first species to colonize the exposed silt plains immediately after the retreat of the monsoon floods and constitutes a very important source of food for the greater one-horned rhinoceros (*Rhinoceros unicornis*) and other large mammals such as the Indian elephant (*Elephas maximus indicus*).

Today the Royal Chitwan National Park in southern Nepal is home to over 500 one-horned rhinoceroses, accounting for around half the entire estimated population of the species. It is also inhabited by the chital or axis deer (*Axis axis*), which is the preferred prey of the Bengal tiger (*Panthera tigris tigris*), one of the eight subspecies of tiger. There are four Tiger Conservation Units (TCU) in the Terai-Duar region. This system of reserves is the most important transboundary area of the entire Indian subcontinent devised specifically for the conservation of the tiger. However, it is also home to an important leopard (*Panthera pardus*) population and a small population of the rare clouded leopard (*Neofelis nebulosa*).

129

Following the monsoon season the waters retreat, leaving the soil covered in mud. This is the ideal habitat for *Saccharum benghalensis* and other herbaceous species that are kept short by intense grazing

131 The tiger is an excellent nocturnal hunter. It starts seeking its prey at dawn or dusk, and will continue all night if necessary. Once it has sighted its victim the large feline presses its body close to the ground, before suddenly pouncing.

by numerous herbivores, such as the barasingha (*Cervus duvaucelii*), a type of deer with particularly branched antlers, and the rare endemic pygmy hog (*Sus salvanius*).

One of the reasons for the Terai-Duar's inclusion among the Global 200 Ecoregions is the specific diversity of the ungulates that inhabit its various grasslands and forests, along with its high level of biomass. At higher altitudes the alluvial terrain gives way to the deciduous tropical forest, where common species include the sal tree (*Shorea robusta*), a tropical species belonging to the Dipterocarpaceae family, from which vegetable fats are obtained.

Three bird species are endemic to the Terai-Duar: the spiny babbler (*Turdoides nipalensis*), the gray-crowned prinia (*Prinia cinereocapilla*) and the Manipur bush-quail (*Perdicula manipurensis*). Other important examples of bird species include the intermediate egret (*Mesophoyx intermedia*), the banded bay cuckoo (*Cacomantis sonneratii*), the coppersmith barbet (*Megalaima haemacephala*) and the red-breasted flycatcher (*Ficedula parva*).

WWF has launched numerous conservation projects throughout Nepal and particularly in the Terai-Duar ecoregion. These include the recent agreement, signed in Katmandu in March 2006 by the Ev-KÇ-CNR Committee in collaboration with WWF Nepal for the conservation of endangered species in the area of the Sagarmatha (Mt. Everest) National Park. Under this agreement, the two organizations have joined forces to research, monitor and protect the snow leopard – the big cat at the greatest risk of extinction – and its prey.

One of the most important conservation schemes is the *Terai Arc Landscape Project*, launched in 2003 in a key area lying between Bhutan, India and Bangladesh.

The area involved is not only one of the Global 200 Ecoregions, but also one of the priority landscapes of the *Save the Tiger* Fund and home to two UNESCO *World Heritage* Sites. It covers 8600 sq. miles (22,275 sq. km) and comprises four protected areas: the Parsa Wildlife Reserve, the Royal Chitwan National Park, the Royal Bardia National Park and the Royal Suklaphanta Wildlife Reserve. The project has raised the awareness of the local populations and involved them in the successful prevention and repression of poaching. It has also restored 1325 acres (536 hectares) of forest, started to create natural corridors between the protected areas through regeneration and reconversion schemes, and achieved the sustainable management of over 600 acres (242 hectares) of pastureland.

The *Terai Arc Landscape Project* involves a series of activities both inside and outside the protected areas, which are aimed at the conservation of the environment and its wildlife – primarily the greater one-horned rhinoceros, but also the Bengal tiger and the Indian elephant. In Nepal the local communities help WWF to maintain the integrity of the natural corridors in the forests, which are key areas for the survival of the tiger.

132 top The long snout of the false gavial or tomistoma (from the Greek "sharp mouth") has evolved as a consequence of its specialized diet, which consists mainly of fish.

132 center The sambar is a largely solitary and nocturnal deer. Stags have large six-pointed antlers with well-developed tines. During the rut they gather a small harem of females around them.

132 bottom Although the Indian elephant's appearance is different from that of its African counterpart, its behavior is similar. It too lives in herds of 8-20 individuals led by a matriarch and feeds on grass, fruit and bark.

132-133 The Indian, or greater one-horned, rhinoceros hides among the thick swampy jungles of northern India. It can be distinguished from the African species by the presence of a single horn on its nose.

133

134 top The red panda feeds at night on bamboo, fruit, leaves, roots and occasionally insects and small vertebrates and sleeps during the day. This small carnivore is classified among the 100 species at greatest risk of extinction.

134 bottom The snow leopard roars loudly if angered. It is thought that this seriously endangered species is distributed between southern central Russia, the Pamirs, Tibet and the Himalayas, probably reaching northward as far as the Altai and Sayan Mountains, Mongolia and western China.

135 left The chital is an agile deer with an unmistakable reddish coat with white spots, which is widespread in wooded regions of Sri Lanka and India. Its diet consists mainly of grass, although it also feeds on the tender parts of trees.

135 right The sloth bear has a long, shaggy coat and a distinctive "V"-shaped white mark on its chest. Its long snout, bare lips and lack of upper incisors are adaptations to its particular diet, constituted mainly of ants and termites.

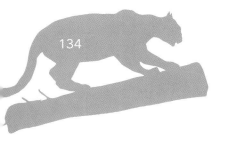

135

THE SUNDARBANS MANGROVES

"India is a geographical term.
It is no more a united nation than the Equator."
Winston Churchill

Situated along the coast of Bangladesh and eastern India, this ecoregion covers an area of about 1400 sq. miles (3626 sq. km). It is bounded to the north by the Bagerhat, Khulna and Satkhira districts; to the south by the Bay of Bengal, to the east by the Baleshwar (or Haringhata) River and the Perojpur and Barisal districts, and to the west by the Raimangal and Hariabhanga rivers that form part of Bangladesh's frontier with the Indian state of West Bengal.

The Sundarbans is at risk of becoming a ghost region. Hundreds of years of exploitation by one of the world's most densely populated areas have taken a heavy toll on the habitat and biodiversity of this ecoregion. The ecoregion is situated on the immense Ganges and Brahmaputra delta, whose alluvial deposits make it exceptionally fertile, and it has suffered so heavily from the constant expansion of agriculture that it is impossible to imagine the area's original composition.

The Sundarbans are coastal forests which grow in areas with brackish waters and rich sediment, are principally constituted by mangroves, and appear as low-growing vegetation with clearings. Mangroves are evergreen trees and shrubs whose aerial roots (pneumatophores) emerge from the mud to absorb oxygen, making them ideally adapted to salty and swampy habitats.

The water of this region is always brackish and is regenerated during the rainy season, when fresh water from the Ganges and Brahmaputra flushes out the salty pools that stagnate among the mangroves, depositing a layer of sediment in them. This form of "recycling" is essential for the metabolism and health of the ecosystem.

The monsoon season, from June to September, is marked by frequent and often violent rains. The Bay of Bengal is repeatedly scourged by storms and cyclones, which destroy its villages and natural landscapes. Annual rainfall can reach 140 inches (355 cm) and temperatures can rise to 120° F (49° C), making the area so humid that it is practically uninhabitable.

Although it is impossible to be sure of the original composition of this ecoregion and while the vegetation is not only sparser than in the past, but also very fragmented, a range of typical species of the Sundarbans (in addition to mangroves) can nonetheless be identified. It includes *Heritiera minor*, *Xylocarpus moluccensis*, *Bruguiera conjugata*, *Avicennia officinalis*, *Sonneratia caseolaris*, *Pandanus tectorius*, *Hibiscus tiliaceus* and *Nipa fruticans* along the coast.

The rainforest is the realm of the tiger (*Panthera tigris*). This mammal has adapted both behaviorally and environmentally to the habitat of the mangroves and swamps. However, it requires constant protection as the progressive disappearance of the forest continues to reduce its chances of survival, which are further jeopardized by hunting and poaching. The Sundarbans are currently home to 500 species of mammals, although none of these is endemic. They include the capped leaf monkey (*Trachypithecus pileatus*), rhesus monkey (*Macaca mulatta*), smooth-coated otter (*Lutrogale perspicillata*), oriental small-clawed otter (*Amblonyx cinereus*) and large Indian civet (*Viverra zibetha*). The region is also home to the leopard (*Panthera pardus*) and many other smaller predators, such as the jungle cat (*Felis chaus*), leopard cat (*Prionailurus bengalensis*) and fishing cat (*Prionailurus viverrinus*).

Approximately 190 species of birds have been recorded in this ecoregion although, as with the mammal species, none of them are endemic. However, several are essential to the aquatic ecosystems because of their role as predators, including the osprey (*Pandion haliaetus*) and the gray-headed fish eagle (*Ichthyophaga ichthyaetus*).

The aquatic habitat is home to many endangered species at the center of conservation projects, such as the Ganges river dolphin (*Platanista gangetica*) and three species of crocodiles: the mugger (*Crocodylus palustris*), the saltwaterf crocodile (*Crocodylus porosus*) and the Indian gharial (*Ghavialis gangeticus*). This area is afflicted by numerous environmental problems. Poaching and the loss of habitats – due to deforestation and other factors of destruction associated with human impact – have led to the extinction of many key species of the ecoregion, such as the barasingha (*Cervus duvaucelii*). Others, such as the tiger and gharial are rapidly disappearing.

Oil spills from ships that sail up the river to the port of Kolkata (Calcutta) and pollution from the large cultivated areas – due to the use of chemical fertilizers, for example – are just some of the most widespread and significant threats to the health of the environment. The Ganges is 6th on WWF's list of the world's most threatened rivers. The deviation towards India during the dry season of over a third of the Ganges' currents by the Farakka Barrage, whose construction in 1951 created much tension (it was completed in 1974), further depletes water resources in the areas that are no longer washed by the river. In 2004 the Bangladeshi government accused the dam, built by the Indian government, of having caused the drying up of over 80 rivers. Furthermore, the survival of many plant species of these regions is dependent on the level of salinity of the water. The absence of fresh water in the Ganges is causing the advance of a saline front that threatens the fish and the mangrove forests, and both the Bengal tiger and the Ganges river dolphin are in danger of extinction. In his latest book, *The Hungry Tide*, Indian novelist Amitav Ghosh denounces the fact that what was once one of most of the extraordinary rivers in the world now resembles a mere rivulet at low tide.

Conservation activities in this ecoregion are aimed chiefly at identifying and protecting the remaining plant and animal species. One of the most important projects focuses on the conservation of the Ganges river dolphin and has involved painstaking surveying to achieve precise mapping and distribution criteria of this freshwater mammal. An Indian River Dolphin Committee has also been established, which has drawn up a plan of action for the conservation of this endangered species and an educational program aimed at increasing awareness of the problem. The project also has the objective of monitoring any activities that could damage the habitat and living conditions of the dolphins.

Other projects have been established for the conservation of typical species, such as the swamp francolin (*Francolinus gularis*), as well as tigers, crocodiles and gharials, and several monitoring programs have been set up to assess the quantity and quality of the remaining mangroves.

138 top The liontail macaque or wanderoo is an endemic monkey of the Western Ghats. This mountain range still preserves rainforests at elevations between 1600 and 4000 ft (88 and 1220 m), which are the typical habitat of this species.

138 center The Borneo pygmy elephant is one of the world's most endangered animals, for the conversion of forests to farmland is rapidly bringing this subspecies to the verge of extinction.

138 bottom The Ceylon python is endemic to Sri Lanka. This is the smallest subspecies of the Indian python, reaching a maximum length of 10-11.5 ft (3 and 3.5 m).

138-139 In southwestern Bangladesh the Sundarbans region is formed by a mass of islands and islets where the fresh water transported by the rivers mingles with the salt water of the sea. These are ideal conditions for the growth of huge and highly evocative mangrove forests.

140 top The greater one-horned rhinoceros inhabits the swampy areas in the north of the Indian subcontinent. Although it is a powerful and heavily built animal, its survival is seriously threatened by poaching.

140 center Sambars graze the aquatic vegetation, while a heron eats a small frog. The sambar is widespread throughout the Indian subcontinent and Southeast Asia.

140 bottom The fishing cat is perfectly adapted to aquatic habitats, whose resources it exploits more efficiently than any other feline species. Its diet consists of amphibians, small reptiles and fish, which it scoops out of the water with its paws.

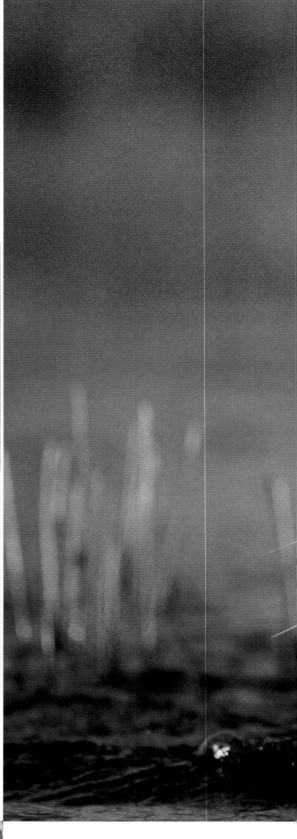

140-141 The Bengal tiger is fond of water and can also be found in swampy habitats and among the thick mangroves. It needs to kill every 3-5 days to feed, and will cover distances of up to 12 miles (19 km) a day in search of prey.

BORNEO'S PEAT SWAMP FORESTS

"[T]he program of scientific experimentation that
leads you to conclude that animals are imbeciles
is profoundly anthropocentric. It values being able
to find your way out of a sterile maze, ignoring
the fact that if the researcher who designed the maze
were to be parachuted into the jungles of Borneo,
he or she would be dead of starvation in a week."
J. M. Coetzee

Borneo (286,915 sq. miles/743,106 sq. km) is the third largest island in the world. It is bounded by the South China Sea to the north and west, the Sulu Sea to the northeast, the Celebes Sea and the Makassar Strait to the east, and the Java Sea and the Karimata Strait to the south. The island is surrounded, from west to east, by Sumatra, Java, Sulawesi and the Philippines. The peat swamp forests ecoregion covers an area of about 27,000 sq. miles (70,000 sq. km).

Due to its remoteness in relation to the rest of the world, the island of Borneo was long ignored by traders and immigrants, who preferred the busier and more dynamic Indian routes. It was not until the 16th century that Spanish and Portuguese explorers and traders first reached its coast, closely followed by the Dutch and English, who ruled the island from the 17th until the 20th century. Indonesia was granted independence in 1949 and Malaysia in 1957.

Today Borneo's population is formed by non-Muslim Dayaks and Islamic Malays, as well as Chinese and Europeans. The island is home to an array of indigenous tribes, each of which has its own language and culture. The largest of these remaining native groups is the Iban, once sadly renowned as headhunters, who have now adopted a tamer lifestyle as farmers and hunters. Due to their frequent raids along the coast – now made for solely commercial purposes – they are also known as the Sea Dayak. They live in the hills and the middle and lower basin of the watercourses of Sarawak, in a region of the interior dotted with swamps – some very large – that incorporates Lake Mahakam and Lake Kapuas and merges with the rainforest. The native villages are built on sites laboriously cleared of vegetation but perennially threatened by the encroachment of the living and unexplored forest, which the indigenous people call *Ulo*, meaning "unknown world." This is a very intense and intricate environment, which is difficult to explore.

Due to its size and great variation in altitude, the island of Borneo has been divided into nine ecoregions, with flat areas dominated by rainforest, but also mountains, heath forests, swamps, mangroves, wetlands and peat bogs. The latter two habitats belong to the peat swamp forests ecoregion.

The swamps form a sodden maze where the ground is so soft that it feels as if one were walking on a sponge. The origins of this carpet lie in the organic matter that builds up behind the coastal mangroves. In time these mounds can reach a height of 65 ft (20m), forming domes of plant detritus. The subsoil on which the peat rests is nonetheless poor in mineral nutrients, such as silicon, and is characterized by high acidity. Despite the scarcity of nutrients, ecologists have managed to distinguish six habitat types, each characterized by dozens of plant species.

Borneo is a true naturalist's paradise. It is the home of the orangutan (*Pongo pygmaeus*), whose name means "man of the forest" in Malaysian, and is not only an ecoregion with exceptionally high biodiversity, but also one of the last frontiers of science, as it is the source of a continuous stream new discoveries. In 2006 alone, 56 new animal and plant species were found in this region, while it has been calculated that an average of 3 new species have been discovered each month over the past 10 years. Many of these creatures, hitherto unknown to science, are truly amazing: a miniature fish (the world's second smallest vertebrate), measuring less than 0.5 inches (1.27 cm) in length, which inhabits the highly acidic blackwater peat swamps; six species of Siamese fighting fish, including one with a beautiful iridescent blue-green marking; a catfish with protruding teeth and an adhesive belly that enables it to stick to rocks; and a tree frog with striking bright green eyes. For plants, the number of ginger discoveries more than doubles the entire number of the *Etlingera* species found to date, and the rich flora of Borneo known to science has been further expanded by three new tree species of the genus *Beilschmiedia*.

The fact that this habitat was formed recently means that it has very few endemic species. They include the Borneo roundleaf bat (*Hipposideros doriae*) and two birds: the Javan white-eye (*Zosterops flavus*) and the hook-billed bulbul (*Setornis criniger*). Although this habitat is different from that of the rainforest, the humidity that envelops the peat swamps creates a labyrinthine and variegated world, which is home to a considerable number of plant and animal species. Gibbons and orangutans are present throughout these swamp forests, albeit at low densities, while long-tailed macaques (*Macaca fascicularis*) can be found in large groups near the rivers. This is the preferred habitat of the proboscis monkey (*Nasalis larvatus*), a unique large-nosed monkey endemic to Borneo. Here it is able to swim, despite the presence of crocodiles, and find the fruit and leaves that form its diet.

The ecoregion is also home to many bird species, over 200 of which have been recorded in the Tanjung Putting National Park, a large tropical peat swamp in Kalimantan. The maze of fresh watercourses that soaks the peat swamp is inhabited by one of the most desirable and rare aquarium fish, the arowana (*Scleropages formosus*), as well as otters, false gavials and crocodiles.

As noted above, Borneo continues to yield new species. The latest, and most hotly discussed, is the Bornean clouded leopard. In fact, scientists have discovered that the feline that inhabits the islands of Borneo and Sumatra does not belong to the same species that is found in mainland Southeast Asia. The new species has been called *Neofelis diardi*, to distinguish it from its mainland "cousin" (*Neofelis nebulosa*) described for the first time in 1821 by British naturalist Edward Griffith (1790-1858). For over 100 years nobody realized that the Bornean leopard was unique. However, this is indeed the case and the two species differ in the size and distribution of their markings and even in the color of their coat, which is lighter in the case of the mainland species. The Bornean clouded leopard population is estimated at 5000–11,000 individuals in the forests of Borneo, and 3000–7000 on Sumatra. However, more research is required in order to obtain reliable figures. These felines inhabit the extensive forests of the islands, from the coastal areas to the more mountainous ones of the interior. Their preferred habitats, where most animals have been found, are the lowland forests and hill rainforests. They usually avoid open areas with few trees and are very sensitive to human disturbance. Bornean clouded leopards feed on monkeys and several species of forest pigs and deer, which they stalk on the ground or pounce upon from the branches of the trees. Occasionally they eat birds and reptiles (such as monitor lizards) as well.

More than thirty palm species have so far been found in the peat swamp forests, including the red-stemmed sealing wax palm (*Cyrtostachys lakka*).

In Borneo deforestation has been increasing since 1996 and has now reached an average rate of 7750 sq. miles (20,000 sq. km) per year. The tropical peat swamps, which up until a few years ago covered a large area in Sarawak and Sabah, have been reduced to around half their original size. Fortunately, those of Brunei and the Belait River are still intact. The greatest threats are represented by fires used to clear forest for the cultivation of commercial tree crops such as rubber, palm oil and cellulose. The peat swamps are particularly vulnerable to fire, and during burning they produce large amounts of fine particulate matter that contributes to the atmospheric pollution of the whole of Southeast Asia, extending as far as Bangkok. Many proboscis monkeys and unknown numbers of birds, reptiles, amphibians, primates and other mammals died in the fires or shortly after due to the scarcity of food. Hundreds of orphaned orangutans that survived the fires were sold to the international pet trade, while several females were even used to satisfy the tastes of the clients of brothels in nearby Thailand.

In order to preserve the region a system of 11 protected areas has been established, covering an area of 1660 sq. miles (4300 sq. km). However, work has only just begun. The conservation of this corner of the world is considered one of the global priorities. Consequently, on January 12, 2007, the governments of the three countries of Borneo (Brunei Darussalam, Indonesia and Malaysia) signed a declaration for the protection of this extraordinarily rich biodiversity and WWF guaranteed its support for the practical application of this commitment, which is important not only for the future of plants and animals, but also for our own.

146

143 The orangutan's long and powerful arms and opposable thumbs make it very well adapted for life in the trees. Its way of moving around by swinging between the branches is known as "brachiation."

146-147 Thick vegetation, majestic rivers and walls of creepers: the impenetrable jungle of Borneo is ideal for elusive and mysterious animals such as the pygmy elephant.

146 bottom Striking limestone pinnacles rise in the Gunung Mulu National Park, which is home to the world's largest, and still partly unexplored, system of natural caves.

147 top Despite their primeval appearance, the forests of the Gunung Palung National Park are among the habitats most seriously threatened by deforestation.

147 center The Tanjung Puting National Park provides refuge for many species of primates, including orangutans fleeing from areas transformed into palm oil plantations.

147 bottom *Rafflesia arnoldii* produces the largest individual flower in the world (over three feet across), but lacks chlorophyll. Consequently, it lives as a parasite on the lymph of a host plant.

GLOBAL 200

148 top The long-tailed macaque is widespread throughout much of Southeast Asia. It has learned to supplement its diet of fruit and leaves with crabs and shrimps that it catches in rivers, as it is an excellent swimmer.

148 bottom Following a gestation period of nine months the female orangutan normally gives birth to a single young, to which she dedicates her full attention. The newborn baby is completely helpless and clings to its mother's fur as she suckles it.

GLOBAL 200

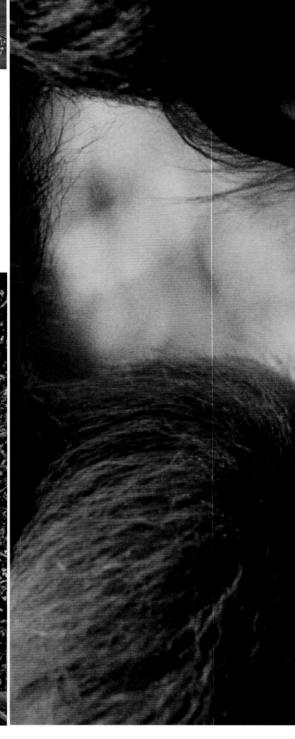

148-149 Orangutans are highly social animals. During infancy the interaction between mother and baby is vital for the young animal to learn to find food, avoid danger and establish proper social relations.

BORNEO'S PEAT SWAMP FORESTS

150-151 Wallace's flying frog is a treefrog that inhabits the rainforests of Borneo and Malaysia. Its webbed hands and feet allow it to glide gracefully among the treetops or to the ground.

151 left The Oriental whipsnake (*Ahaetulla prasina*) lives in wooded and rural areas, feeding on small vertebrates, including lizards, small amphibians and birds. Its beauty and elegance makes it one of the reptiles most sought after by collectors. However, it does not survive long in captivity

151 right The larvae of the Limacodidae family of moths are brightly colored. This is a powerful warning sign, for these insects have stinging hairs capable of inflicting great pain on predators.

THE DAURIAN STEPPE

*"On the steppe each blade of earth bends beneath the weight of the sky.
On the steppe everything is flat to make more room for the great sky.
On the steppe each man carries the sky on his shoulders."*
Anton Quintana

The Daurian steppe is a large ecoregion covering an area of over 420,000 square miles (1.08 million sq. km) in Mongolia, China and Russia. It is bounded by the semicircular Khentii mountain range.

The steppe is an area of grassland with few or no shrubs and trees. Often portrayed as a place where solitude and melancholy assume epic proportions, this ecosystem of vast plains or uplands is fairly widespread throughout the world and can be found in the tropical, subtropical and temperate regions. Areas where grassy expanses constitute the predominant vegetation have different names depending on the continents on which they are found and the cultures that inhabit them. Although they are often very different in terms of climate and geomorphology, they are all characterized by a flat, even landscape dominated by herbaceous vegetation. We thus have the South American pampas, Mediterranean garrigue, North American prairies, Eurasian steppe, South African veldt, Hungarian puszta, Australian outback, African savanna, Californian chaparral, and so on.

The Daurian Steppe ecoregion is one of the best and most intact examples of steppe and grasslands, forming a mosaic of grass and forest extending along the border between Russia and Mongolia. Genghis Khan was born in this region in the 12th century and made it the center of his empire. The heirs of his world still live as though time had stood still, their lives marked by the slow movements of the herds, and sharing their homeland with huge populations of large vertebrates.

The region has many rivers. The main ones include the Onon and the Ulz. The plentiful water supplies support large forested areas dominated by larches, and huge mixed woodlands with pines and beeches. The average elevation is about 5250 ft (1600 m) above sea level and the average annual temperature approximately 32° F (0° C). In winter the temperature can fall below -5°F (-20° C), while summer temperatures never rise above 77° F (25° C). Rainfall is low, and the annual average rarely exceeds 6 inches (15.2 cm).

Although most of the plants of the Mongolian steppe are fairly common locally, there are also several threatened species. In fact, 15 plants are considered rare and 8 endemic. Many of these are medicinal or have been exploited by man in other ways. The names of several of these species recall their origin: e.g., *Rhododendron dauricum*, *Caryopteris mongolica*, *Adonis mongolica*.

The Daurian Steppe still preserves an array of exceptionally important natural treasures and is home to unique animal species. Some scholars claim that the eastern Mongolian steppes, including the Chinese and Russian regions, are one of the world's largest undisturbed habitats, and indeed the presence and impact of humankind are almost imperceptible here.

The many mammal species include the characteristic Mongolian gazelle or dzeren (*Procapra gutturosa*), which closely resembles the small antelopes of the African savanna, although it is slightly more heavily built. Its coat is a buff color, but varies in shade according to the season, affording it efficient camouflage. Only males have horns, which are black and curved. During the rut the males can also be identified by their swollen throats, which give the species its scientific name (*gutturosa* in Latin means "swollen throat"). The gazelles spend autumn and winter in the cold grazing grounds, feeding on all the edible plant species during the early hours of the morning and at dusk, and sheltering from the wind by crouching in small depressions or behind shrubs for the rest of the day.

These gazelles are very fast and agile animals (they can maintain speeds of over 35 miles (53 km) per hour over long distances). They are also good swimmers and are able to leap higher than 6.5 ft (1.9 m). Their physical stamina and need for food allow them to migrate over long distances in spring and summer like the African antelopes (e.g., the wildebeest). These migrations involve up to 8000 individuals, which manage to cover distances of over 150 miles (240 km) per day. In June the huge herds reach their summer grazing grounds and the first births commence, following a gestation period of approximately six months. The young remain hidden and motionless for the first few days, starting to follow the herd after a week. The Mongolian gazelle is not currently endangered, but its range has greatly diminished over the last decades and the species is now entirely confined to the eastern area.

The undisputed "kings" of these steppes are the cranes. Elsewhere these birds are fairly rare or circumscribed to particular areas, but this ecoregion is home to six different species: the white-naped crane (*Grus vipio*), the Manchurian crane (*G. japonensis*), the common crane (*G. grus*), the demoiselle crane (*Anthropoides virgo*), the Siberian crane (*G. leucogeranus*) and the hooded crane (*Grus monacha*). All crane species are migratory and breed on open steppes or plains on all continents. Most of them prefer open spaces with good visibility, while some species also require nearby wetlands with shallow waters. Cranes always try to remain a long distance from human settlements, as they suffer from the disturbances caused by man, who is still deeply fascinated by these birds. Indeed, cranes have long inspired myths, legends and traditions. In Asia they also play a well-defined role in religious beliefs, while in China they are a symbol of longevity and are believed to carry the souls of the dead to heaven. Nonetheless, all 15 of the world's crane species are threatened to varying degrees, thus constituting one of the most endangered families of birds.

The most characteristic carnivore of this ecoregion is undoubtedly Pallas' cat (*Felis manul*), a feline about the same size as a domestic cat, with a thickset body and a long, thick, streaked gray coat. Be-

154 The Daurian Steppe is a rare example of intact Eurasian grassland and is home to large herds of wild mammals and a rich community of birds, including six different species of cranes.

155 The loss of wetlands due to agricultural-economic development is responsible for the decline of the white-naped crane. Some 5500-6500 of them live in northeastern Mongolia, China and some areas of Russia.

cause of its long hair, it was once thought to be the ancestor of the domestic Persian cat breed. Pallas' cat usually inhabits the semi-desert and rocky areas of eastern Asia, feeding on other vertebrates that it catches using the same techniques as its domestic "cousins": skill, ambushes and quick reflexes.

In this region inhabited by nomadic herders the impact of humankind has always been relatively limited. Only recently have several groups of nomads become more sedentary in habit, spending several months of each year close to towns and villages. This new trend has led to overgrazing in several areas where overly large herds remain too long. However, this is just one of the many threats to this fragile and unique ecoregion. The steppe, where for centuries the horse was the most widespread and efficient means of transport (and is still used by the postal service today), now faces the threat of urbanization and the accompanying infrastructures.

As elsewhere in the world, the construction of new roads not only promotes mobility, but also new settlements, for communication routes now allow towns to be established in areas that were once very difficult to reach. This leads to a change in land use, and nomadic herders may become sedentary livestock breeders or traders. Eventually they all become "town dwellers," thus increasing their impact on the delicate equilibrium of the steppe.

The current system of protected areas scattered over a very large territory is not yet sufficient to protect the biodiversity of this ecoregion. Consequently, WWF has launched a project to improve the management of the system of protected areas, with the long-term goal of creating a plan able to reconcile sustainable development and biodiversity with the participation and collaboration of the various countries of Central Asia.

156 top The red-crowned crane, considered a symbol of luck and fidelity, is one of the rarest crane species, with an estimated wild population of fewer than 2000. The patch of skin on its head becomes bright red when the crane is angry or excited.

156 center Although its numbers are declining elsewhere, the demoiselle crane populations of eastern Asia are stable or rising.

156 bottom Following arrival at their wintering grounds, common cranes commence a complicated ritual dance with which they synchronize their reproductive cycles.

156-157 The Orkhon Valley nestles between the mountains and larch forests. This area has many lakes and rivers and is still inhabited by nomadic Mongol herders with their horses, oxen, yaks and sheep.

157 bottom The goitered or Persian gazelle inhabits the desert regions extending from Mongolia to the Caucasus, as far as Asia Minor.

THE EAST SIBERIAN TAIGA

"Siberia: it fills one twelfth
of the land-mass of the whole Earth,
yet this is all it leaves
for certain in the mind.
A bleak beauty, and an indelible fear.
The emptiness becomes obsessive."
Colin Thubron

This ecoregion lies between the Yenisei River and the Verkhoyansk Mountains in Russia. It covers an area of over 1.5 million sq. (about 3 times the size of Alaska). Its northern border reaches the Arctic Circle, while its southern one extends to 52°N latitude.

Taiga is a Russian word meaning "forest" The largest forest in the world, which comprised the Scandinavian Peninsula as far as eastern Canada, once formed an unbroken blanket of green woods that covered much of the northern hemisphere before humankind commenced its struggle for survival "against" nature. The taiga occupies the far northern areas of the planet, separated from the pole by an even colder habitat with even fewer resources: the tundra.

Although water is present throughout this biome, it is frozen and thus unavailable for much of the year, while snow constitutes the sole form of precipitation. These habitats are thus dominated by plants that have developed alternative resources for resisting the cold and the absence of water for long periods: conifers.

The East Siberian taiga ecoregion is still one of the largest forests in the world and one of the most intact examples of this widespread biome. The tree-cover of this area of over 1.5 million sq. miles (3.9 million sq, km) is mainly made up of tree species with needle-like foliage, dominated by the Dahurian larch (*Larix gmelini*), concentrated in areas with lower snowfall.

Survival in the taiga requires the ability to withstand cold and solitude. Indeed, the bitterly cold climate and scarcity of resources make life difficult for all living organisms, particularly in the winter. Some animals hibernate during the cold season, while others migrate to less inhospitable areas. However, several species are forced to withstand and cooperate with the environment and, even though special adaptations may help them to get through the winter, spring remains a vain hope for many.

The average temperature remains constantly below freezing point for at least 6 months a year, and during winter the temperature may fall below -60° F (-51° C). Minimum summer temperatures are also well below freezing, while maximum temperatures rarely rise above 68° F (20° C). Summer – if it can be called that – consists of a maximum of 100 ice-free days and is the only period during which water is readily available, particularly for plants. Such a harsh climate does not permit the explosion of rich, diverse and abundant life forms of the tropical and subtropical areas. However, in the summer the populations of the few species able to survive in this ecoregion multiply, as in the case of insects, millions of which are present during this season, although they belong to just a few separate species. Thousands of birds of different species nest and breed here.

The dominant plant species are evergreen conifers. However, evergreens here are not able to continue their vital functions throughout the year, like those of warmer climates. Indeed, the transitional seasons, and particularly spring, are so short that the trees would have neither the time nor the nutritional resources necessary to change their entire foliage. In this case the process is different: the leaves and other green parts of the plants, which are the only ones able to use the sun's energy for photosynthesis, must be able to exploit this energy as soon as the adverse climatic conditions start to improve. Even the first rays of sun of an early spring day are sufficient to trigger the transformation of carbon dioxide into carbohydrates within the dark evergreen leaves, allowing the production of new foliage, fruits and seeds, and branches, as the tree grows towards the sun. Evergreen trees tend to be tall and slender, with drooping branches, which allow the snow to slide off rather than accumulating and breaking them. They are also able to sprout and grow close to each other, forming thick forests, in which the trees are protected from the cold and the wind.

Fire represents a serious threat for the forests of the taiga, and one of its natural causes is lightning. However, the trees have relatively thick bark and generally manage to survive fires of limited proportions. On the other, hand fire thins the branches, allowing light to reach the forest floor. When this happens the undergrowth, which is otherwise very dark beneath the foliage, receives the energy necessary for the growth of new plants and shrubs, providing new food sources for herbivorous animals.

However, lightning is not the only cause of catastrophes in this ecoregion. Many decades ago it was devastated by an enormous fire, whose cause remains largely unknown. At 7:17 (local time) on June 30, 1908, near the Tunguska River, over 60 million trees in an area of 830 sq. miles (2150 sq. km) were destroyed by an explosion that, despite not having left the slightest trace of a crater, is reported to have been heard at distances of over 600 miles (965 km). Several witnesses 300 miles away claim to have heard a dull rumble and seen a cloud of smoke on the horizon. On the basis of the evidence gathered, it is believed that the force of the explosion was between 10 and 15 megatons (1000 times greater than the atomic bomb dropped on Hiroshima). The most likely hypothesis is that it was caused by the airburst of an asteroid measuring 200 ft (70 m) across at a height of 5 miles (8 km) above the Earth's surface.

Fortunately the Tunguska event did not claim any human lives, for the area was almost uninhabited, but its effects were widely felt. A shower of incandescent debris hit a train on the Trans-Siberian Railway, 300 miles (482 km) away. A series of magnetic disturbances were also triggered, which even reached the radio operators of the transatlantic liners, whose equipment unexpectedly stopped working. Almost all over the world people realized that "something had happened" in Russia. During the following days a strange orange glow lit the sky for miles and miles around the area of the fire, also illuminating the night. However, the only objective indication of the extraordinary event was an alteration of the seismographs in the Siberian city of Irkutsk, which recorded the presence of a moderate earthquake in the region. Despite many scientific expe-

ditions to the area, including several recent ones, a definitive explanation has yet to be found. Today nothing of this mysterious gargantuan fire remains, not even the burnt trees.

The taiga is home to only a modest variety of animals, but those that do inhabit this region share an unusual characteristic: they are heavily built and rather stumpy, with either short, or long and slender necks and legs. This is because they need to conserve their body heat, and so their surface area is limited, resulting in heavily built animals with short limbs or with very long and slender legs.

The wolverine (*Gulo gulo*) is a carnivore and the largest member of the Mustelidae family (that includes the otter, weasel and marten), which can weigh up to 77 lbs (35 kg). It is a heavyset, squat and extremely strong animal, capable of fending off much larger predators, such as bears. As food is scarce in its habitat, the wolverine conducts a solitary and nomadic life, covering large distances within its extensive territory. It is a voracious hunter with an extremely varied diet, which may also include domestic animals, carrion and plants if necessary.

The moose (*Alces alces*, Linnaeus 1758) is the largest member of the deer family, Cervidae, and is distinguished from other species by the antlers of the males. They grow as cylindrical beams projecting on each side at right angles to the middle line of the skull and dividing in a fork-like manner after a short distance. The lower prong of this fork may be single, or divided into two or three tines, with some flattening. In the East Siberian subspecies (*Alces alces bedfordiae*) the posterior division of the main fork divides into three tines, with no distinct flattening. In the common moose (*Alces alces alces*) this branch usually expands into a broad palmate structure resembling a spoon, with one large tine at the base, and a number of smaller snags on the free border. The moose's long legs give it a decidedly lanky appearance. Its muzzle is long and fleshy, with only a small naked patch below the nostrils, and the males have a peculiar sac, known as a "bell," hanging from their neck. The moose's short neck does not allow it to graze and its chief food consists of shoots and leaves of willow and birch, and water plants. The average weight of adult bulls is over 1200 lbs (544 kg), while cows often weigh over 880 lbs (400 kg). Calves weigh around 33 lbs (15 kg) at birth but quickly increase in size. Height at the shoulder is generally between 7 and 7.5 ft (2.1 and 2.2 m). Only the males have antlers, with an average spread of 64 inches 1.62 m) and a weight of about 44 lbs (20 kg).

A huge tract of the original habitat of the East Siberian taiga still remains. Part of it is located in protected areas, including the nature reserves of Stolby, Olekminskii, Tugusskii and Tsentralno-sibirskii (Eniseisko-Stolbovoy uchastok), Lenskie Stolby National Park and numerous nature monuments. Nevertheless, experts stress that the existing network of nature reserves is not sufficient for such an extensive region. Indeed, the diversity of the taiga ecosystem is not adequately represented and the protected areas are too isolated. Despite their relative intactness, due principally to the remoteness of several areas, many threats weigh on these forests, including fires, poaching and illegal felling of trees.

There is also a series of plant associations requiring priority protection, including among others *Pinus sylvestris, Duschekia fruticosa, Vaccinium vitis-idaea, Scorzonera radiata, Limnas stelleri, Picea ajanensis* and *Pinus pumila*.

161 At the beginning of the early Russian autumn, the vast deciduous forests of the Bryansky Les Zapovednik assume fiery hues that are reflected like gigantic prisms in the water.

162 Steller's sea eagle is a majestic bird of prey distributed along the coastal areas of the Sea of Okhotsk. It feeds on salmon and other fish that it skillfully catches.

162-163 Karymsky is a volcano of the Kamchatka Peninsula that has been constantly active since 1996. This activity generally consists of moderate lava flows alternating with impressive throw-outs of ash.

163 bottom Karymsky Lake is situated at the foot of the volcano of the same name. It is currently the largest acid lake in the world, due to the underwater eruption that occurred in 1996.

164-165 The antlers of the adult male moose have an annual growth cycle, at the end of which they are shed. In late summer the vascularized tissue (known as "velvet") that covers them peels off and the moose may eat the newly removed skin.

165 top The golden eagle is a large bird of prey with a wingspan of up to 6.5 ft (10.4 km). Its range is now chiefly restricted to mountains, due to the transformation of its habitat.

165 center The northern hawk owl builds its nest in hollow trees in the taiga. This bird is widely distributed across the boreal regions. Its diet consists mainly of small rodents.

165 bottom The ermine is a carnivore belonging to the Mustelidae family. Its thick fur makes it well adapted to the cold climate of the Siberian taiga.

166 top The physical conformation of Avachinskaya Bay, surrounded by the vast marshes of the southeastern Kamchatka Peninsula, affords it protection from inclement weather.

166 bottom The Altaisky Zapovednik has been declared a UNESCO World Heritage Site. Here the brown bear still finds virgin forests and clearings in which to breed.

166-167 The Kuznetsky Alatau Zapovednik, north of the Altai Mountains, comprises coniferous taiga forests and, beyond the tree line, mountain meadows and tundra.

THE EAST SIBERIAN TAIGA

THE BERING SEA

"The ice and the moonlit
polar nights, with all their yearning,
seemed like a far-off dream from another world
– a dream that had come and passed away.
But what would life be worth without its dreams?"
Fridtjof Nansen

The Bering Sea ecoregion extends from the Alaskan coast to Russia, across the Aleutian Islands, covering an area of over 385,000 sq. miles/1 million sq. km). This area comprises the Bering Strait, between Cape Dezhnyov, the easternmost point of the Eurasian landmass, and Cape Prince of Wales, the westernmost point of mainland North America. The strait is about 55 miles (88 km) wide and between 100 and 165 feet deep, and connects the Chukchi Sea (part of the Arctic Ocean) to the north with the Bering Sea (part of the Pacific Ocean) to the south. It was named after Vitus Bering, a Danish explorer in Russian employ, who sailed through it in 1728.

During the Ice Age the Bering Strait could be crossed on foot. The Asian peoples used this icy bridge on several occasions, starting 14,000 years ago, in order to reach the American landmass and then spread southward.

The Bering Sea ecoregion is thus a threshold area, suspended between and contended by two very different zones, and is characterized by sea, islands, coasts, coastal lagoons and ice. The area is inhabited by approximately 100,000 native people, generically referred to as Inuit (previously as Eskimos), meaning "eaters of raw meat"), comprising the Aleut, Cupik, Yupik Chukchi and Inupiat. It has witnessed successive waves of European "invaders," starting with whalers in the 17th century, followed by explorers in the 18th century and trappers in the 19th century. However, since the end of the 19th century economic interest in the area has been aimed at the planned exploitation of its natural resources, including coal and oil deposits.

Technological development, brought to the region by the Trans-Siberian Railway, has altered its fragile equilibrium, causing unchecked population growth. For centuries the extraordinary wealth and productivity of the Bering Sea has influenced the life and culture of the peoples that depend on it.

This ecosystem has a very high level of biodiversity. Although the Arctic regions may not be teeming with life in comparison to certain other areas of the world, the Bering Sea possesses an amazing variety of inhabitants, with over 450 species of fish and 26 species of marine mammals

The area is home to 70 percent of the world population of northern fur seals (*Callorhinus ursinus*) and over 80 percent of breeding female polar bears (*Ursus maritimus*). The Arctic region is also inhabited by the walrus (*Odobenus rosmarus*). This large marine mammal can grow up to 13 ft (3.9 m) long and weigh up to 3000 lbs (1360 kg). Like most of the life forms present in the region, the walrus has developed special adaptations to the harsh climate. Its perfect temperature control system allows it to divert blood from the parts of its body in contact with icy surfaces, avoiding heat loss, while it can activate circulation in those exposed to the sun, allowing the heat to spread to the rest of its body. Its size ensures that it has few enemies, just the killer whale, polar bear and – of course – humankind, the deadliest of the trio, hunting it for its hide, blubber and beautiful long ivory tusks. Despite being threatened with extinction worldwide, the walrus still has many breeding colonies in the Bering Sea.

One of the most important areas of this ecoregion is the delta of the Yukon River in Alaska, which is the breeding ground for 750,000 swans and wild geese, 2 million ducks and 100 million shorebirds, making it the area with the highest concentration of nesting seabirds, ducks and shorebirds in the whole of North America. The noise is often deafening along the rugged rocky coasts and on the islands and islets. Flocks of thousands of birds gather and nest here during the summer, when fish and crustaceans are most plentiful. However, with the arrival of the first snow at the end of August, most of them migrate south. Those that remain include the northern fulmar (*Fulmarus glacialis*), the rock ptarmigan (*Lagopus mutus*) and willow ptarmigan (*Lagopus lagopus*).

The area is also exceptionally important for plant species and supports the majority of the world's eelgrass beds. Eelgrass grows in subtidal lagoonal and coastal areas and on the seabed, where it forms meadows. This grass has long ribbon-like blades, produces flower spikes and propagates by vegetative reproduction, by means of long underground rhizomes. Phanerogams play a vital role in the oxygenation of the water, but also offer important anchorage for animal and vegetable organisms and provide nursery areas for larvae and young fish.

Unlike the other principal marine ecosystems – particularly those that are highly productive fisheries, which have been showing worrying signs of degradation and impoverishment in recent years – the Bering Sea still displays an extraordinary vitality and possesses the necessary conditions to avoid an environmental crisis.

170 The Svalbard Archipelago, whose name means "cold coast," is largely covered with ice, even though the presence of the North Atlantic Drift mitigates the Arctic climate, making the surrounding sea navigable almost all year round.

171 The polar bear's range extends throughout the northern Arctic region, encompassing Canada, Alaska and Siberia. Unlike other Arctic mammals, it does not change its white coat in summer. The bear's body is insulated from the cold by its fat reserves.

However, several problems have also started to afflict this area. Scientists agree that the effects of climate change are dramatically visible in the Arctic regions, where the increasingly early thawing of ice is threatening species and entire ecosystems. Other worrying signals are apparent from the monitoring of the animal populations: 7 species of whales are endangered and the population of Steller's sea lion (*Eumetopias jubatus*) has fallen by 80 percent over the past 20 years.

The situation is compounded by problems of a commercial nature. Both the United States and Russia intensively exploit the region's fishery resources, are exploited generating a global turnover of $600 million er year.

Many species of crabs have been overexploited and their numbers have declined sharply or have practically disappeared, while the populations of herring, once the dominant fishery resource, are dwindling dramatically.

Other typical and widespread problems include the introduction of allochthonous species, pollution (closely bound up with climate change) and whaling. A further serious problem is posed by the accumulation of toxic substances in the fat of the great predators: polar bears, whales and also man. Indeed, many substances, such as persistent organic pollutants (POPs) have been found not only in wildlife, but also in humans.

There is also the problem of the introduction and diffusion of non-native species, and rats, foxes, jellyfish and other marine organisms are wreaking a devastating toll on the ecosystems of the Bering Sea.

Fifteen years ago, recognizing the great opportunity to work on a strategic plan for the future of the Bering Sea aimed at reconciling the conservation of biodiversity and the interests of the local populations, WWF and The Nature Conservancy (TNC) launched a large-scale venture that has established long-term goals through the creation of local partnerships and shorter-term projects. The involvement of over 60 American, Russian and Japanese experts has enabled the construction of a detailed picture of the biodiversity of the ecoregion and the identification of 20 priority areas.

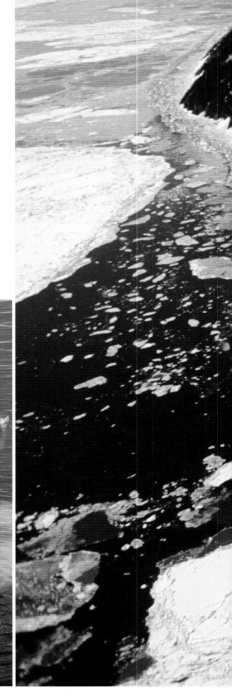

172 top Much of the Arctic Ocean is covered with ice and the area is characterized by long winters with endless nights. Although the days are much longer in summer, temperatures do not rise much.

172 bottom The erosive action of the sea models the ice, creating sculptures that emerge from the water. The area is the breeding ground of kittiwakes, identified by the tremendous noise they generate.

172-173 The Bering Strait is about 55 miles (88.5 km) wide. It sepatares Cape Deshnev, the easternmost point of the Eurasian landmass, and Cape Prince of Wales, the westernmost point of mainland North America.

174-175 A family of polar bears on the move. This species is seriously endangered by the melting of the ice caused by climate change.

175 left The killer whale is a social animal found in all cool oceans. All the members of the pod participate in hunting and their prey depends on their lifestyle, with resident populations feeding on fish and transient ones on marine mammals.

175 right Belugas are renowned for their frequent and intense vocalizing and live in pods of 3-20 individuals. In summer, during the feeding periods, gatherings of over 1000 of these cetaceans have been sighted near estuaries and rivers.

176 top In winter the male tufted puffin dons its splendid plumage in preparation for the breeding season. During this time it grows showy yellow plumes above its eyes, which it sheds at the end of summer.

176 center The tusks of the male walrus continue to grow throughout its life and can reach over 3 ft (0.9 m) in length. Following promulgation of the "Walrus Act" by the United States, which the USSR also agreed to respect in 1956, the walrus population in the Bering Sea rose from 40,000 in 1960 to 250,000 in 1980.

176 bottom A sea otter eating a crab. This species was once hunted for its luxuriant fur, with up to one million hairs per square inch, and is now considered endangered by the IUCN.

176-177 The natural arches and rugged coasts around Cape Pierce in Alaska offer spectacles of rare beauty and are home to unique species of plants and animals.

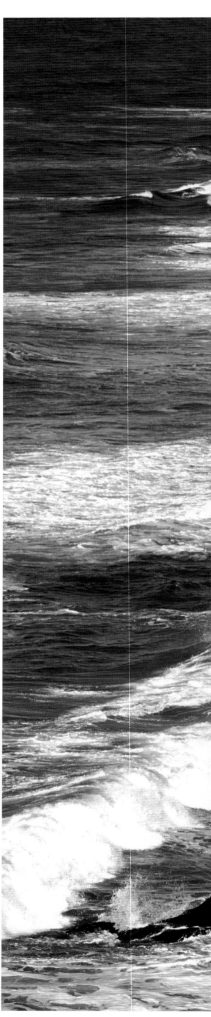

THE NORTHWESTERN AUSTRALIAN DESERTS

"A man raised in one part of the desert would know its flora and fauna backwards. He knew which plant attracted game. He knew his water. He knew where there were tubers underground. In other world, by naming all the "things" in his territory, he could always count on survival."

Bruce Chatwin

This vast region is divided between the Australian states of the Northern Territory and Western Australia. It covers an area of almost 487,000 sq. miles (1.26 million sq. km) and is completely uninhabited by humankind. Tall parallel dunes of red sand extend for hundreds of miles in the western part, while vast sandy plains are broken by low hill ranges to the east. The largest and most famous feature on the landscape is Uluru, better known by its English name of Ayers Rock. It is an awesome red sandstone monolith rising about 1100 ft (335 m) above the surrounding desert plain, which constitutes the last remaining block of an ancient mountain range that has been almost completely eroded. The rock is about 2.2 miles (3.5 km) long and has a perimeter of approximately 5.5 miles (8.8 km).

In 1873 the English explorer William Gosse named the symbol of this region Ayers Rock after Sir Henry Ayers, the premier of South Australia. However, in 1993, a dual naming policy was adopted that also featured the traditional Aboriginal name, thus acknowledging the rock's great religious significance for the Aboriginal peoples and cultures. Indeed, the morphology and the surface corrosion of Uluru are explained by the Dreamtime mythology, which underlies Indigenous Australian culture. Scholars consider the Dreamtime stories "formation myths" (where the term "formation" literally means "to take form"), as they provide an explanation of the origin of the world and its geographical and topographical features. During the Dreamtime the world was undifferentiated and inhabited by mythological figures, represented as gigantic creatures with the forms of plants or animals. As they walked, hunted, danced or simply sat on the ground, these fantastic beings left their traces on the physical world. Mountains, valleys, lakes, rocks, waterholes, rivers and all other natural features thus take on a sacred meaning in Aboriginal culture, and it comes as no surprise to discover that the lifestyle of these people takes pains to avoid damaging the desert and its resources in any way. The landscape, understood as the true "body" of nature, is sacred and untouchable.

According to Bruce Chatwin in *Songlines*, the Dreamtime stories are handed down through the generations as songs, each of which describes the path of an ancestral creature's original journey, and has a musical structure that corresponds to the morphology of the territory crossed, like a sort of map. Even today, each Aboriginal group or nation still preserves a certain number of stories, for which it is responsible. However, the dual effects of colonization and the secrecy of the traditions, unfortunately mean that only a tiny part of the Aboriginal mythology is known to anthropologists.

Like all desert regions, this area of Australia has limited and sporadic rainfall. Vegetation is sparse and dominated by a few species that have adapted to the particular conditions of their habitat. These plants are chiefly sclerophyll shrubs with leathery leaves or thorns. The most widespread species is spinifex. This name is used to refer to a group of tussock-forming grass belonging to the *Triodia* genus that is incredibly adaptable. Indeed, these species are able to grow in very arid and nutrient-poor soil and are resistant to fire. Spinifex represents around 20 percent of Australian vegetation and comprises numerous species (more than 60), which generally form thick hemispherical tussocks with wiry blades, earning it the alternative name of porcupine grass.

During the southern summer, temperatures reach 105° F (40° C), even in the towns. The winters are usually very short and fairly warm, with temperatures rarely falling below 75° F (24° C). In order to live in this ecoregion the animal species have learned to feed during the cooler nighttime hours. The greater rabbit-eared bandicoot or bilby (*Macrotis lagotis*) is an omnivorous marsupial. It spends the day in burrows up to 10 ft (3 m) deep, in which it also breeds, emerging in search of food after dark. It was named for its long, wide ears, which probably act as "radiators" for efficient heat dispersion, a strategy adopted by several other vertebrates. The mulgara (*Dasycercus cristicauda*) is a small carnivorous marsupial threatened with extinction. It too is nocturnal and digs deep burrows that it uses for both shelter and breeding. This species is able to accumulate fat reserves at the base of its tail, which

179

thus assumes a distinctive pear shape that is wider close to its body and tapers towards the tip. Of course, life in the desert is very difficult, and the natural equilibrium is very delicate.

Any disturbance that alters the environmental or ecological conditions to which the desert species have laboriously adapted through the course of their evolution, can seriously threaten their survival. As a result, many species of this ecoregion are at risk and 14 species of marsupials are now considered extinct, including the crescent nail-tailed wallaby (*Onychogalea lunata*). This wallaby weighed up to 7.5 lbs (3.4 kg) and spent the day hidden in the vegetation, emerging to feed on plants at dusk. It was once widespread in all the desert areas of west and central Australia, but it disappeared around 1960, following a very rapid decline. Today all that remains of the species are drawings and a few stuffed examples in museums. Another species of marsupial survives only in captivity: the mala or rufous hare-wallaby (*Lagorchestes hirsutus*), which can thus be considered extinct in the wild. Then there are the marsupial moles, including the Southern marsupial mole (*Notoryctes typhlops*), which spend their entire lives underground, catching insects and other soil-dwelling invertebrates, and several bird species, such as Alexandra's parrot (*Polytelis alexandrae*), which is now more commonly found in aviaries throughout the world than in its natural Australian desert habitat. However, there are also a fair number of "new" species, such as the wongai ningaui (*Ningaui ridei*), a small, mouse-like, carnivorous marsupial weighing just 0.5 oz (14 gr), which hunts among the spinifex scrubland at night. While it is fairly common, it was not mentioned in the scientific literature until 1975.

Although the apparent repetitiveness of the landscapes would suggest otherwise, the desert has plenty of surprises in store and these areas are even home to a small amphibian despite the scarcity of water. The metallic toadlet (*Uperoleia micromeles*) is brown with lighter markings on its back. It spends its time beneath the soil, emerging only on occasion of the very rare rains. Its unusual habits make it very difficult to estimate its population and exact distribution. However, the species does not seem to be endangered or suffering from any evident problems.

One of the most serious problems for the Australian deserts is constituted by alien species introduced by humankind. Foxes, cats and rabbits are now widespread in these habitats and constitute dangerous rivals for species that, despite being better adapted for life in the desert, are ill equipped to deal with interference. The introduced species, on the other hand, are hardy and easily adaptable, allowing them to find food in both natural habitats and more urbanized settings. As they are accustomed to living alongside man, they are not disturbed by human presence and are thus able to survive in conditions of high anthropic stress.

The desert fauna also includes introduced Arabian camels, which have formed feral populations. The wild dromedaries are the descendents of domestic camels imported from Afghanistan and used for desert caravans until around 1920, when they were replaced by motor vehicles. As is always the case for imported species, these camels constitute a serious threat for the biodiversity of the desert because they degrade the natural vegetation. Other threats are posed by the expansion of livestock farming and mining. Tourism has also started to constitute a problem over the past few decades, particularly in the area of Uluru.

The desert is a fragile habitat that requires protective measures aimed at limiting activities that cause the erosion of its soil and its scarce resources. The long-term conservation of such a characteristic and unique group of ecosystems, animal and vegetable species, specialized communities and endemisms, represents a challenge that an advanced and civilized country like Australia cannot ignore or risk losing.

The life of the Aboriginal populations that – lulled by the songs and beliefs of the Dreamtime – still manage to live on the minimal subsistence offered by the desert, depends on the choices made by the "Western" people, who are now the dominant population in terms of both number and power. We can but hope that the encounter of such diverse worlds will result in a productive alchemy that marries the traditional Aboriginal respect for nature with the drive for progress of the richer nations. It will thus finally be possible to continue our evolutionary course without damaging the place where it started: the Earth.

182-183 and 184-185 Ayers Rock, or Uluru, is a monolith about 1150 ft (350 m) tall and 5.5 miles (8.8 km) around. Its conformation has a strong religious significance for the Aboriginal people.

183 bottom left The bilby is a small desert marsupial with long ears that also act as "radiators" to disperse heat.

182 top Australia has the largest number of venomous snakes in the world, but the woma is not one of them. This nocturnal python feeds on rodents and may grow up to 5 ft (1.5 m) in length.

182 center left Uluru is part of a much larger underground rock formation. Its distinctive red color is caused by the oxidation of the iron contained in the rock.

182 center right Uluru has a myriad of cracks and fissures, some of which widen to form canyons large enough to require half an hour to be explored on foot.

THE NORTHWESTERN AUSTRALIAN DESERTS

182 bottom The thorny devil is a small endemic reptile of the Australian desert, which feeds on ants and is perfectly camouflaged against its arid habitat.

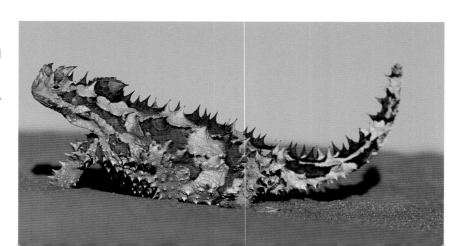

183 bottom right The desert around Uluru, the Aboriginal name of Ayers Rock, is not devoid of life as one might expect. When it rains the shrubs and herbaceous plants burst into flower, offering splendid displays of color.

183

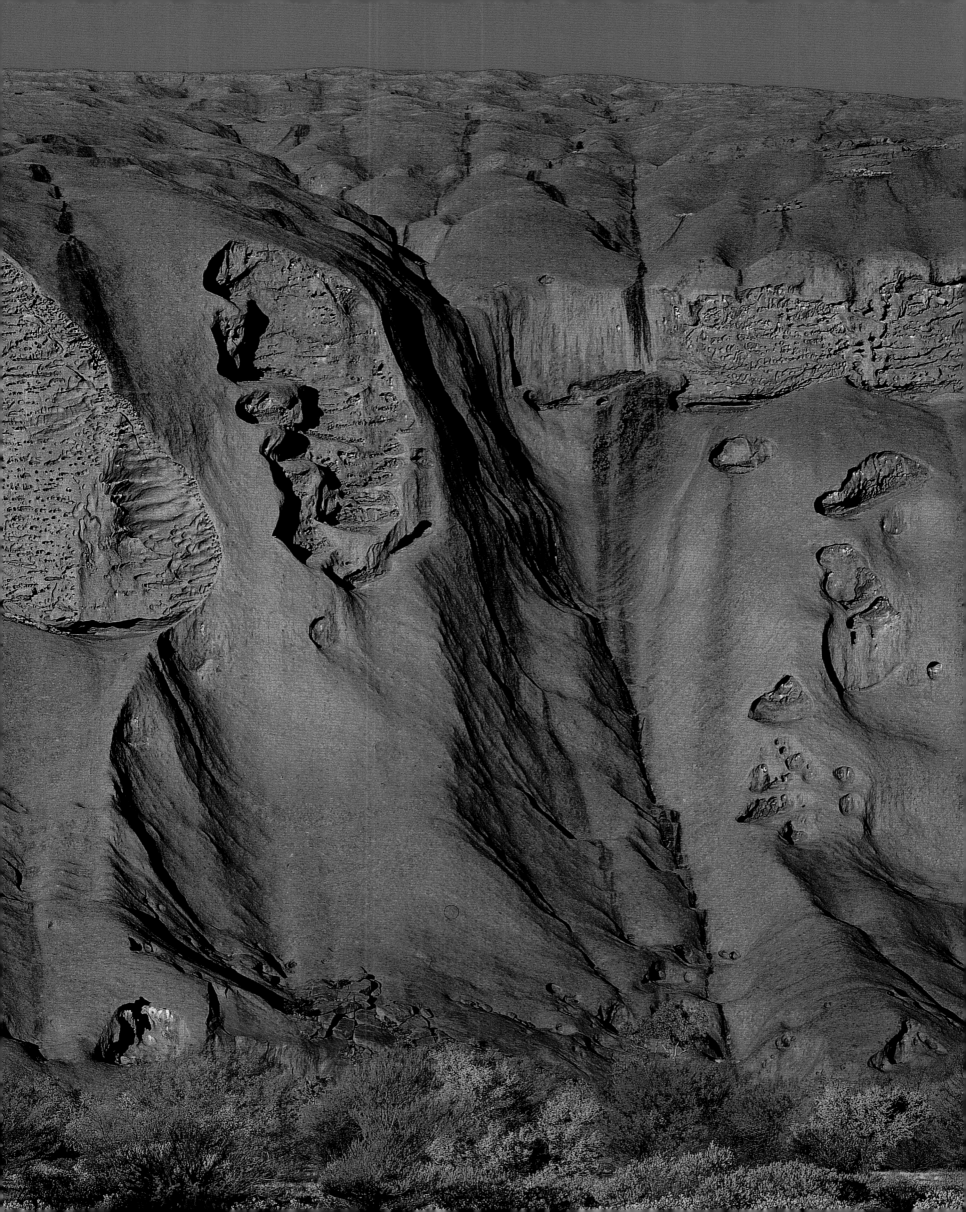

THE GREAT BARRIER REEF

"Life, in its constant formation and destruction,
seems to me never better framed for the human eye,
than between the hedges of blue titmouses of aragonite
and the treasure bridge of Australia's Great Barrier Reef."
André Breton

The Great Barrier Reef extends for over a thousand miles along the Queensland coast in northeastern Australia, from Cape York to Brisbane.

Just one dive is enough to appreciate the fragility of this ecosystem, which is the result of slow, complex and incredible processes that have taken place over thousands of years.

The coral reefs and atolls form an impressive but very delicate barrier that is a prime example of the marvel of nature at work. Immersed in the transparent water, the polyps labor with silent dedication, requiring specific physical conditions for their development, such as shallow, clean waters, temperatures between 65 and 85° F (18 and 29.5° C), a solid substrate on which to grow, and normal light and salinity. However, the optimal combination of these conditions is rarely encountered, explaining their limited distribution and inestimable value.

Considered one of the greatest natural wonders of the world, the Great Barrier Reef with its multicolored coral and fish extends for 1250 miles (2110 km)) along the northeastern coast of Australia in a succession of 2100 different reefs. Unique in terms of biodiversity, it is home to around 1900 species of fish, 350 species of coral, over 4000 species of mollusks and more than 400 species of sponges. It was proclaimed a national marine park in 1975 and a UNESCO World Heritage Site in 1981.

Coral, which boasts an extraordinary variety of species, forms colonies constituted by millions of individual organisms, known as polyps. Each of these contributes to the growth of the general structure of the reef, depositing a layer of calcium carbonate on top of the existing layers. Coral can be considered a true community, a kind of extended family where each member contributes to making its home bigger and stronger.

The skeleton of each coral species is structured in a different way and growth varies from a few fractions of an inch to 6 inches (15 cm). However, even within the same species growth varies according to the physical conditions of the environment. It is the combination of these factors that gives rise to diverse reef forms and iridescent colors, with their consequent wide range of habitats.

The single-cell algae that inhabit the tissues of the coral play a vital role during the formation of a reef. The photosynthesis performed by these algae provides the polyps with the oxygen that they require for the secretion of calcium carbonate. Without the algae, the polyps would have to rely on the nutrients present in the water alone and the construction rate would be up to 30 times slower. Coral spawning is a spectacular and apparently chaotic orgy, when the reef's usual silent and diligent labor becomes a dance of procreation: the polyps of the colony release eggs and sperm directly into the water on the nights following the full moon, where they spin and whirl like snowflakes in a storm.

There are several types of coral: soft corals (Alcyonacea) and stony corals (madrepores), constituted by a calcareous external skeleton that supports the living tissue, and thus also known as "true corals."

It is currently estimated that the other flora and fauna of the reef are composed of around 1500 known tropical marine species plus many others that have yet to be classified. The complex physical structure of the coral reef generates a wide variety of habitats, which are easily overlooked by any attempted "censuses" and conceal priceless hidden treasures.

Each of the corals offers food and shelter to countless species of animals and plants, making the reef – together with the tropical forests – the habitat with the highest biodiversity in the world. Corals, sea slugs, sponges, octopus, turtles and fish of indescribable beauty populate the crystal-clear waters of this part of the world, making them an unforgettable explosion of light and color.

The species supported by this ecosystem include the dugong (*Dugong dugon*), of the order Sirenia, which is the only exclusively herbivorous marine mammal and the sole surviving species of the family Dugongidae, and the saltwater crocodile (*Crocodylus porosus*), which at 21.5 ft (6.5) long is the largest reptile in the world and the only crocodile that leaves river estuaries to roam the nearby sea coasts.

One of the most exciting experiences during a dive is an encounter with a sea turtle. Australia is home to the world's largest population of green sea turtles, although the numbers of this species have declined dramatically in recent years, due to this turtle's attractiveness as a gourmet food. Although the sale of turtle meat is illegal, it is still highly sought after for the classic soup. However, the list of species could be endless. The unusual disk-shaped longnose butterfly fish (*Forcipiger longirostris*), for example, swims

189 Australia's Great Barrier Reef is one of the ecosystems with the highest biodiversity on Earth. Here many organisms assume gigantic dimensions, such as the sea fans that cover the coral reefs to depths of hundreds of feet.

among the coral, using its pointed snout to pull off the little polyps. The brightly colored clownfish (*Amphiprion* spp.) lives in symbiosis with the sea anemone. This fish hides among the anemone's stinging tentacles, defending itself from attack by covering itself with its host's mucus, making it immune to the poison that can be fatal to other species The surgeonfish (*Acanthurus* spp.) is a chameleonic inhabitant of the reef. It invites "cleaner" species, which feed on the mucus and dead skins cells of other fish, to approach by changing its color.

The Great Barrier Reef's vibrant life is threatened by a series of factors that constitute very real threats to the survival of the ecosystem. The first of these is represented by eutrophication (caused by the chemical contamination of water) that is a direct consequence of the development of agriculture (e.g., sugarcane cultivation, which is particularly widespread in this area). It has been calculated that millions of tons of chemical sediment and compounds reach the sea each year, infiltrating the coral reef. These foreign bodies increase the density of the water and the level of sedimentation, suffocating the reefs and reducing their dimensions in terms of both area (the coral stops reproducing, and thus growing) and biodiversity, for the reduction in the number and availability of refuges causes the death of the organisms that inhabit the reefs.

WWF not only works ceaselessly for the creation of protected areas with the authorities of the marine park, but has also been developing medium- and long-term conservation projects with a series of concrete local activities for many years. One of the latest, launched following the Seventh Meeting of the Conference of the Parties to the Convention on Biological Diversity held in Malaysia in April 2004, is aimed at the conservation of corals, mangroves and sea turtles.

A new project was also commenced July 2004, with the objective of attaining a role of greater responsibility and involvement for WWF Australia in the conservation of the reef. This project, which was concluded in February 2006, identified a series of key points associated with specific threats and developed activities designed to stem the dangers menacing the seafloors of this ecosystem. These include the Reef Water Quality Protection Plan aimed at improving the water quality of the inshore reefs, the extension of the Great Barrier Reef Marine Park, and the international widening of knowledge connected with this ecosystem through the WWF network and the consequent development of the best methods to protect it.

There are also more specific programs, such as the Tropical Seas project, focusing exclusively on the sea, which was launched in January 2003 and is expected to continue until June 2010. It is essential to keep the water clean because the algae need sunlight to survive; the corals and their inhabitants need the algae; and humankind needs a healthy natural environment and pleasant surroundings.

190 top The Great Barrier Reef resembles complex tracery when viewed from above. The coral formations, atolls and lagoons vary in color according to the depth of the ocean. The reef extends for over a thousand miles along much of the Queensland coast.

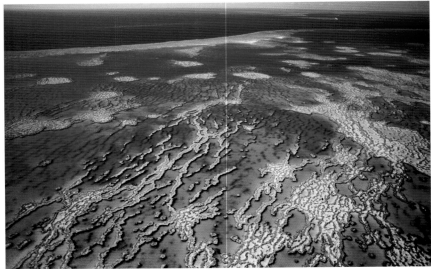

190 center At Cairns the Great Barrier Reef is over 25 miles from the coast, forming a sort of natural barrier against the open sea.

190 bottom left Lying just off the Queensland coast, the Whitsunday Islands are a group of over 70 islands discovered by Captain Cook in 1770.

190 bottom right The forest extends almost to the sea, covering the sand dunes behind Maheno Beach, on Fraser Island, off the eastern coast of Australia.

191 The sea and vegetation create bizarre forms and hues on the atolls of the Great Barrier Reef, in this case the Capricorn Islands, lying on the Tropic of Capricorn.

192-193 and 193 top left Sea fans and e soft corals are just some of the thousands of species of organisms that contribute to the incredible biodiversity of the Great Barrier Reef.

193 top right Life other reef fish, the pink anemonefish has developed a symbiotic relationship with the stinging sea anemone.

193 center left The green sea turtle breeds on the reef and lays its eggs on the sandy beaches of the atolls and islets. It is easily sighted as it feeds on the sea floor or coral reef, often in just a few feet of water.

193 bottom The potato cod can grow up to 9 ft (2.7 m) long and weigh over 650 lbs (295 kg). It inhabits the lagoons or coral reef and can be observed at depths ranging from a few feet to over 300 ft (91.5 m).

194 top The dugong, or sea cow, is a herbivorous marine mammal that lives along the northern coast of Australia, from the Great Barrier Reef to Shark Bay. Here over 10,000 of them (10 percent of the world population) live.

194 bottom During the summer months humpback whales gather along the Queensland coast, particularly towards the southern end of the Great Barrier Reef, to breed and nurse their newborn calves.

194-195 The great white shark lives in the open sea. It generally frequents cooler waters, like those of the southern coast of Australia, but it is also a sporadic visitor to the Great Barrier Reef.

195 bottom Despite its name, the saltwater crocodile – the largest species in the world – also lives in rivers and estuaries. Its small-scaled skin is considered particularly valuable, causing serious consequences on the population of the species.

NEW CALEDONIA'S MOIST FORESTS

"The return to tradition is a myth.…
Our identity is before us."
Jean-Marie Tjibaou

The islands of New Caledonia are situated in the Pacific Ocean about 750 miles (1210 km) east of Australia and 900 miles (1450 km) northwest of New Zealand. The main island, known as Grande Terre by the inhabitants, has an area of approximately 6500 sq. miles (16,835 sq. km).

Huge expanses of white sand, mountains covered with virgin forests and deep skies dotted with fluffy spun-sugar clouds: when Captain Cook landed here in 1775 the landscape reminded him of his homeland, Scotland, whose Latin name (Caledonia) he subsequently gave to the newly discovered islands.

Officially a French overseas territory, the islands have been ruled by France since 1853. The geographical position of the archipelago, surrounded by a long coral reef, gives it distinctly tropical characteristics: crystal-clear sea, luxuriant and brightly colored vegetation and breathtaking beaches, combined with a slight *ambiance française*. This is perhaps the most jarring aspect, for the sweet aroma of baguettes freshly baked in the alleys and streets of these scraps of land, lava and coral set in the middle of the Pacific Ocean could not seem more out of place. It is a reminder of old colonial ambitions, whose painful after-effects can still be felt at the beginning of the third millennium.

Unlike the small islands of recent volcanic origin, Grande Terre broke off from Australia 85 million years ago, and has been separated from the continent by a wide expanse of ocean ever since. Consequently the ecoregion has a high degree of endemism. Almost 80 percent of the plant species are endemic and five plant families (Amborellaceae, Oncothecaceae, Papracrypyiaceae, Phellinaceae and Strasburgiaceae) are found only in this area of the world. The islands have the highest level of endemism in the entire Pacific after Hawaii (89 percent) and New Zealand (82 percent). However, Hawaii has only 956 autochthonous plant species, compared with New Caledonia's 2973. The ancient nature of plants in particular is exemplified by *Amborella trichopoda*, the only species in the family Amborellaceae, thought to be one of the closest living relatives to the first angiosperms (flowering plants). New Caledonia also has a remarkable diversity of gymnosperms (primitive non-flowering plants that include conifers): 44 species, 43 of which are endemic. The forest landscape has changed little since the times of the dinosaurs.

The fauna too is represented by unique species. There are no native amphibians and just three species of snakes, none of which live on Grande Terre, but on the small volcanic islands. Mammals are represented by nine species of bats, most of which are endemic and several endangered

(*Notopteris macdonaldi, Pteropus ornatus, Pteropus vetulus*). All 68 lizards of New Caledonia (60 of which are endemic) belong to just 3 families: Gekkonidae Diplodactylidae and Scincidae

There is also an ancient endemic family of birds (Rynochetidae), which is currently represented by a single species: the kagu (*Rhynochetos jubatus*). The kagu is the national bird of New Caledonia and is distinguished from all other species by the little "nasal corns" that cover its nostrils. It is capable of emitting a range of different sounds, many of which can last up to 15 minutes. Sadly, the kagu is an endangered species, along with the Australasian bittern (*Botaurus poiciloptilus*), the New Caledonian lorikeet (*Charmosyna diadema*), and the New Caledonian owlet-nightjar (*Aegotheles savesi*). Another seriously threatened species is the New Caledonian rail (*Gallirallus lafresnayanus*). Some of the vertebrate species of New Caledonia are oversized, such as the New Caledonian imperial-pigeon (*Ducula goliath*), the largest arboreal pigeon in the world; *Rhacodactylus leachianus*, the world's largest gecko; and the giant skink (*Phoboscincus bocourti*), although this species has not been sighted since the 1870s and may be extinct.

The New Caledonia rainforests are the richest part of the French territory and one of the world's priority regions for biodiversity conservation. However, in recent years they have suffered large losses of native habitat, with coverage falling from 70 percent of the land area to just 21.5 percent. Much of this loss is due to mining, for New Caledonia produces about half of the world's nickel and is home to 40 percent of the world's known nickel deposits. Deforestation and open mines have resulted in serious soil erosion, and scrubland is now colonizing areas that were originally covered by rainforest. The construction of roads has made the forests more accessible to hunters and several species, including the New Caledonian imperial-pigeon, are now endangered.

Introduced animals, such as pigs, goats, cats, dogs, and rats, are becoming an increasing problem for native species. Java deer (*Cervus timorensis*) have also been introduced to New Caledonia for hunting. In addition to damage caused by trampling and grazing, fires are often started by hunters, making both the deer and their hunting serious threats for the survival of the forest habitats. Alien species also include the Neotropical ant (*Wassmannia auropunctata*) that was accidentally introduced with Caribbean pine cultivation and now poses a serious threat to local ant species.

In 2002 WWF and several partners launched a program for the recovery and conservation of the New Caledonia forests. This ambitious project involves both reforestation and the reintroduction of autochthonous species.

198

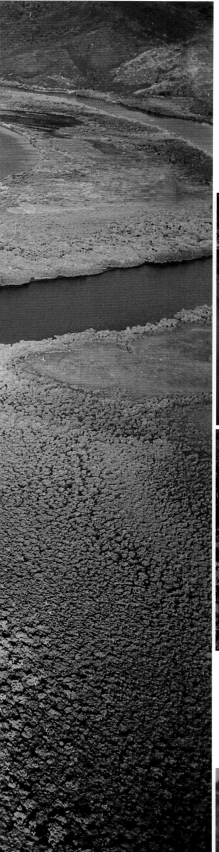

198-199   Viewed from above, the thick primary forest that covers the northern part of the island of New Caledonia appears as a sort of bizarre maze of meanders and swamps, formed by the slow-flowing waters of the La Foa River.

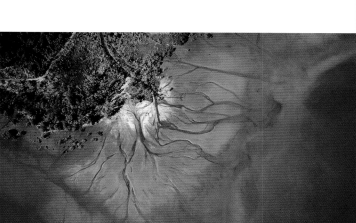

199 top right   In the Parc Territorial de la Rivière Bleue it is still possible to admire virgin forests of araucaria and kauri pines, pure lakes and a great variety of birds, including the kagu, which is the symbol of New Caledonia.

199 top left   The mingling of the nutrient-rich rivers with the salt water of the sea creates the jarring color contrasts of Canala Bay.

199 center left   Isolated from the neighboring islands and continents since time immemorial, New Caledonia's rainforest formed during the Cretaceous, and is still partly unexplored. The island's flora boasts great biodiversity with over 76% of endemic species, and habitats including evergreen and sclerophyll forests and low scrubland

199 bottom   Guichenot's giant gecko is also known as the eyelash gecko due to the hair-like projections above its eyes, which proceed along its neck and back to form a crest. This species has no eyelids and so uses its tongue to clean its eyes.

200 top Numerous little islands are dotted inside the coral reef of the Isle of Pines, where the calcareous skeletons of the coral have formed a stony barrier.

200 bottom Nekaawi is one of New Caledonia's tiny coral islands. The local reef is the second largest in the world after the Great Barrier Reef and stands out not only for its exceptionally high level of biodiversity, but also for the presence of many rare and endemic species.

200-201 One of the main attractions of the Isle of Pines is Oro Bay, an estuary famous for its sheltered position, knee-high turquoise waters and towering pines that surround the lagoon.

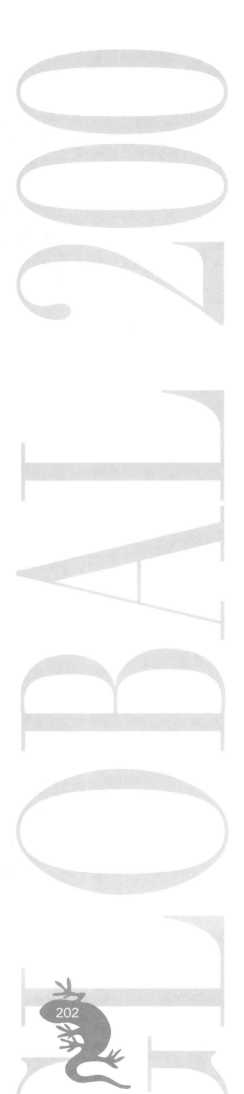

THE HAWAIIAN FORESTS

"Hawaii is not a state of mind, but a state of grace."
Paul Theroux

The Hawaiian Islands form a tropical archipelago situated between latitudes 23° N and 18° N. The group is composed of the island of Hawaii, seven other main islands, including Oahu with the capital Honolulu, and many minor islands, rocks and coral atolls. The archipelago is situated about 2500 miles (4025 km) from both the coast of the United States and Tahiti. It belongs to Oceania geographically and the United States politically.

Exploring these islands means coming face to face with breathtaking waterfalls, admiring foam-dotted slabs of slate rising out the ocean, and immersing oneself in a cloud of steam, like a natural sauna, on the peak of volcanoes. This is Hawaii, a land that was once the stuff of dreams, conjuring up images of an earthly paradise, but which is now sometimes overlooked, lost among the many exotic destinations of mass tourism. However, the Hawaiian Islands are a classic with undying charm, and the sound of their name alone brings to mind images of luxuriant vegetation and spectacular natural scenery. This reputation is well deserved, for the archipelago is blessed with the highest level of biodiversity in the entire Pacific. There are two main reasons for this: the mountainous nature of the islands, where the differences in elevation have led to the formation of various habitats, and the volcanic eruptions. Indeed, lava streams can act as impenetrable barriers for certain animal species poorly adapted for dispersion, thus isolating them and sometimes triggering new processes of diversification.

Visitors must imagine themselves inside a casket within a casket (as in a game of Chinese boxes), and then select an even smaller area within this exceptionally rich and variegated world. They will find themselves in the Hawaiin moist forests ecoregion.

It covers an area of 2600 sq. miles (6733 sq, km) and is constituted by rainforests, moist shrubland and bogs, located at altitudes between 2450 and 5600 ft (546 and 1710 m), constantly swathed in mist and sodden with the water of the tropical rains.

The inaccessibility of the loftiest peaks has allowed the survival of relatively intact habitats with a high number of endemic tree species and tiny flowers that constitute the diet of many tree snails and bird species, such as the Hawaiian honeycreeper family, of the family Drepanididae. This endemic group evolved from a single ancestor in the same way as Darwin's finches in the Galápagos Islands. Today the group is composed of 23 species, although it was far more numerous before man's arrival on the islands. The ones that survived were those that managed adapt themselves in unique ways to exploit the available food resources, such as the scarlet Hawaiian honeycreeper or i'iwi (*Vestiaria coccinea*) and the now extinct akialoa (*Hemignathus obscurus*), specialized in sucking nectar. Others, like the akiapola'au (*Hemignathus wilsoni*), which resembles a woodpecker, sifted through the seeds in the forests or pecked the bark of trees to capture larvae and insects.

The Hawaii moist forests are also the principal habitat of other birds, such as the Hawaiian hawk (*Buteo solitarius*), one of the few endemic predators of the archipelago, the Hawaiian crow (*Corvus hawaiiensis*), which now survives only in captivity, and the Hawaiian thrush or oma'o (*Myadestes obscurus*). The islands were also once home to many species of birds known as Hawaiian honeyeaters, which are now extinct.

This ecoregion witnessed the adaptive radiation – a sort of multidirectional evolutionary explosion – of many plant species, honeycreepers, Hawaiian *Drosophila*, and other invertebrates. The Hawaiian *Drosophila* belong to a genus of small fruit flies that originated from a small colonist group. Entomologists estimate that Hawaii is home to over 1000 different species of these insects. The Hawaiian *Drosophila* have even been defined as "the world's supreme example of evolutionary process."

Finally, the islands are inhabited by the Hawaiian goose (*Branta sandvicensis*), also known as the nene, which favors high, windy spots. It is has been included on the list of the Convention on International Trade in Endangered Species (CITES), for the number of birds remaining in the wild is rapidly dwindling, due to the disappearance of their habitat.

The main plant species of the forest canopy are acacia trees (known locally as koa) and *Metrosideros* (Ohia'lehua). The rainforests of the mountainous areas are dominated by *Metrosideros polymorpha*, accompanied by other tree species (e.g., *Cheirodendron, Ilex, Antidesma, Melicope, Syzygium, Myrsine, Psychotria and Tetraplasandra*), tree ferns (*Cibotium* spp.) and a variety of shrubs and epiphyte plants, such as *Clermontia, Cyanea, Gunnera, Labordia, Broussaisia, Vaccinium, Phyllostegia* and *Peperomia*, which cover the forest floor and the trunks and branches of the trees. Numerous ferns and mosses, as well as Hawaii's three native orchids, also occur in the rainforest.

Lowland and foothill moist forests have been largely destroyed by fire to make room for pastures and farmland. The isolated remnants of the ancient tropical Hawaiian forests still exist in mountainous areas on the larger islands, but are seriously endangered by feral pigs

204 Colorful flowers and fruit stand out among the luxuriant green vegetation. Pollen and seeds rely on animals for their dispersion, so the more visible they are, the greater their chance of being "chosen" by these carriers.

205 The forest canopy, formed by the tallest and largest trees, makes the vegetation appear misleadingly monotonous. However, this uppermost layer conceals the exceptionally rich and varied flora below.

and deer species originally from North America, and by the introduction of alien plant species. The negative effects of grazing by wild ungulates, invasive plant species and the growth of tourism are most acute on these fragile island habitats.

Both WWF International and WWF-USA have drawn up conservation projects for the area in the past. The area is currently comprised in WWF's Global Marine Programme, aimed at countering overfishing and promoting sustainable fishing, which will run until June 2007. This project is also working toward the creation of a network of Marine Protected Areas, covering at least 10 percent of the world's seas, including offshore areas.

Nonetheless, many problems remain. Several relatively intact tropical forest areas have not yet been declared protected and satisfactorily safeguarded. These include the Waianae Mountains of Oahu, the East Molokai Mountains, the West Maui Mountains, the East Mountains of Lanai, the Kohala Mountains, and the Hamakua-Hilo and Kona subregions. Biologists and conservationists are drawing the attention of local government to the need to establish new protected areas on the islands and to combat invasive alien species.

206 top The streams caused by the equatorial rains create spectacular waterfalls.

206 center The soil of volcanic islands is always fertile and rich in nutrients.

206 bottom River valleys form along pre-existing fractures and discontinuity lines, created by the original conditions of geological formation. The water carves out deep valleys with a characteristic "V" shape.

206-207 The Hawaii are geologically young formations and their rocky slopes are rugged, rather than smoothed by erosion. The hot and humid climate is ideal for the growth of vegetation and the landscape is always green and teeming with life.

208-209 A waterfall thunders among the lush vegetation of the underbrush. Although humidity is high, the lack of light may restrict the growth of plants. Consequently, they have large, dark leaves that are capable of absorbing every ray of sunlight.

209 top left A small, camouflaged forest lizard suddenly appears well defined and "defenseless" on a red flower. The Hawaii moist forests are home to several plant and animal species adapted to the tropical climate.

209 top right The iiwi is one of many endangered species. Its long, curved bill allows it to feed on the nectar of particular flowers, such as lobelias.

209 bottom Ferns and other plants of the undergrowth have covered every scrap of bare ground in the forests on the slopes of the Hawaiian volcanoes.

209

RAPA NUI

"In Easter Island ... the shadows of the departed
builders still possess the land.
[T]he whole air vibrates with a vast purpose and energy
which has been and is no more.
What was it? Why was it?"
Katherine Routledge

Rapa Nui, or Easter Island, is located in the Pacific Ocean, approximately 2250 miles (3620 km) west of mainland Chile and about 1300 miles (2090 km) east of Pitcairn Island in Polynesia, and has a total area of 63 sq. miles (163 sq. km). It is one of the most isolated inhabited islands in the world.

Rapa Nui is a sort of living Atlantis, which preserves the traces of a mysterious and fascinating remote past. Perhaps surprisingly, due to its administrative status as a Chilean dependency and the theories that maintained that the Incas were the first people to have set foot on the island, its discoverers and earliest inhabitants were actually Polynesians. This has been proven by genetic tests performed on the skeletons of the ancient inhabitants, which revealed characteristics exclusive to these people. The island was subsequently "discovered" by the Dutch admiral Jacob Roggeveen on Easter Sunday, 1772, who thus named it Easter Island. However, from the 19th century its inhabitants started calling it Rapa Nui ("Big Rapa"), as Tahitian sailors had noticed its resemblance to the Polynesian island of Rapa, 2400 miles (3860 km) to the west.

The nearest land to Rapa Nui is a four- or five-hour flight away, and since the construction of a landing strip, few ships sail to this remote scrap of land set like a gem in the immense ocean. However, this extreme and oppressive isolation allowed the development of a singular culture. The sculpture of the island's ancient inhabitants survives in the form of unique and perfectly preserved statues, which have become the symbol of vanished civilizations and all that we can we can admire yet whose essence escapes us. These statues have become the symbol of our relationship with the past. They are the famous *moai* figures, colossal stone busts with stylized faces. Over 1000 of these statues are scattered all over the island, rising from the earth as though in an attempt to re-establish an ancient form of territoriality, and many more remain to be discovered. On the basis of their particular location, mainly along the coast, archaeologists have surmised that they were symbolic markers of the boundary between the "home" and the "outside" and served to protect the island, like silent guards, against an external world that was perceived as simultaneously distant and looming.

Among the reed-dotted lakes, rolling hills, caves and gorges, and magnificent ranks of *moai*, lie various traces of rock art and remains of houses, structures or simply floors dating from remote times, making the island a huge natural archaeological site. Indeed, as explained by Paul Bahn and John Flenley, the authors of the famous book entitled *Easter Island, Earth Island,* "The present-day Easter Islanders live amid the ruins of their ancestors' remarkable accomplishments." This charismatic and controversial past "weighs" not only on the island's culture, but also on its geological history, fauna and flora.

Rapa Nui is situated on a so-called "hotspot," meaning that it was formed by copious flows of hot lava released from the Earth's crust. If it were not for the sea, which hides much of its structure, we would be able to see the island for what it really is: an imposing mountain almost 10,000 ft (3050 m) high. The land is dotted with hills surmounted by craters, the largest of which, on the peak of Rano Kau, is almost a mile across. The island's volcanic origins have also given rise to a great variety of rock formations. The three principal peaks, Terevaka (1673 ft/510 m) above sea level), Poike (1509 ft/460 m) and Rano Kau (984 ft/300 m) are formed of basalt, which is solidified lava. Many caves were formed by lava, which solidified on the outside to create walls as it cooled, while the incandescent molten rock continued to flow on the inside, carving out these tubular cavities. They are the reason behind the island's aridity, for they drain off most of the rainwater. Despite the fact that the island has a mild climate, with an average temperature of around 69° F (20° C), it is consequently rather dry. Rainfall is irregularly distributed throughout the year, with the rainiest periods being April and June and periods of drought during the other months, particularly September.

The island's flora and fauna are very limited. In 1956 the Swedish botanist Karl Skottsberg observed that no other oceanic island of similar size, geological conformation and climate has such a poor native flora. This is due not only to the aforesaid climatic conditions, but also to Rapa Nui's extreme isolation, compounded by the fact that it appears never to have been connected to any continental land mass. It has no mammal species, except for several introduced carnivores and rodents, such as the Polynesian rat (*Rattus exulans*), which was later ousted by the European rat. The colonists also imported many domestic animals, such as cats, dogs and rabbits (although the latter two species were eaten to extinction), sheep, pigs, horses and cattle. Introduced birds include the chimango caracara, the Chilean tinamou, a species of quail and

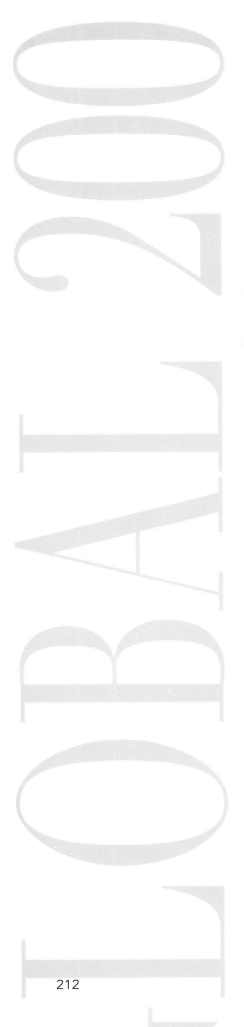

chickens, many of which became feral and developed a curious characteristic: they lay pale blue eggs. Only two terrestrial reptiles, *Lepidodactylus lugubris* and *Ablepharus boutoui poecilopleurus*, are found on the island. There are several micro-lepidoptera, most of which are cosmopolitan or widespread in the Indo-Australian islands. Only one species (*Asymphorodes trichograma*) appears to be endemic.

Rapa Nui was once a haven for migratory birds, many of which nested on the island before the arrival of man. However, today the nesting sites are the three islets of Motu Nui, Motu Iti and Motu Kau, about a mile off the coast. These are gathering points for petrels, sooty terns, gray noddies, gannets, frigatebirds and other tropical bird species. Apart from the odd sea turtle, there are few marine animals and the waters around the island are inhabited by little more than a hundred species of fish. As there is no coral reef, there are consequently also few crustaceans. Invertebrates include a limited number of spider, insect, isopod and worm species, a single type of snail, and introduced scorpions and crickets.

In 1967 the botanist Sherwin Carlquist estimated that over 70 percent of Rapa Nui's plant species had been transported to the island by birds, explaining its current sparse vegetation, due to the lower variety and presence of birds. Another factor that caused the impoverishment of the original vegetation was the arrival of Europeans, whose requirements and settlements damaged the environment. The state of the flora in general is still difficult to assess. It has been suggested that marine currents transported the seeds of several species distributed in tropical or subtropical coastal areas, which arrived on the island intact and thus created new colonies. However, seeds may also have been borne by the wind or birds.

Although paleobotanical studies of fossil pollen and volcanic soil indicate that the island hosted an extensive array of trees, shrubs and ferns, distributed in zones at different elevations – especially on the flanks of the volcanoes Rano Aroi and Rano Raraku – prior to the arrival of the first Polynesian settlers, it is now almost completely grass-covered, except for a few shrubs and introduced ornamental trees. The distribution of the plant species has varied over time, due to the climatic fluctuations that occurred during the final phases of the Pleistocene and the beginning of the Holocene. Some of the tree species that dominated these ancient forests included a now-extinct palm, related to the Chilean palm, and the toromiro. The toromiro (*Sophora toromiro*) has an intriguing history. This endemic species, belonging to the Fabaceae family and discovered by Skottsberg, can grow up to ten feet tall. Its exceptionally hard, blood-colored wood was the preferred material for the construction of ritual objects. The introduction of grazing animals spelled ecological disaster for the toromiro and the last example was found by Thor Heyerdahl in 1956, in the crater of Ranu Kau. No other botanist has since found a single plant. However, the toromiro has not died out completely. Heyerdahl gathered several seeds from the last surviving example in the wild and planted them in the Gothenburg Botanical Garden in Sweden, allowing the propagation of new plants, with precious examples also in the Val Rahmeh Botanical Garden in Menton, in France. The shrubs surviving on the island include the hau hau (*Triumfetta semitriloba*). Ferns are among the species that can be considered indigenous to Rapa Nui. However, just 4 of the 15 reported species are endemic: *Doodia paschalis, Polystichum fuentesii, Elaphoglossum skottsbergii*, and *Thelypteris espinosae*. Ornamental plant species, such as the nasturtium and lavender, have recently been introduced to the island. Cropping plants cultivated locally include avocados and French beans, while tree species comprise the blue gum eucalyptus and Monterey cypress.

The Rapa Nui National Park, a protected area that currently covers an area of over 27 sq. miles (70 sq. km), was declared a UNESCO World Heritage Site in 1995. However, islanders do not recognize the authority of the Chilean government and commonly ignore park regulations. The situation is further aggravated by the problem of alien species, which have altered the island's ecological equilibrium, in some cases irreversibly. One of the most visible effects has been deforestation, caused by grazing animals and fires. Other environmental problems include damage from archaeological excavations and tourism. Chile has recently announced plans to accelerate the protection of the habitats of Rapa Nui and in the past WWF International has promoted and backed research into the island's endangered plant species. However, much still remains to be done.

Rapa Nui can be considered a small-scale model of the Earth. The history of the island – climatic change, the arrival of peoples bringing alien species and a "civilized" lifestyle, causing the destruction of this earthly paradise – seems to echo the history and course of the whole planet. Consequently, it is vital to take action immediately and to redress the balance. In this respect, the words of Bahn and Flenley have a prophetic ring: "(. . .) It would be a truly spectacular sight if all the statues could be re-erected on their platforms. Nevertheless, Nature, despite the abuse she has suffered on the island, will eventually reclaim everything: quite apart from the possibility of a volcanic eruption, it is inevitable that not only will all the statues be worn away, dissolved back into the soil by the sun, rain and wind, but, in some millions of years, the waves and the wind will batter the island itself to nothing." (Paul Bahn and John Flenley, *Easter Island, Earth Island*).

214 top According to researchers, some moai busts once had white eyes made from coral, like those that can still be seen at Ahu Tahai, giving them an even more disquieting appearance.

214 bottom Recent research has confirmed that the statues had headdresses carved from red rock. Many busts have been restored and replaced in their original positions, gazing in the same direction.

214-215 Hundreds of Moai busts, of which many are unfinished, still lie on the slopes of Rano Raraku. This volcano is home to the quarries where the great statues were carved.

215 bottom Between 500 and 600 Moai busts are situated along the coasts of Rapa Nui. Many are arranged in series, while others are isolated, their severe gaze fixed on the horizon.

216 top Rapa Nui's first settlers probably reached the island following a journey of thousands of miles aboard small boats, encountering the unexpected sight of this windswept scrap of land pummeled by the waves in the midst of the Pacific Ocean.

216 bottom The crater of Rano Kau, like that of Rano Raraku, has a small lake at the bottom. The Rano Kau crater is situated about 330 ft (100.5 m) above sea level and is covered in rich marshland vegetation.

216-217 Rapa Nui is a volcanic island composed principally of black eruptive rock. However, in some spots this has been eroded by the sea, giving rise to typically tropical beaches, such as Ovahe Beach.

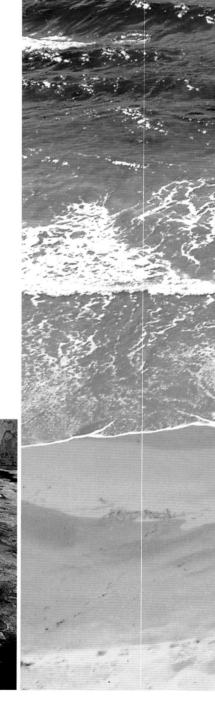

THE GALÁPAGOS ISLANDS

"The inhabitants, as I have said, state that they can distinguish
the tortoises from the different islands;
and that they differ not only in size,
but in other characters."
Charles Darwin

The Galápagos Islands form an archipelago of 13 large islands, 19 smaller ones, over 40 islets and many emergent rocks some of which are still unnamed. These volcanic islands emerge from the sea about 600 miles (965 km) west of the mainland of Ecuador, to which they belong. The main island is called Isabela and has an area of approximately 1750 sq. miles (4532 sq. km). The four next largest islands – Santa Cruz, Fernandina, Santiago and San Cristóbal – are all bigger than 200 sq. miles (518 sq. km). In total, this arid and barren archipelago, set in the middle of the Pacific Ocean, has a land area of around 3000 sq. miles (7770 sq. km). The majority of the islands are mountainous, with volcanoes – some of which still active – towering up to 5500 ft (1976 m) above sea level. Although they straddle the Equator, their climate is unusually dry for the tropics.

Ever since their chance discovery by the bishop of Panama in 1535, the Galápagos have aroused great interest, particularly for their unusually trusting wildlife, earning them the name of Islas Encantadas ("Enchanted Islands"). The archipelago comprises two ecoregions: an arid terrestrial one and a marine one. However, as is often the case, the ecosystems know no boundaries and thus overlap each other, establishing complex environmental relationships.

The climate is characterized by a hot rainy season from January to June and a cool dry one (*garua*), from June to December. As they are situated far from the mainland, the islands are strongly influenced by the ocean currents, in particular the cold Humboldt Current. Periodically, the temperature of the water rises unusually, causing intense rain. This phenomenon is known as El Niño and is most common around the end of the year.

The islands boast a variety of species that are not found anywhere else in the world, such as the equatorial albatross, the equatorial penguin, the marine iguana and the flightless cormorant. The mingling of the cool Humboldt Current with the warm equatorial ones gives rise to a phenomenon known as upwelling, i.e., the rising of nutrients, which creates and maintains a rich food chain, allowing the waters to support sea turtles, sharks, dolphins, killer whales and a wide array of fish worthy of a coral reef.

The giant tortoises, after which the islands are named, constitute another important aspect of the wildlife. They played a vital role in the theory of evolution developed by the British naturalist Charles Darwin, who visited the archipelago in 1835. Indeed, the tortoises captured the

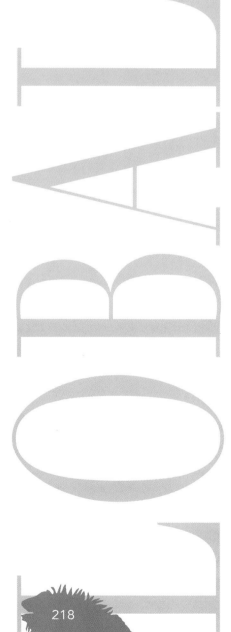

218

young Darwin's attention, for the shape of their shells varied from island to island, allowing them to be distinguished from each other. Following his return to England, as he reordered his notes and the specimens collected during his five-year round-the-world expedition, Darwin developed his theory of natural selection to explain evolution.

Seabirds predominate in the islands' birdlife, with many endemic species, such as the Galápagos penguin (*Spheniscus mendiculus*), the only equatorial penguin; the flightless cormorant (*Nannopterum harrisi*); the swallow-tailed gull (*Creagrus furcatus*), the world's only nocturnal gull, which probably developed its habits to escape from the insistent attacks of kleptoparasites (animal species that "steal" the food of others); and the lava gull (*Larus fuliginosus*), probably the rarest gull in the world. Other examples include the waved albatross (*Diomedea irrorata*), 12,000 pairs of which breed on Espanola Island; Audubon's shearwater (*Puffinus lherminieri*); storm petrels; the red-billed tropicbird (*Phaeton aethereus*); the brown pelican (*Pelecanus occidentalis*); the greater frigatebird (*Fregata minor*) and the magnificent frigatebird (*Fregata magnificens*); and three species of boobies that form colonies composed of hundreds of pairs: the blue-footed booby (*Sula nebouxii*), the red-footed booby (*Sula sula*) and the masked booby (*Sula dactylatra*). Other endemic species of the Galápagos include the lava heron (*Butorides sundevalli*), which frequents the rocky cliffs; the Galápagos hawk (*Buteo galapagoenis*); the Galápagos barn owl (*Tyto punctissima*); the Galápagos rail (*Lateralus spilonotus*); the Galápagos dove (*Zenaida galapagoensis*); the Galápagos flycatcher (*Myiarchus magnirostris*); the Galápagos martin (*Progne modesta*), four species of mockingbird (*Nesomimus* spp.); and, of course, Darwin's finches.

The 13 species of finches of the Galápagos Islands constitute one of the most famous examples of speciation (i.e., the formation of new species). When Darwin collected several specimens and presented to them to the ornithologist Gould for classification, he had no idea of their significance. More recently Darwin's species have been studied extensively by Peter and Rosemary Grant, who discovered how these birds are living proof of evolution in action, changing their appearance from generation to generation in order to adapt to environmental changes.

However, the islands are also home to mammals of great conservational importance: the Galápagos sea lion (*Zalophus californianus wollebacki*) and Galápagos fur seal (*Arctocephalus galagapoensis*) form noisy colonies along the sandy and rocky coasts. The ocean surrounding

the islands is so rich in cetacean species that the archipelago was once used as a base by many whalers.

The Galápagos Islands are not all arid desert. The slopes of the volcanic mountains are covered with tropical rainforest, with ferns, mosses, lichens and bromeliads. The islands are also home to unique dry forests of palo santo (*Bursera graveolons*) and *Sesleria* spp.), which belongs to a family of species that is very widespread, particularly in arid areas. Other common species include cacti, and in particular a typical species of recent lava fields known as the lava cactus (*Brachycereus nesioticus*), and *Jasminocereus thouarsii*, which can grow up to 23 ft tall (7 m). The coast is also home to mangrove forests, which offer refuge to many animal species.

The causes of the degradation of the ecosystems of the Galápagos Islands are connected with their popularity, which in recent years has led to the exponential growth of tourism and the consequent increase in the local population, attracted by the new economic possibilities associated with the growing flow of visitors. The increased human presence (both residents and tourists) has caused problems of pollution and the introduction of invasive species, which pose a threat to the survival of the native flora and fauna. The situation is further complicated by accidents ensuing from increased shipping in the area. The latest, and most serious, of these occurred in January 2001, when the oil tanker *Jessica* ran aground off the island of San Cristóbal.

Many organizations are actively engaged in limiting the threats and protecting the incredible biodiversity of the islands. The most important of these include WWF, Fundación Natura, the World Conservation Union (IUCN), The Nature Conservancy and the Galápagos National Park Service. Their activities are related to the management of tourism, the limiting of human encroachment on the islands with larger settlements (Santa Cruz and San Cristobál), the management of sea cucumber and lobster fishing, and the control of invasive species, particularly domestic ones, such as pigs, dogs, cats, donkeys and goats. The government of Ecuador has enacted the "Galápagos Special Law" and the future of the islands (the conservation of their biodiversity and opportunities for the local people to participate in the management of the territory) will depend on its effective application.

THE GALÁPAGOS ISLANDS

223 top The islands off the coast of Ecuador were named after the giant tortoises (*galápagos in Spanish*) that inhabit them. There are many of these reptiles, which have evolved into distinct subspecies on different islands.

224 top The Galápagos Islands often witness spectacular lava flows that empty into the sea, generating huge columns of white steam and underscoring the volcanic origins of the archipelago.

224 center The bluish cliffs of the Galápagos are inhabited by red crabs known as Sally lightfoot crabs, because they scuttle about the shore in search of food avoiding the surf.

224 bottom The sea lions of the Galápagos Islands are very trusting and are not particurarly afraid of humankind. Indeed, they often swim around tourists snorkeling off the beaches.

224-225 The Galápagos Islands are home to the world's only species of marine iguana. It feeds on algae and its claws allow it to grip the submerged rocks in order to avoid being washed away by the currents.

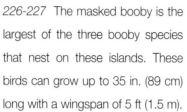

226-227 The masked booby is the largest of the three booby species that nest on these islands. These birds can grow up to 35 in. (89 cm) long with a wingspan of 5 ft (1.5 m).

226 bottom With a wingspan of up to 7.5 ft (2.9 m), the magnificent frigatebird is an expert flier, which specializes in stealing food from other seabirds. During courtship the males inflate their red throat pouches.

227 top The Galapagos brown pelican is a subspecies of the bird widespread in much of America and the Caribbean.

227 bottom left The blue-footed booby is an incredibly trusting bird. The distinctive color of its feet acts a message to the female during courtship.

227 bottom right The female waved albatross lays a single large egg. Española Island is home to 12,000 pairs of this species, constituting almost the entire world population.

228 top Marine iguanas grip the submerged rocks when feeding on algae. They can reach depths of 50 ft (15 m) and remain underwater for half an hour.

228 top center The Galápagos penguin is the only species found at the Equator, as all the others live in Antarctica or along the coasts of the southern continents.

228 bottom center The whale shark is found around the Galápagos and is the largest fish in the world. It can grow up to 60 ft (18.2 m) long and weigh up to 24 tons.

228 bottom The hammerhead shark is the most fearsome of the many sharks found in the waters around the Galápagos. However, the great richness of the marine food chain ensures that predators do not go hungry, thus reducing the risk of attacks on man.

229 Sea lions inhabit the waters around the Galápagos Islands, enlivening them with their underwater dances.

THE NORTHERN PRAIRIE
of NORTH AMERICA

"So in America when the sun goes down....
and [I] sense all the raw land
that rolls in one unbelievable huge
bulge over to the West Coast,
and all that road going,
all the people dreaming in the immensity of it,
and in Iowa I know by now the children must be crying
in the land where they let children cry,
and tonight the stars'll be out...."
Jack Kerouac

The Northern prairie is the largest grassland ecoregion in North America, covering an area of 246,500 sq. miles (639,000 sq. km). It extends over parts of southeastern Alberta and southwestern Saskatchewan, much of the area east of the Rocky Mountains, central and eastern Montana, western North and South Dakota, and northeastern Wyoming.

The first pioneers to reach these regions found themselves faced with an impressive sight: a huge, apparently endless plain, covered with flowers and inhabited by a wide variety of game species. However, following the arrival of the European colonists, who flocked to the area in ever-increasing numbers, year after year, the landscape changed rapidly as the first farms appeared. The animals started to be hunted using more advanced weapons, no longer simply for food but also for sport. The rich prairie soil was systematically cultivated or used as grazing land for cattle. Much of the forest was felled and the land plowed up. These events marked the beginning of the history of the modern countries of Canada and the United States, which was accompanied by the progressive disappearance or relegation to reservations of the witnesses of the area's earlier history: the Native Americans. Today these indigenous people continue their struggle to defend a culture that thrives on and is fueled by contact with the nature that – despite the impact of the colonists – continues to dominate the endless Great Plains.

Four major features distinguish this ecoregion from other grasslands: the harsh winter climate, with frequent snowfalls (and temperatures falling as low as 14° F (-10° C); a short growing season; periodic droughts; and the type of vegetation.

In the northeastern regions of North America the flora is composed chiefly of broad-leaved forests, which are gradually replaced by conifer forests at higher elevations. There are also many grasses, such as grama (*Bouteloua* spp.), needlegrass (*Stipa* spp.) and wheatgrass (*Agropyron* spp.). Further north into Canada the natural vegetation is characterized by spear grass (*Poa annua*) and, to a lesser extent, June grass (*Koelaria* spp.). A wide vari-

ety of herbs and shrubs also occurs, while yellow cactus and prickly pear (*Opuntia* spp.) can be found in more arid areas. Aspen (*Populus* spp.), willow (*Salix* spp.), and box elder (*Acer negundo*) grow in the valleys and on the river terraces.

Around 1850, the Northern prairie was the most extensive habitat of the North American bison. However, today these animals are reduced to small herds on Native American lands and private ranches. The population of black-footed ferret, once very widespread, has also declined sharply. Several projects are underway for the reintroduction of this species, which is necessary not only for its own conservation, but also to control the abundant prairie dogs (*Cynomys* spp.) on which it preys. Numerous efforts are also being made to "recover" the swift fox (*Vulpes velox*) population in the northern part of the ecoregion.

Although we immediately think of the prairies as an immense expanse of grass, a sort of endless and identical meadow, they are actually surprisingly rich and varied. For example, they have an unusually rich population of mammals for an ecoregion so far north. In addition to the bison and the black-footed ferret, they are also home to the coyote (*Canis latrans*), whose range is actually expanding, unlike that of other predators, and the purity of the species is threatened by its willingness to mate with other canines, such as wolves or domestic dogs, generating hybrids that constitute a threat for biodiversity. Other inhabitants include the red fox (*Vulpes vulpes*), the Northern raccoon (*Procyon lotor*), the American black bear (*Ursus americanus*), the woodchuck (*Marmota monax*), the gray squirrel (*Sciurus carolinensis*), the striped skunk (*Mephitis mephitis*), the white-tailed deer (*Odocoileus virginianus*), the star-nosed mole (*Condylura cristata*), the American beaver (*Castor canadensis*), the Canada lynx (*Lynx lynx canadensis*) and the gray wolf (*Canis lupus*). Amphibians include the gray treefrog (*Hyla versicolor*) and the American bullfrog (*Rana catesbeiana*), while reptile species comprise the common garter snake (*Thamnophis sirtalis*).

The bird species of this ecoregion include the boreal owl (*Aegolius funereus*), the blue-winged teal (*Anas discors*), the blue jay (*Cyanocitta cristata*), the American woodcock (*Scolopax minor*), the great horned owl (*Bubo virginianus*) the Oriental scops owl (*Otus sunia*), the great blue heron (*Ardea herodias*) and the golden eagle (*Aquila chrysaetos*).

232 and 233 A flash of lightning heralds the arrival of a storm. Incredibly violent tornados with tremendous destructive power may develop on the prairies of the Central United States.

The Northern prairie contains the largest breeding sites of the endangered piping plover (*Charadrius melodus*), which are situated around alkaline lakes. Other threatened birds include the burrowing owl (*Athene cunicularia*) and the ferruginous hawk (*Buteo regalis*). WWF and other environmental associations are concentrating their conservation efforts on both of these species.

Almost all (over 85 percent) of the ecoregion is now grazed by livestock or dedicated to crop cultivation. In the Canadian portion, it is estimated that only 2 pecent remains as natural, intact habitat. On the United States border hay crops and cattle grazing have almost entirely replaced the native grasslands. However, the potential for recovery of this ecoregion is exceptionally high (possibly the highest in the whole of North America). Consequently numerous restoration projects are underway, aimed at the protection and repopulation of the native species. One of these, launched in 2003 by WWF-Canada, has two goals. The first of these consists of the restoration and conservation of a large area of grassland by 2025, along with the conservation of its threatened species. The second – following the compilation of a list of the "basic characteristics" required by this type of habitat – is the reintroduction and care of endangered species, such as the North American bison and the black-footed ferret, within the framework of an ambitious transboundary project.

One day it may again be possible to contemplate a landscape very similar, if not identical, to that sighted by the first adventurers, allowing us to view North America through their eyes and experience the same sensation of freedom and the same thrill of authentic, healthy and virgin nature.

234 top The western frontier of North America's Great Plains is formed by the Rocky Mountains. The population density of this area is still low, although it experienced a boom during the second half of the 19th century with the Rocky Mountain gold rush.

234 center The spring flowers transform the huge North American prairie into a blaze of color.

234 bottom The North American bison (often referred to as the buffalo) is the best-known symbol of the Great Plains. Bison live in herds, which are often very large.

234-235 The Missouri is the longest river in the United States, flowing about 2350 miles (3782 km) from the Rocky Mountains in Montana to join the Mississippi just north of St. Louis in Missouri.

235 bottom The Crow Nation is comprised of over 10,000 Native Americans of the Apsáalooke tribe, chiefly dedicated to stockbreeding.

235

236-237 A coyote howls on the North American prairie. Coyotes have a huge repertoire of calls that they use to communicate with each other. These include howls similar to those of the wolf.

237 top The pronghorn antelope is the sole surviving species of the Antilocapridae family and the fastest animal in the world over long distances, reaching speeds of up to 60 mph (96.5 k/hr) per hour.

237 center American cattle ranchers have long waged indiscriminate war on the prairie dog, and still do, claiming that this species competes with their herds for grasses and roots.

237 bottom The black-footed ferret is one of the most characteristic
small mammals of the prairie and
the most endangered mammal of
North America. Considered extinct
on several occasions, its continued
survival is due solely to the success
of breeding and reintroduction programs.

238 top The dam-building beaver is one of the very few animals capable of creating a new ecosystem.

238 center left The raccoon is a small North American carnivore that is often found around lakes, rivers and wetlands.

238 center right A female white-tailed deer accompanied by her fawn. This species lives in large herds in woodlands and parklands. It is particularly fond of prairies and open spaces.

238 bottom Parental care is always very important in mammals, particularly in canines, such as the red fox.

239 The American black bear is the largest carnivore of the North American prairie. Cubs remain with their mother for at least a year after birth in order to learn all her "tricks."

240 top The boreal owl is a resident and territorial bird that is largely nocturnal and flies noiselessly. It lives in pairs and builds its nests in holes in trees abandoned by large woodpeckers

240 center A bison crossing Yellowstone Park. This is the last remaining area where the herds still migrate today.

240 bottom Hunting of the lynx is still permitted in the United States, even though it has drastically reduced the population of the species.

GLOBAL 200

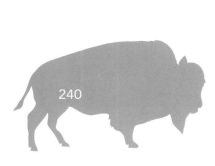

240-241 The wolf was brought to the verge of extinction in the continental United States by persecution by man, who considered it a dangerous competitor and a predator of livestock. The first conservation programs were launched only a few decades ago.

241 bottom The fox is an opportunistic hunter that adapts to the habitat in which it lives. Its diet includes birds, insects, earthworms, fruit, berries, carrion and even fish.

THE CHIHUAHUAN DESERT

"The house, the stars, the desert –
what gives them their beauty is something that is invisible!"
Antoine de Saint-Exupéry

The Chihuahuan Desert ecoregion extends across the border between the United States and Mexico. It occupies the valleys and central basin of New Mexico and Texas west of the Rio Pecos in the United States, as well as the northern half of the Mexican state of Chihuahua. It covers a total area of approximately 200,000 sq. miles (518,000 sq. km).

Chihuahua is believed to derive from the Nahuatl word *Xicuahua* meaning "a dry, sandy place." The Chihuahuan desert is a frontier land in more than one sense. It marks the imaginary biogeographic line that separates the Nearctic region (North America and Alaska) from the Neotropical region (the rest of the Americas), on either side of which the flora and fauna change as one moves north or south. However, this area also served as the "bridge" that allowed contact between the Spanish, arriving from the south, with the awesome Mesoamerican civilizations, and later the European colonists (with their settlements, roads, railways, mines and livestock), arriving from the north, with the fragmented remaining native populations.

The Chihuahuan desert is a cold desert with elevations ranging from 3500 to 5000 ft (1066 to 1524) above sea level. Although its climate is characterized by dry summers and occasional winter precipitation, this desert has more rainfall than other warm desert ecoregions (6-16 inches/15.2-40.6 cm). Indeed, the imposing canyons of the region were eroded over the course of millions of years by water, which in the past took the form of rivers and fast-flowing torrents. They include the Barranca del Cobre, the largest canyon in the world, which cuts through the Sierra Madre Occidental, the mountains of the Tarahumara Native American people, to a depth of around 4600 ft (1400 m).

The Chihuahuan desert is one of the three desert ecoregions with the greatest biodiversity in the world, along with the Great Sandy-Tanami Desert of Australia and the Namib-Karoo of southern Africa. It is home to over 250 species of butterflies, 250 species of birds, 100 species of mammals, 100 species of reptiles and 20 species of amphibians. It is thus a very special desert.

Caught between two profoundly different countries, the Chihuahuan desert has retained its highly distinctive physiognomy, also in relation to neighboring desert regions, such as the Sonoran Desert and the Sierra Madre Mountains. Indeed, this ecoregion has remained completely isolated for the past 10,000 years, allowing the development of many endemic species, particularly plants. These are mainly cacti and succulents, which are so peculiar as to have become famous throughout the world. The Chihuahuan desert is home to around 3500 plant species, about a third of which are endemic. The dominant plant species is the creosote bush (*Larrea tridentata*), accompanied by viscid acacia (*Acacia neovernicosa*) and tarbush (*Florensia cernua*) in the northern part of the desert, and yucca and opuntia, in the southern areas. The southernmost area is inhabited by Mexican fire-barrel cactus (*Ferocactus pringlei*) and Arizona rainbow cactus (*Echinocereus polyacanthus*).

Cacti constitute one of the plant families with the greatest level of endemism: *Coryphanta* and *Opuntia* are among the five genera that have the most species of the world's entire flora.

Due to the region's recent geological origin, few warm-blooded vertebrates have had time to form new species. However, the Chihuahuan desert supports many mammals that have disappeared elsewhere and require large open areas, such as the pronghorn antelope (*Antilocapra americana*), with only a couple of dozen individuals recorded in the state of Chihuahua; the gray fox (*Unocyon cineroargentinus*); the American black bear (*Ursus americanus*); the jaguar (*Panthera onca*); the collared peccary (*Pecari tajacu*); the kangaroo rat (*Dipodomys* spp.); the Mexican prairie dog (*Cynomys mexicanus*); and the common prairie dog (*Cynomys ludovicianus*). It is also home to the mule deer (*Odocoileus hemionus*), the black-tailed jackrabbit (*Lepus californicus*), the kit fox (*Vulpes macrotis*) and the coyote (*Canis latrans*). Birds include the great horned owl (*Bubo virginianus*); the elf owl (*Micrathene whitneyi*), which is the smallest owl in the world, with a wingspan of just four inches; and the Gila woodpecker (*Melanerpes uropygialis*). There are also many lizards, geckoes and snakes, including the notorious western diamondback rattlesnake (*Crotalus atrox*); tortoises, such as the desert tortoise (*Gopherus agassizii*); and amphibians, like the Chiricahua leopard frog (*Rana chiricahuensis*). The region is also home to various species of butterflies, scorpions and pollinating insects that are not found anywhere else in the world.

Over the past couple of centuries vast portions of the Chihuahuan desert have been irreversibly altered by human activities. Pressure from agriculture and urbanization has transformed much of the habitat into secondary vegetation. The soils preferred by farmers are those occupied by desert plants capable of retaining water, such as the tree yucca (*Yucca filifera*). Heavy grazing, fires and depletion of water sources are all altering the native vegetation in favor of invasive species. Large vertebrates have practically disappeared. The Mexican wolf (*Canis lupus baileyi*), once widespread in the area, has been literally wiped off the landscape. The Rio Grande, which runs through the innermost areas of the ecoregion, is increasingly polluted. Finally, illegal trade in animal and plant species has brought many unique cacti to the verge of extinction.

The Chihuahuan desert suffers from the lack of legal protection. There are several nature reserves, but they are not large enough to protect the many species threatened with extinction Consequently, the principal efforts of conservationists are currently concentrated on petitioning the local authorities to establish new protected areas.

In 1993 WWF-Mexico launched an innovative conservation project that made this ecoregion a model for the experimentation of a new approach to biodiversity conservation. Its main goals are the protection of several priority areas and the sustainable utilization of resources and wetlands. For example, while goat grazing can be detrimental to vegetation, soil properties, and the diversity of vertebrates, relatively minor adjustments in management procedures can reduce this harmful impact, as well as enhance productivity for goat ranchers. Consequently, a manual for sustainable goat grazing has been developed in collaboration with the leading authorities. This WWF-Mexico project has also developed water management guidelines and is currently identifying key wetlands on which to concentrate its efforts.

244-245 The Chihuahuan Desert landscape is formed by ancient river valleys, deep canyons and rocky ridges affording breathtaking views over vast and desolate expanses.

245 top The Barranca del Cobre (Copper Canyon) of the Chihuahuan Desert covers an area of 25,100 sq. miles (65,000 sq. km) and is the largest and deepest in the world.

245 center The saguaro is part of the flora of the Mexican deserts.

245 bottom Prairie dogs are rodents that live in large colonies.

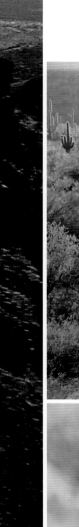

THE CHIHUAHUAN DESERT

246 left The jaguar (*Pantera onca*) is a predator capable of killing large animals such as deer and peccaries. It lives in jungles, but also in open habitats or wetlands.

246 right The mule deer (*Odocoileus hemionus*) is easily distinguished by its long mule-like ears and its short, black-tipped white tail. It is able to adapt to arid and semi-desert habitats.

247 The range of the American black bear (*Ursus americanus*) extends from the forests of North American to Mexico, where it can be found in many different habitats, preferring cool, forested areas.

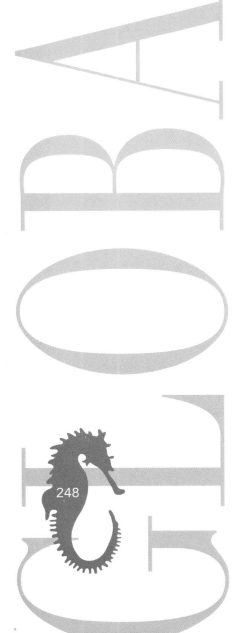

THE GREATER ANTILLES: CUBA

"Write to me, for you know that the loneliness of Havana
is as great as that of the icy wastes."
José Lezama Lima, letter to a friend

Situated in the Caribbean Sea, in Central America, Cuba is formed by the island of Cuba itself, Isla de la Juventad ("Isle of Youth") and around 1600 small islands, covering a total area of 42,804 sq. miles (110,861 sq. km). The main island, whose capital is Havana, is divided into 14 provinces: Pinar del Rio, La Habana, Ciudad de la Habana, Matanzas, Cienfuegos, Villa Clara, Sancti Spíritus, Camagüey, Las Tunas, Holguín, Granma, Santiago de Cuba, Guantánamo and Ciego de Ávila. It is separated from Haiti (48 miles/77 km to the east) by the Windward Passage and is situated 130 miles northeast of Mexico. Jamaica lies about 95 miles (152 km) south of Santiago de Cuba, while the United States is approximately 90 miles (144 km) north of Havana, across the Straits of Florida.

Cuba is a fascinating and contradictory land. This is immediately apparent upon arrival, when the visitor is assailed by a pungent smell of gasoline and sulfur, mingling with the sweeter undertones of tropical vegetation. The landscape; the colonial-style architecture and the Fifties cars that give it the flavor of a suspended and nostalgic world; the plethora of posters celebrating the revolution, the past and a freedom that now have a legendary feel; the run-down palaces and luxury hotels; the dazzling Caribbean sun and the dim electric lighting all confirm the contrasting sensations evoked by this land. These aspects are combined with an exceptionally gentle, imaginative intelligent people who possess a boundless vitality, a unique musical heritage and a history of struggles, exploitation, hunger and the desire to escape from the ever-present shadow of colonial domination.

Blessed with excellent ports (Havana, Gibara and Santiago de Cuba), which once made it an important base for the Spanish treasure fleets, today Cuba is a popular tourist destination, due to both its fascinating history and its natural beauties. The country boasts 3570 miles (5745 km) of coast, 289 natural beaches, one of the largest coral reefs in the world, thousands of breathtakingly beautiful islands and islets, and magnificent underwater scenery.

Cuba's natural history is also a story of dependence and separation of varying intensity. Indeed, the island is home to the greatest number of endemic plants in the Caribbean, suggesting that it was once connected to the American mainland by a strip of land or a chain of islands that allowed the spread of the pioneer species that generated its current flora. This theory seems to be confirmed by the fact that the Cuban flora is far more similar to that of Central America, than to that of the rest of the Antilles.

Cuba is home to 8000 botanical species, which are scattered over the entire country. Around 6700 of these are vascular plants (made up of 500 pteridophytes – ferns and related plants – and 6200 anthophytes – flowering plants) and about 3100 are endemic. There are 74 endemic genera of flowers.

The island's vegetation is mainly of the secondary type (woods, scrub and meadows, but chiefly grasslands and sugarcane plantations), although there are also broad-leaved and conifer woods and swamps.

Cuba boasts 300 different species of palms. The most famous of these is the royal palm (*Roystonea regia*), which is a national emblem (it is featured in the Cuban coat of arms and even in the logo of a locally produced beer). It has a slender, smooth gray trunk and fronds 10 to 15 ft (3 to 4.5 m) long. Then there is the coconut palm (*Cocos nucifera*), which can reach a height of 100 feet with leaves up to 20 feet long. The fruits are initially green, turning to yellow and then brown when mature. These palms line the island's beautiful white, sandy beaches, tempting tourists with their refreshing coconuts, which the local people pluck directly from the trees, pierce and offer as a drink with a straw. Other species include the Cuban belly palm (*Colpothrinax wrightii*), with its distinctive bottle-shaped trunk, and the cork palm (*Microcycas calocoma*), which is actually a member of the Zamiaceae family, but closely resembles a palm. Mangroves (belonging to the Rhizophoraceae family), account for 26 pecent of the island's forests and their densely tangled roots protect the coastal soil from erosion and offer shelter to countless small fish and birds.

Cuba also has pine forests and, at higher altitudes, rainforests of ebony and mahogany, now interspersed with an allochthonous eucalyptus species.

The city of Santiago de Cuba has botanical gardens of ferns and cacti, while Pinar del Rio boasts orchid gardens. The national flower is the butterfly ginger (*Hedychium coronarium*), locally known as *mariposa* for its butterfly-like white flowers, with large petals, which are popularly used for weddings.

Cuba's fauna also has a high rate of endemism, for the same geological reasons as its flora. The island is home to 350 different species of birds, including the incredible bee hummingbird (*Mellisuga helenae*), known locally as the zunzuncito, which is the smallest bird in the world, just 2.5 inches (6.35 cm) in length, making easily mistaken for an insect.

The Cuban trogon (*Priotelus temnurus*), whose local name is tocororo, is the national bird, as its red, white and blue plumage of echoes the colors of the Cuban flag. The ivory-billed woodpecker (*Campephilus principalis*), believed extinct following the last sighting at Baracoa during the late 1980s, is now thought to survive in Cuba.

There are few native mammals and the largest remaining one is the Cuban solenodon or almiqui (*Solenodon cubanus*), an insectivore about 18 inches long.

Invertebrates include the glasswing (Greta oto), known locally as the *mariposa de cristal*, which is one of just two transparent-winged butterflies in the whole world. The polymita snail (*Polymita* spp.) has a

249

251 The island of Cayo Paredón Grande is joined to Cayo Largo by a road running along the top of a dam. The Diego Velázquez lighthouse, named after the Spanish conquistador, stands on the eastern tip. The view from the top is simply unforgettable: dazzling white beaches, deep blue sky and crystal-clear waters extend as far as the eye can see.

brightly colored shell and can now be found only in the nature reserves, or in the form of necklaces on market stalls in the Baracoa area. In addition to iguanas, chameleons, crocodiles and lizards, reptile species include the Cuban boa (*Epicrates angulifer*) a nocturnal snake that does not attack man.

Cuba's marine life is also exceptionally rich and includes the West Indian manatee (*Trichechus manatus*), the whale shark (*Rhincodon typus*), and four species of turtle: the loggerhead sea turtle (*Caretta caretta*), the leatherback sea turtle (Dermochelys coriacea), the green sea turtle (*Chelonia mydas*) and the hawksbill sea turtle (*Eretmochelys imbricata*). The green moray (*Gymnothorax funebris*), is the largest moray of the region and can reach a length of over 6.5 ft (1.9 m).

Cuba is a country on the verge of great change, not only political and economic. In recent years the government has acknowledged the great importance of tourism and has endorsed all projects aimed at promoting and boosting it. One of the results was the establishment of a National System of Protected Areas, constituted by 263 protected natural areas, covering around 22 percent of Cuban territory, 77 of which are considered of national significance: 7 Natural Reserves, 14 National Parks, 25 Ecological Reserves, 6 Outstanding Natural Elements, 9 Managed Floral Reserves, 8 Faunal Reserves and 8 Protected Areas. Cuba's four mountain ranges, the Sierra Maestra, Nipe-Sagua-Baracoa, Guamuhaya and Guaniguanico are Special Regions of Sustainable Development. This type of protected area also includes the Cienaga de Zapata wetlands and the Canarreos and Sabana-Camagüey archipelagos. Marine parks include Punta Francés off Isla de la Juventud, Cayo Piedras del Norte, Cayo Mono and the Península de Hicacos at Varadero, and several areas of the Península de Guanahacabibes.

The relatively recent creation of these kinds of areas means that they are managed differently than their counterparts in the United States or Europe. Many nature trails and visitor centers are still under construction and a growing number of courses are held for tourist guides in the parks and hotels. In the light of the considerable success achieved by environmental conservation policies (schemes for the development of wind energy generation, forest management and reforestation, and the reduction of atmospheric and inland water pollution), WWF has declared Cuba the only country that meets both of its criteria for sustainable development, with a good level of human development and an acceptable ecological footprint.

252 top Cayo Largo, with its 16 miles of white sand gleaming in the bright sun, is a true earthly para-dise.

252 center The Cayo Largo reef separates the open sea from the inner lagoons, creating tidal chan-nels that color the waters many marvelous shades of blue.

252 bottom The rich marine fauna of Cayo Coco offers diving enthusi-asts a memorable experience of rare beauty.

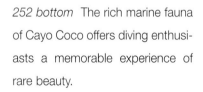

252-253 Cayo Coco is considered the jewel of Cuba, due to its beautiful sea and tropical landscapes. The island is also an important bird-watching spot and home to Cuba's largest colony of flamingoes.

253 bottom Playa Juraguá, in the province of Santiago de Cuba, not only boasts clear waters and scenic cliffs, but also offers unrivaled views of the Sierra Maestra mountains.

254 top and 254-255 The crystal-clear waters of Cayo Largo conceal a coral reef teeming with life and color, inhabited by silent corals and sea fans.

254 top center The bull shark has a massive body, a rounded head and very small eyes. It is the only shark species able to live in both saltwater and freshwater habitats, and is found in tropical seas, lakes and rivers.

254 bottom center Manatees or lamantines are rare and mysterious marine mammals that gracefully swim in these seas. Along with the dugongs, they gave rise to the legend of the mermaid, for sailors sighting them peeping out of the water mistook them for fascinating creatures half woman and half fish. The West Indian manatee grazes on sea grasses on the seafloor, grasping them between its muscular lips.

254 bottom The common eagle ray can be found at depths of up to 200 ft (61 km), where it searches for fish, crustaceans and mollusks on the seafloor.

256-257 The Hanabanilla River runs through the luxuriant tropical forest of Sancti Spiritus, creating a series of waterfalls, some of which are higher than 1000 feet.

257 top The Cuban crocodile (*Crocodylus rhombifer*) lives exclusively in a couple of swamps on the Caribbean island after which it is named

257 center right The Hanabanilla River, which forms spectacular waterfalls, rises in the Sierra de Escambray.

257 center left The hypnotic charm of a chameleon enchants visitors who venture among Cuba's luxuriant vegetation.

257 bottom The common Cuban slider can often be seen sunning itself in groups in streams and rivers in the morning. This particular behavior is known as basking.

THE LLANOS SAVANNAS of COLOMBIA and VENEZUELA

"I can read a dark sob in the stone, echoes suffocated in towers and buildings, I use the sense of touch to study a land full of rivers, scenery and colors and yet I cannot manage to reproduce it."

Eugenio Montejo

Llanos is the Spanish term used to refer to the vast plain with typical savanna vegetation situated in northern South America. This system of grasslands, occupying a huge region of Colombia and Venezuela, extends northwest of the Orinoco River basin and is bounded by the Amazon River basin to the south. The overall area, including the huge Apure-Villavicencio dry forests (26,400 sq. miles/68,375 sq. km), exceeds 175,000 sq miles (453,150 sq. km). About 60 percent of the Llanos belongs to Venezuela and accounts for over 30 percent of its entire area.

This region is the land of the Llanero cowboys and is dotted with ranches (known locally as *hatos*). It is inhabited by a wide variety of animal and plant species and boasts one of the most developed and characteristic continental freshwater systems in the world. Here rivers flow slowly through grassy plains, are interrupted by sudden falls, plummet over sheer rock faces, and finally break among luxuriant forests, creating clouds of shimmering water. The plain alternates periods in which it is dotted with shiny, marshy pools, and others in which it is dry and green. Fire and water are two sides of the same coin and the main and contrasting elements of the same region. During the wet season (summer and autumn) heavy rainfall causes floods and the rivers burst their banks, while the long drought and strong sun of the dry season give rise to many natural fires.

This ecoregion is one of the best examples of tropical savanna in South America. The Llanos is located in a large depression in the Earth's crust between the Andes and the Guiana Plateau. It is incredibly flat, with a very low gradient (0.02 percent). Toward the east the highest land stands just 260 ft (79 m) above sea level, while the central region, drained by the Orinoco River basin, is occupied by flooded savannas. The geological substrate of the Llanos is thus principally formed by recent alluvial deposits (no more than two million years old), which are highly permeable and constituted by sediment from the erosion of the Andes. From a geological point of view, these ecosystems are fairly "young."

The Llanos can be divided up into four distinct environmental zones: flooded alluvial plains, eolic plains, highplains, and foothill savannas.

The flooded alluvial plains can be divided into *banco, bajio*, and *estero* savannas, each of which exhibits different characteristics in terms of vegetation, soil and elevation. The *bancos* form along the banks of rivers, about 6.5 ft (1.9 m) above the surrounding areas. The soil is poor and badly drained, dominated by gallery forests of palm species such as *Copernicia tectorum, Pithecellobium saman, Genipa americana* and *Cordia collococa*. Occasionally they may also be home to exceptionally tall trees, such as *Terminalia amazonica* and *Ceiba pentandra*, which can reach a height of 165 ft (50 m). The *bajios* form at lower elevations, situated further from the rivers, in an area reached by only the finest clay sediments. Consequently, these soils are badly drained and flood during the rainy season. The poorer soils support sparse trees. These areas are characterized by the presence of palm forests (dominated by *Mauritia flexuosa*), known locally as *morichales*, and are the zones most widely used for human activities. The *esteros* constitute the lower part of the savannas and are covered with very fine sediment that forms almost waterproof beds, where water stagnates in pools until the end of the dry season. In these areas there are almost no trees, except for a few isolated palms, and the vegetation in dominated by floating aquatic species, with freely hanging roots, such as the common water hyacinth (*Eichhornia crassipes*) and the anchored water hyacinth (*E. azurea*), both of which are very widespread. Other common floating species are *Salvinia, Pistia stratiotes*, and *Ludwigia*, while terrestrial plants include *Thalia geniculata, Ipomoea crassicaulis, Ipomoea fistulosa, Eleocharis* and *Cyperus*.

The eolic plains extend to the south of the aforesaid areas and consist of large systems of fossilized dunes modeled by the wind, which formed during recent ice ages. They are extremely arid and covered with vegetation consisting of coarse grass species (e.g., *Paspalum* and *Trachypogon*), while trees grow only on the banks of the few rivers.

The highplains are characterized by the presence of low hills that break up the otherwise flat profile of the Llanos. The vegetation is constituted mainly by coarse grasses, while the wetter areas support scrubland dominated by *Caraipa llanorum*. As these regions are periodically flooded, they do not allow the growth of shrubs (which would be completely submerged). The ground is thus covered with annual herbaceous species.

The foothills are situated at the base of the Andes. Here the soil is deep and fertile, allowing it to support the richest forests of the Llanos. Agriculture and cattle-raising are thus chiefly concentrated in this area. The most typical tree species are the same as those of the *bancos*.

The Llanos has a high degree of biodiversity. The flora includes over 3500 species, with a low

number of endemic species (approximately 40). Many typical plant species have developed forms of adaptation to defend themselves from fire. For example, the bark of *Curatella americana, Byrsonima crassifolia, Bowdichia virgilioides* and *Palicourea rigidifolia* is very thick (up to 1.5 inches/3.8 cm) and suberized, similar to that of the cork oak. The fauna of this ecoregion includes important endemic species such as the Llanos long-nosed armadillo (*Dasypus sabanicola*), the Orinoco crocodile (*Crocodylus intermedius*), the Orinoco sword-nosed bat (*Lonchorhina orinocensis*) and O'Connell's spiny rat (*Proechimys oconnelli*). The most remarkable of these is undoubtedly the Orinoco crocodile, which can reach a length of up to 20 ft (6 m), making it one of the largest crocodile species. Its limited distribution has led to its classification as "critically endangered" by the World Conservation Union (IUCN). Another important species is the green anaconda (*Eunectes murinus*), the largest snake in the world, which is found in the rivers and the permanently flooded *baijos*. However, the commonest and most typical animal species is undoubtedly the capybara, represented in the ecoregion by the Llanos subspecies (*Hydrochaeris hydrochaeris hydrochaeris*). It is the largest rodent in the world and can weigh in excess of 175 lbs (80 kg). It is very common in the flooded plains and the canals and rivers of the Llanos, where it spends most of its time cooling off in the water or mud, making it one of the easiest preys of the anaconda.

The Llanos is also home to numerous indigenous populations. The 2000 census revealed the presence of at least 16,000 indigenous people, belonging to several ethnic groups. The largest of these are the Kariña, the Pumé (or Yaruro), the Sikuani and the Warao. Even today only a few individuals speak Spanish, and the groups continue to live a traditional subsistence lifestyle, supporting themselves by hunting, fishing and the intermittent cultivation of crops, including yucca. The total human population of the Llanos is around one million, with an average density of 5.26 inhabitants per sq. mile (2 per sq. km).

Despite the low population density, human encroachment remains one of the main threats to this ecoregion, especially with regard to fires, most of which are caused by humans. Indeed, burning is used to create short-lived fresh pastures, or used during hunting by the indigenous peoples. Other threats are constituted by large-scale cattle raising, fishing along the rivers, and the introduction of alien domestic species, such as rats, cats and dogs. However, most of the ecoregion has survived in its natural state and at least 80 percent of the total area can be considered "wild." The main changes to the environment and habitats caused by human activities, such as the building of dams and infrastructures and deforestation, have not yet had widespread effects on the Llanos. As the Venezuelan novelist and journalist Adriano González León wrote, "El encanto del Orinoco o del mar Caribe sobre Margarita no me hace olvidar los problemas" [the magic of the Orinoco or the Caribbean Sea on Margarita Island has not made me forget the problems]. On the basis of this motto and in order to guarantee a future for these lands, WWF has developed a project aimed at the conservation of the Llanos and the entire Orinoco River basin. The hope is that this "wilderness" will be able to remain intact, benefiting nature, the local populations and all the world's inhabitants.

262-263 Unlike the undergrowth, the forested areas of Venezuela and Colombia are able to survive for long periods submerged.

263 center When the water retreats during the short dry season, the soil is covered with a thin layer of nutrient-rich silt.

263 top The waters of this tributary of the Orinoco River are brown and cloudy due to their high content of organic matter, which will provide precious nutrients for numerous ecosystems before reaching the sea.

263 bottom A giant otter in the Pantanal region, eating a freshly caught fish. These highly social animals live in groups of 3-9 individuals in the tropical regions of South America.

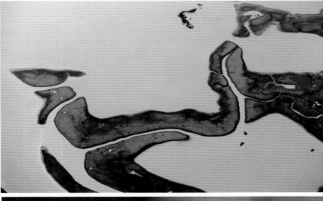

GLOBAL 200

263

264 top A caiman basks in the warm South American sun. The butterflies seem to sense that the reptile has no interest in such small prey.

264 bottom The jaguar is the largest predator of the rainforests of Central and South America. It generally captures its prey by ambushing it, and the victim's surprise is surpassed only by its terror.

264-265 The capybara is a typical rodent of the Llanos savannas of Venezuela. It moves agilely and confidently around the flooded plains and other creatures, such as the bird perched on its head, use it to spot their prey from above.

265 bottom The anaconda is the largest snake in the world. It moves agilely and silently among the submerged plants of the flooded plains and ambushes its prey, which rarely escapes.

266 A roseate spoonbill is about to land in a pool. This species uses its specially adapted bill to sieve the small creatures that it eats from the water.

267 top Herons and ibis choose the same trees for nesting, coloring them white and red.

267 bottom right A scarlet ibis perching in a tree. This individual has a metal ring around its leg, allowing researchers to identify it.

267 bottom left A flock of white-faced whistling ducks and black-bellied whistling ducks takes off from a lake in the Llanos.

THE AMAZON RIVER
AND FLOODED FOREST

"It was like a virgin whose flesh
had never known the call of passion.
Like a virgin, it was lovely,
Mysterious as the body of a woman
that has not yet been possessed,
it too was now ardently desired."
Jorge Amado

The Amazonian rainforest covers an area of around 2.3 million sq. miles/5.9 million sq. km (more than the entire United States) and occupies vast areas of several South American countries, especially Brazil, with which it is often associated. However, it also extends into Venezuela, Colombia, Ecuador, Peru, Bolivia, Suriname and French Guiana.

A dense network of waterways crisscrosses this huge green blanket. The relative humidity of 90 percent and an average annual rainfall of around 120 inches (305 cm) ensure that the area is permanently sodden, to the extent that the forest can be likened to a sponge. This is the land of the Amerindians, a land, to use the words of the poet Marcia Theophilo, of "famished" and "dazzled trees," but also a land of water and fire, a land where the rivers are "gold," the forest green and all around is a jumble of colors, songs, calls and cries of birds. Life here is not easy: until recently the Amazon region was considered a paradise by naturalists from all over the world, but a hell by those who had to cross it. Although it remains one of the areas of lowest human population density on Earth, today it is dotted with rapidly expanding cities and areas that attract farmers, stockbreeders, miners, gold and precious-stone seekers, woodcutters and oil workers.

However, despite the dizzy progress of colonization and deforestation, the entire Amazon Basin is still home to an enormous number of animal and plant species, making it one of the world's most precious treasure troves of biodiversity. Considering aquatic life alone, the Amazon River is inhabited by the largest number of freshwater fish in the world, estimated at over 3000 species, along with mammals, such as the pink river dolphin and the giant otter.

It is also the habitat of over 60,000 species of plants, 1000 species of birds and over 300 species of mammals. However, the list of records continues. At almost 4000 miles (6440 km), the Amazon is the second longest river in the world after the Nile. However, in terms of volume, it is the largest river on Earth, carrying 20 percent of the world's fresh water. It transports this enormous mass of water from the highest peaks of the Andes to the Atlantic Ocean, where it forms a huge estuary with countless branches, separated by huge islands with changing coastlines. The largest of these is the island of Marajó that covers an area of 18,500 sq. miles/47,900 sq. km (one and a half times the size of Belgium).

Each year, during the rainy season, the level of the river rises over 30 ft (9.1), flooding and submerging the forest and the neighboring habitats. The nutrient-laden waters enrich the land on which the forest grows, the lake basins that dry out during the dry season, and the grasslands. Freshwater fish swim among the underwater forests, often feeding on the fruit that falls from the trees. The flood areas represent a world of extreme biodiversity, where the boundaries between terrestrial and freshwater ecoregions are very transient. The environment is constantly "rewritten," testifying not only to the regenerative power of nature, but also to its intrinsic indifference to all attempts at classification.

During the period in which the river floods and submerges the surrounding areas, the Piramutaba catfish – one of the many large catfish of the Amazon – migrates a distance of about 2050 miles (3300 km) from its nursery grounds in the Guianan-Amazon mangroves to its spawning grounds in the upper Amazon. Each year fish, reptiles and other aquatic animals migrate across these submerged habitats to feed and breed, returning to the main riverbeds when the floodwaters subside.

The animals, including many species of monkeys, depend on the food resources offered by the habitats shaded by the forest canopy. The reproduction of many trees is dependent on the dispersion of seeds by frugivorous animals, including numerous species of fish. Typical fish species of the Amazon ecoregion include the guppy, piranha, tambaqui, arawana, pirarucu (10 ft (3 m) long and 220 lbs (100 kg) in weight), Lepidosiren paradoxa and tucunaré. Mammals include the pink river dolphin, gray river dolphin (or tucuxi), manatee and monkeys, such as the rare uakari. The region is also home to the largest South American river turtle (*Podocnemis espansa*) and the black caiman (*Melanosuchus niger*).

In September 2002 the Brazilian government launched the Amazon Region Protected Areas (ARPA) program in conjunction with WWF. Specific partnerships were set up for the forests, including one with the World Bank, with the objective of tripling the protected areas within a decade. The program aims to expand the 80 envisaged parks and WWF has already directly contributed to the protection of over 13,000 sq. miles (33,700 sq. km) of territory. One of the most encouraging successes was the establishment of the Tumucumaque Mountains National Park, which is the world's largest tropical forest park.

The numerous projects implemented in the area include the Manu project in the Peruvian nation-

269

al park of the same name, established in the 1970s to protect a wide variety of species, and the Jupará project, named after a nocturnal species of marten that spreads the seeds of the forest trees and cacao plants, thus unwittingly contributing to the conservation of its habitat. This project is aimed at halting the clearing of the last green areas and providing incentives for the organic cultivation of pepper, cloves, guarana and cocoa beans. The Projeto Castanha (Brazil Nut Project), which WWF supports in the northwestern Brazilian state of Acre, is aimed at helping Brazil nut producers – through training and equipment – better organize themselves, get their product certified and find new markets. Most importantly, the project endeavors to increase the income of local communities living off the harvest of this commercially valuable crop. The Paragominas project, on the other hand, aims to demonstrate that sustainable forestry is not only possible, but also more economically viable. The increasingly widespread Forest Stewardship Council (FSC) label certifies the provenance of timber from well-managed forests.

All WWF projects in the Amazon region are aimed at environmental and social sustainability, through constant collaboration with the local populations. The native fishermen, for example, are valuable allies in the battle to protect the flood forests of the lower course of the Amazon. Together, WWF experts and fishermen choose the areas to protect, replanting trees along the riverbanks and establishing catch quotas for the more sought-after fish.

271 Extending from Brazil to Venezuela, Colombia, Ecuador, Peru, Bolivia, Guyana, Suriname and French Guiana, the Amazonian rainforest is the world's largest tropical forest and the ecosystem with the greatest biodiversity.

272-273 The Amazon River rises in the Peruvian Andes and – after having covered a distance of about 4000 miles and been swollen by many tributaries – empties into the Atlantic Ocean.

273 top The San Rafael Falls are Ecuador's highest and most imposing waterfall, where the Quijos River drops 500 feet to join the Napo River, before merging with the Amazon.

273 center The white-faced capuchin, with a head somewhat like a
white-cowled Capuchin monk), lives
in central and northern South America. Its diet consists mainly of fruit,
berries, nuts and small insects.

273 bottom Known for the slowness
of its movements, the sloth is a very
sedentary animal, which often never
leaves the tree in which it was born.
The brown-throated three-toed sloth
may live in very different habitats.

GLOBAL 200
THE AMAZON RIVER

274 top left A capybara scans the horizon. This species inhabits the tropical and temperate wetlands of South America and is a favorite prey of the predators of the Amazon Basin.

274 top right The common caiman is widespread throughout South America, and particularly the Pantanal, due to its adaptability and its omnivorous food habits.

274 center The giant anteater feeds on ants and termites, which it locates using its excellent sense of smell and captures with its long tongue.

274 bottom The giant otter is the largest of the 13 extant species of otters and one of the main predators of the tropical freshwater habitats of South America. It is now an endangered species.

274-275 The jaguar's name is derived from a Guaraní word. This large feline lives near rivers, swamps and forests, where the thick vegetation allows it to ambush its prey without being seen.

276-277 A flock of red-and-green macaws penetrates the vegetation of the forest. This parrot has a red body and tail, blue and green wings, white cheeks and lores with red stripes, and dark legs and feet.

277 top left Colored clouds of Amazonian butterflies swirl around the areas where water gathers, alighting in the spots where minerals accumulate.

277 center left The toco toucan, whose long, bright orange beak has the purpose of frightening predators and impressing females, lives in small groups, seeking fruit and small prey in the forest.

277 bottom left The white-lined leaf frog is a nocturnal treefrog. Some species of tree frog produce a waxy secretion that reduces moisture loss by evaporation, thus preventing dehydration.

277 top right The hummingbird is known for its ability to remain almost still while hovering in the air to feed on nectar by inserting its long beak into flowers.

277

THE PATAGONIAN STEPPES

"The end of the world is the beginning of everything"
Writing on a house in Ushuaia, Tierra del Fuego

Patagonia covers an area of over 300,000 sq. miles (777,000 sq. km) between latitudes 37° S and 55° S in Argentina and Chile. The cities of Carmen de Patagones and Viedma are the gateways to the region.

The highway connecting Buenos Aires to Bahia Blanca cuts through the pampas for over 370 miles (595 km). Continuing south, beyond Puerto Madryn and toward Ushuaia, the southernmost city in the world, the landscape becomes a sterile and desolate desert. The road runs straight, with only the windswept grasslands either side. These are places that arouse sensations of oblivion and stupor; places that touch your heart.

In the final chapter of *A Naturalist's Voyage Round the World*, Charles Darwin asked himself why these plains, "pronounced by all wretched and useless" and always described in negative terms, "without habitations, without water, without trees, without mountains…. Why, then, and the case is not peculiar to myself, have these arid wastes taken so firm a hold on my memory?" He concluded that "it must be partly owing to the free scope given to the imagination." Or perhaps it can be explained by the *immense tristesse* of these boundless spaces described by Blaise Cendrars, which gives the landscape a fascinating melancholy aura.

This is the Patagonia that we have discovered and learned to love in the travel journals of Bruce Chatwin, Darwin himself, and Francisco Coloane. It is a land of xerophytic steppe with sparse and very low-growing shrubs (able to withstand the strong wind, which would uproot anything taller), thorny bushes and broken grass cover. However, there is another, more varied and unpredictable Patagonia, featuring not only steppe, but also snow, ice, lakes and even forests. Few places on Earth offer such a wide range of scenery in such a small space: the steppe highlands extend to the east of the Andes, while the mountains themselves and the Pacific coast are home to forests, lakes and glaciers. Tierra del Fuego – named after the fires lit by the natives that appeared against the night sky to the explorers who reached the region by sea – has peaks of over 6000 ft (1830), while the eastern side of the Andes is home to plains resembling those of the Atlantic seaboard.

Livelier scenarios can be witnessed along the coast, such as the Punta Tomba penguin rookery, which is the largest breeding colony of penguins in South America, second only to those of the Antarctic. Here male and female Magellanic penguins (*Spheniscus magellanicus*) divide their time between hatching eggs and fishing, with the typical dynamism of large colonies of this species. Beyond Punta Tombo lies the steppe, formed by scattered tufts of grass, with no trees at all and a regular succession of service stations and *estancias* – farms constituted by two or three houses that look like villages on the maps – located every 125 miles (200 km) or so.

The entire Rio Santa Cruz area is a desert crossed by the opalescent turquoise river, which winds its way through the landscape, giving it a lunar touch. The basalt plateaus continue as far as the town of El Calafate, where the desert becomes shrubland and isolated boulders, popularly called "devil-stones" (it is not known who or what brought them here), before merging into a wood and then a series of forests formed by different species of beech and larch, and a dense undergrowth of lianas, epiphytes, mosses and bamboo (*Chusquea* spp.). Finally, the vegetation gives way to a white sea – the Perito Moreno Glacier, declared a UNESCO World Heritage Site in 1981. The mystery of the turquoise river is revealed here: the abrasive action of the glacier on the rocks causes the formation of microscopic mineral particles, which float on the surface of the water, giving it its characteristic color. The boulders along the road are also the work of the glaciers that once occupied the area, which left behind their burden of rocks and stones when they melted.

The coastal strip of the far southern end of the Chilean side of the region is home to the Nothofagus forest and the Magellanic forest, with deciduous species and heaths (*Pernettya mucronata* and *P. pumilia*). The age-old division of the Chilean and Argentinean sides by the Andes, and the difference in climate, explains why only 4 or 5 of the 150 species of cactus present in Argentina are also found in Chile.

Here nature bears the signs of time – not the time that we are used to, but geological time, which changes the forms of the Earth, creating or erasing lakes and continents, eroding rocks and carving valleys. Huge plains extending for hundreds of miles often terminate high above the sea, revealing the phases of their history on the bare rock face. The lands of this ecoregion are incredibly dynamic, for they have sunk below the sea and re-emerged many times and bear the traces of each movement, which are still visible in the form of layers of seashells and marine or alluvial deposits. Such movements caused the isolation of animal populations, a phenomenon that allowed the naturalist Charles Darwin to corroborate his theory of evolution. The Rio Deseado Valley, for example, is the gigantic fossil of a tropical forest: 60 sq. (155 sq. km) miles of desert dotted with petrified *proaraucaria* tress (the ancestor of today's *araucaria*) 115 ft (35 ft) tall, whose enormous fronds offered shade to dinosaurs and other prehistoric creatures during the Jurassic. The trees were subsequently covered by volcanic eruptions, until erosion brought them back to light. They are now columns of stone and since 1954 have been part of a protected area and natural park (Monumento Natural Bosques Petrificados).

The fauna of this ecoregion includes endemic and unique species, such as the Andean condor (*Vultur gryphus*), one of the so-called "New World vultures" and the largest raptor, with a wingspan of over 10 ft (3 m), a weight of 25-35 lbs (11-16 kg), and particularly well-developed eyesight that allows it to spy the

280 Rocks remain as the Perito Moreno Glacier was once much larger than it is today. The parts that have now melted left behind their burden of rocks and ice.

281 Los Glaciares National Park is a protected area of over 1700 sq. miles (4400 sq. km) on the Chilean border.

carrion on which it preys; the giant armadillo (*Priodontes maximus*), which has a shorter head than other armadillos and is able to survive in harsh, arid habitats; the Patagonian hog-nosed skunk or Humboldt's hog-nosed skunk (*Conepatus humboldtii*), whose smell can be perceived at a distance of 2.5 miles (4 km); the lesser rhea or Darwin's rhea (*Pterocnemia pennata*), known locally as the petiso or choique, which resembles an ostrich. The male, which is taller than the female, hatches the eggs and cares for the young. The bird can run at speeds of 30 miles per hour, making it very difficult to catch. The guanaco (*Lama guanicoe*) is a member of the camel family, whose range extends from southern Bolivia to Patagonia. It has a very long neck; wary, circumspect behavior; and can reach surprisingly high speeds, despite its elegant gait. The maned wolf (*Chrysocyon brachyurus*), on the other hand, resembles a fox with long legs, which allows it to move among the tall grass.

Other species include the pampas deer (*Ozotoceros bezoarticus*), the bush dog (*Speothos venaticus*), the pampas fox (*Pseudalopex gymnocercus*), the marsh deer (*Blastocerus dichotomus*), the jaguar (*Panthera onca*), the capybara (*Hydrochoerus hydrochaeris*), the puma or mountain lion (*Puma concolor*), the Patagonian kelp goose (*Chloephaga hybrida hybrida*), and the crested caracara (*Caracara cheriway*), to name but a few.

There are also many "invader" animals, originally from Europe, which were introduced at the time of the Spanish Conquest, including European hare and deer, goats, mink, horses and oxen, which have damaged the ecosystem. The area is home to many foreign plants, such as the Aleppo pine and the dandelion, which is now very common in the grasslands. However, the worst threat to this ecoregion is represented by humans, who have brought some species to the verge of extinction through indiscriminate hunting and the destruction of the natural habitat. The guanaco, for example, was a very common sight on the plains and plateaus until 1880. However, its numbers started to fall dramatically with the colonization of the area, which was accompanied by large-scale agriculture, intensive grazing and hunting, and has continued until the present day, when all these factors have become serious problems. Today guanacos can be spotted only in the remotest areas and the pre-Andean regions.

Over the past 30 years Argentina has lost around 60,000 sq. miles (155,400 sq. km) of forest, equivalent to two thirds of its entire forested area. One of the most important projects is thus the Programa Refugios de Vida Silvestre (Wildlife Refuges Programme), which aims to preserve biodiversity by creating a series of Natural Reserves established by means of economic agreements between private individuals, who own 80 percent of land in Argentina, and FVSA (Fundacion Vida Silvestre Argentina). The agreements promote production activities based on the sustainable use of natural resources. In the future these production schemes could become a model for the sustainable development of the country. Since 1987 FVSA has created 16 natural refuges covering a total area of over 450 sq. miles (1165 sq. km).

282 top In the western area, at the foot of the Andes, the Argentinean pampas gives way to a softer steppe landscape, dominated by an umbelliferous plant that tinges the landscape bright yellow.

282 center The guanaco is a protected species in Chile and Peru, but not in Argentina, which exports thousands of pelts each year.

282 bottom The Andes, dotted with glacial lakes and glaciers, rise majestically in the Tierra del Fuego National Park.

282-283 The Patagonian steppe is a windy and arid ecoregion covered with sparse herbaceous vegetation and extending to the Andes.

283 bottom The petrified forest is situated in the northeastern part of Santa Cruz province and has been protected since 1954.

284-285 Punta Tombo is home to a large colony of Magellanic penguins composed of over 1.5 million birds. In winter the penguins disperse into the ocean and along the coasts of Brazil.

285 top The Patagonian coast is home to colonies of elephant seals, fur seals and sea lions. These marine mammals feed on fish, each consuming from 65 to 135 lbs (30 to 60 kg) per day.

285 bottom The South American fur seal breeds between mid-October and December. Many females remain in the colonies all year round, but little is known of the seasonal movements of the males and young animals.

286-287 The Perito Moreno Glacier in Patagonia appears as a sea of turquoise ice. These ice-blinks give the landscape of the Los Glaciares National Park an enchanted lunar air.

GLOBAL 200

THE PATAGONIAN STEPPES

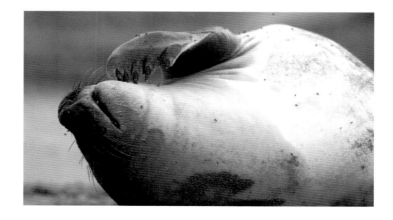

THE ANTARCTIC PENINSULA and WEDDELL SEA

"God manifests himself in the
majestic beauty of nature."
Galileo Galilei

This ecoregion encompasses a large area of sea and coast extending from Cape Adams to the Antarctic Strait. Lying almost entirely inside the Antarctic Circle, it is constituted by the northernmost peninsula of Antarctica, which reaches toward the southern tip of South America, about 600 miles (965 km) away.

Two continents reach toward each other until almost touching. The sea, dotted with icebergs, shimmers in the cold sunlight. Then, suddenly clutches of penguins scatter like flies over the huge icy expanses. A place of ice and light, and blue horizons veined with silver, the Antarctic Peninsula and Weddell Sea ecoregion is a fascinating and magical corner of the Earth, which is also remote and unforgiving. In winter temperatures can fall to -130° F (-90° C) in the interior, while the winds that sweep these barren landscapes can exceed 125 miles (200 km) per hour. This is one of the areas of greatest biodiversity and biological productivity of the Antarctic region, due to the swift marine currents typical of these latitudes and the consequent phenomenon of upwelling, which we will discuss later.

The mountainous snow-covered peninsula is long and narrow, with a ridge reaching points of over 13,000 ft (3965 m) that is a geological continuation of the Andes. Its coasts are highly indented and overlook the Weddell Sea to the east and the Bellinghausen Sea (mostly covered with pack ice) to the west, at the meeting point of the Atlantic and Pacific Oceans. It was discovered in 1820 by an American whaler, Captain Nathaniel Palmer, and was visited in 1832 by another navigator, the Englishman John Biscoe, who called it Graham Land. Consequently, the United States called the region Palmer Peninsula and the British Graham Land, claiming it as a dependency of their Falkland Islands overseas territory. In 1964 it was agreed to rename the region the Antarctic Peninsula, calling its southern section Palmer Land and its northern one Graham Land.

Antarctica and South America are separated by the Drake Passage, which is the stormiest and most fearsome stretch of sea in the world, between Tierra del Fuego and the South Shetland Islands and connecting the Pacific and Atlantic Oceans. The passage is named after the famous navigator Francis Drake (b. 1540, England – d. 1596, off Puerto Bello, Panama), who was renowned as the greatest seaman of his age, receiving first a knighthood and then the rank of admiral from Elizabeth I. However, he never sailed through the passage himself, preferring the "calmer" inner route offered by the Strait of Magellan. The first recorded voyage through the passage was made in 1616 by the Dutch navigator Willem Schouten, who named the southernmost tip of South America after his hometown, the Dutch city of Hoorn. The name later lost one of its two vowels, becoming Cape Horn.

The Weddell Sea is named after the British sailor James Weddell who first explored it in 1823. It supports a rich marine ecosystem, in which huge quantities of krill constitute the fundamental link in a food chain comprising numerous populations of fish, birds and marine mammals.

Euphasia superba (the scientific name of Antarctic krill) belongs to the Euphausiidae family of small marine crustaceans that feed on plankton and live in huge schools composed of millions of individuals, which often saturate many thousands of cubic feet of water. The krill are able to swim, but their main means of propulsion are the marine currents, which they use to descend and ascend to different depths according to their stage of growth. Adults are pink and can grow up to three inches long. They reach sexual maturity at about two years old, which is also their average lifespan. Antarctic krill are very similar to little shrimps and are mainly herbivorous, feeding on microscopic algae or other organisms present in the plankton.

Covered with ice for much of the year, the sea is very cold. The water reaches its greatest density at a temperature of around 39° F (3.8° C), where it is much denser than that at greater depths. This physical characteristic, combined with the action of the surface currents, causes the mingling of huge volumes of nutrient-rich waters that rise from the bottom by means of upwelling. This movement allows the vertical transportation of "energy," in the form of nutrients, from great depths to the surface in a column of water.

The "bloodless" fish of the Channichthyidae family represents one of the natural wonders of these habitats. These species can survive in near-freezing conditions because their blood lacks red cells, and consequently hemoglobin (the molecule that carries oxygen around the bodies of all other vertebrates), making it very thin. Oxygen is highly soluble in water at low temperatures and tends to be more easily absorbed by the branchial blood. These fish also have many capillaries close to their scale-free skin, which help to absorb oxygen and carry it in to their vital organs. The members of the Channichthyidae family feed on krill and other crustaceans and small fish.

The Notothenioids are another group of extremely specialized fish. Their blood not only contains hemoglobin, but also a special substance that lowers the freezing temperature of water – a sort of antifreeze developed by these incredible vertebrates.

Penguins are perhaps the best known and the most characteristic and exclusive animal species of this ecoregion. This generic name is used to refer to a group of flightless seabirds belonging to the Spheniscdiformes order, which inhabits the southern hemisphere. They live in the icy expanses of Antarctica and the subantarctic islands, although several species are native to the coasts of Australia, South Africa, South America and the Galápagos Islands. Most penguins have a white chest and a black or bluish head and back. Many species have red, orange or yellow patches on their head and neck. Their short legs are set relatively far back in rela-

tion to the axis of their body, giving them their typical upright stance. As most of Antarctica's food sources are to be found in the sea, penguins are highly skilled at both fishing and swimming. They use their outstretched flippers like little oars under water. Unlike most birds, penguins do not have different kinds of feathers with different functions (flight, protection, etc.), but are evenly covered with a thick coat of very similar little feathers, whose main function is insulation. However, heat loss is also limited by anatomical features, such as the reduction of body surface in respect to volume. Indeed, penguins have rather stumpy bodies with short limbs (small feet, flippers and head), and a thick layer of subcutaneous fat that acts as insulation.

There are 18 species of penguins, 5 of which are common in the Weddell Sea and the Antarctic Peninsula. The larger ones are the emperor penguin (*Aptenodytes forsteri*), which can reach a height of around 4 ft (1.2 m) , and the king penguin (*Aptenodytes patagonicus*), around 3 ft (0.9 m) tall. The remaining three species are smaller and belong to the same order: the Adelie penguin (*Pygoscelis adeliae*), the gentoo penguin (*Pygoscelis papua*) and the chinstrap penguin (*Pygoscelis antarctica*), none of which exceeds 2.5 ft (0.75 m).

On land, penguins walk, jump or toboggan on their bellies, propelling themselves with their flippers and feet. In the water they are very fast and agile swimmers, whose sole means of propulsion is their flippers, as they use their feet as a rudder. They feed on fish, cuttlefish, crustaceans and other small marine invertebrates. During the breeding season they live in colonies on land, composed of hundreds of thousands of individuals. Although these birds have suffered greatly at the hand of man, who massacred large numbers for their fat and – more recently – their skins, the remoteness of the regions in which they live has helped them to survive.

The emperor penguin breeds in one of the most inhospitable areas of the world, during one of the coldest periods of the year, laying and incubating its eggs at temperatures as low as -80° F (-62° C). Adélie penguins incubate their eggs in the open, on nests made of stones or twigs. The king penguin and the emperor penguin, however, do not build nests, but rest their single egg on their feet, huddling over it so that the skin of their abdomens covers it and keeps it warm.

Both parents usually take care of the eggs and the young. Male Adélie penguins fast throughout nesting, courtship, egg laying and the first two weeks of incubation, while the females build up their fat reserves by feeding in the sea. When the females return to land to take their turn at incubating the eggs, the males go to sea to feed and restore their fat reserves, before returning to the colonies with food for their chicks, which have hatched in the meantime. Both parents share the responsibility of feeding the young. Not all species fast for such long periods as the Adélie penguin during the breeding season. In fact most species nest close to the coasts, in order to be able to visit the sea each day to feed.

An important Antarctic carnivorous predator is named after this sea: the Weddell seal (*Leptonychotes weddellii*). It is a relatively meek animal, which usually gathers in large groups on the pack ice and spends its time in the water hunting fish, cuttlefish and crustaceans. It can dive to great depths (several hundred feet) and remain under water for many minutes in the complete darkness, seeking its prey with the help of its special whiskers (vibrissae). It can even swallow large mouthfuls of food without chewing while under water. The Weddell seal surfaces periodically to breathe or rest using holes that it gnaws in the ice. In fact the main cause of death in elderly individuals is loss of teeth, with the consequent inability to make holes in the pack ice. The males and females make many underwater sounds and it appears that certain types of calls have a territorial function. Weddell seals were once actively hunted by man for their skins, meat and blubber. Fortunately, today hunting has decreased dramatically and their numbers are relatively stable

The ecological conditions of the entire ecoregion remain fairly satisfactory and overfishing represents the only serious local problem. The other problems are global, such as climate change and the continuing depletion of the ozone layer over Antarctica, which constitute two of the most worrying long-term threats. In 2005 WWF launched a conservation program for the Antarctic and Southern Ocean that will continue until 2012. The aim is the protection, restoration and sustainable management of biodiversity in these areas, while attempting to limit the impact of man derived from fishing and climate change.

294 Emperor penguin chicks are almost naked when newly hatched, but soon grow a coat of gray downy feathers, with the exception of the head which takes a black coloring.

295 In May the female emperor penguin lays a single egg, which is incubated by both parents. After hatching, the chick remains with its parents until December, when it leaves the nesting area to forage alone.

296-297 Antarctic prions are monogamous birds that form colonies in the subantarctic regions. Like other members of the Procellariidae family, they have tubular nasal passages on their bill.

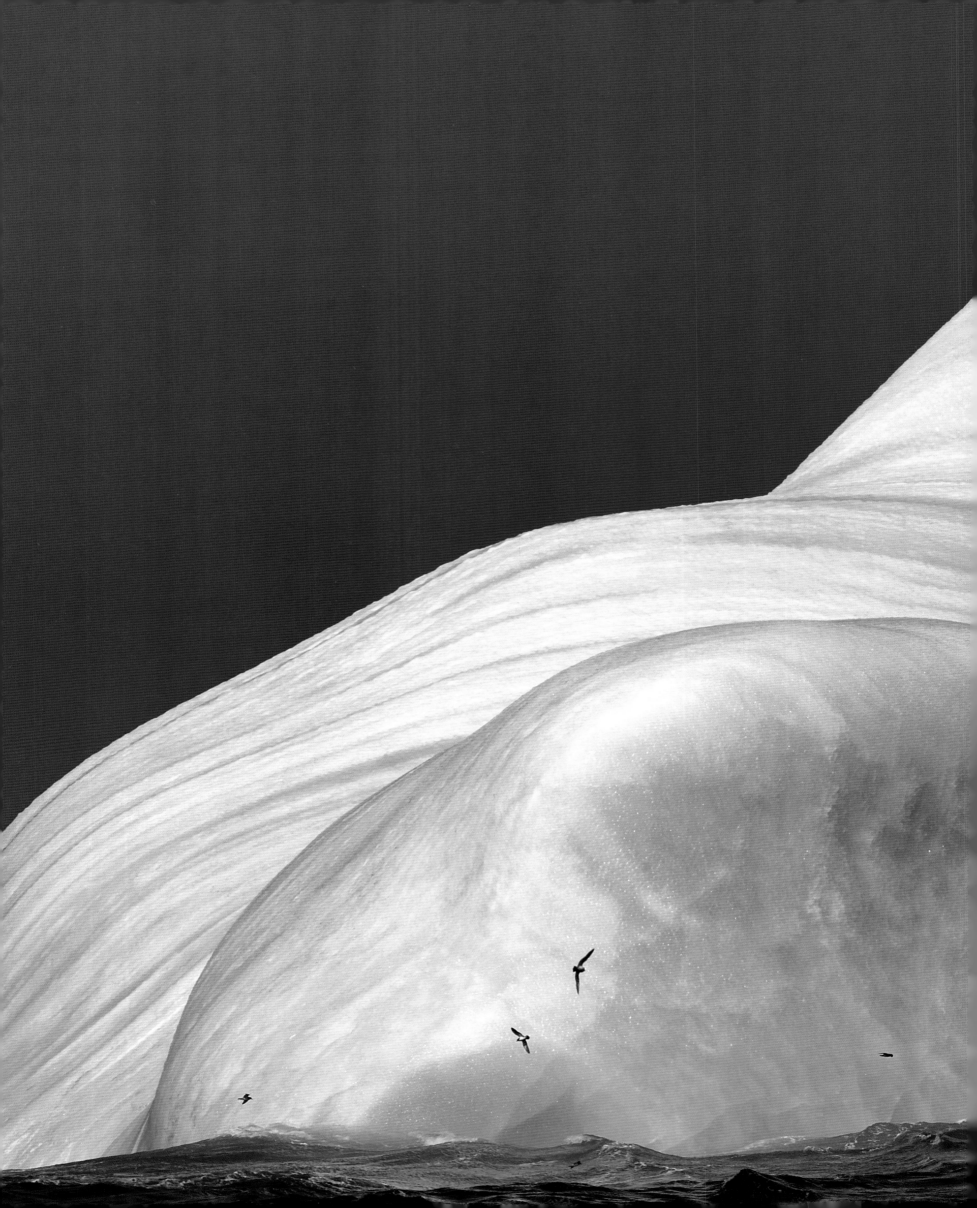

301

page 120 center: Eugen/Zefa/ Corbis
page 120 bottom: A. Ricciardi/Panda Photo
page 121: Getty Images
page 122 top: Marcello Bertinetti/Archivio White Star
page 122 center: Pete Oxford/Nature Picture Library/Contrasto
page 122 bottom: Marcello Bertinetti/Archivio White Star
pages 122-123: Franco Figari
page 124 top: Reinhard Dirscherl/Agefotostock/Marka
page 124 bottom: Reinhard Dirscherl/SeaPics.com
pages 124-125: Kurt Amsler
page 125: Getty Images
pages 126-127: Reinhard Dirscherl/SeaPics.com
page 126: Claudio Cangini
page 127 top: Reinhard Dirscherl/SeaPics.com
page 127 bottom: Kurt Amsler
page 131: DLILLC/Corbis
page 132 top: A.Shah/Panda Photo
page 132 center: Roger Tidman/Corbis
page 132 bottom: Bernard Castelein/ Nature Picture Library/Contrasto
pages 132-133: Wolfgang Kaehler/ Corbis
page 134 top: Getty Images
page 134 bottom: DLILLC/Corbis
page 135 left: Theo Allofs/Corbis
page 135 right: Joe McDonald/Corbis
page 138 top: Elio Della Ferrera/Nature Picture Library/Contrasto
page 138 center: Getty Images
page 138 bottom: David A. Northcott/ Corbis
pages 138-139: Franz-Marc Frei/Corbis
page 140 top: Getty Images
page 140 center: Theo Allofs/Corbis
page 140 bottom: Terry Whittaker/ Frank Lane Picture Agency/Corbis
pages 140-141: Getty Images
page 143: Getty Images
page 146: Robert Holmes/Corbis
pages 146-147: Getty Images
page 147 top: Getty Images
page 147 center: Wayne Lawler/ Ecoscene/Corbis
page 147 bottom: HachettePhotos/ Contrasto
page 148 top: Anup Shah/Nature Picture Library/Contrasto
page 148 bottom: Getty Images
pages 148-149: Getty Images
pages 150-151: Getty Images
page 151 top: Getty Images
page 151 bottom: Getty Images
page 154: Courtesy of the WWF-Canon/Hartmut Jungius
page 155: Herbert Kehrer/Zefa/Corbis
page 156 top: Desireé Astrom
page 156 center: Igor Shpilenok
page 156 bottom: Bernard Castelein/ Nature Picture Library/Contrasto
pages 156-157: Bruno Morandi/ Agefotostock/Marka
page 157: Gertrud & Helmut Denzau/ Nature Picture Library/Contrasto
page 161: Igor Shpilenok
page 162: Desireé Astrom
pages 162-163: Igor Shpilenok
page 163: Igor Shpilenok
page 164 top: Getty Images
page 164 bottom: Robert Pickett/ Corbis
page 165: Staffan Widstrand/Nature Picture Library/Contrasto

page 165 bottom left: Marcello Libra
page 165 bottom right: Getty Images
page 166 top: Yann Arthus-Bertrand/Corbis
page 166 bottom: Igor Shpilenok
pages 166-167: Igor Shpilenok
page 170: Getty Images
page 171: Getty Images
page 172: Lötscher Chlaus/ Agefotostock/Marka
page 172 bottom: Wolfgang Kaehler/ Corbis
pages 172-173: Jacques Langevin/Sygma/Corbis
pages 174-175: Hinrich Baesemann/Dpa/Picture-Alliance
page 175 top: Sue Flood/Nature Picture Library/Contrasto
page 175 bottom: Robert L. Pitman/ SeaPics.com
page 176 top: R. Savi/Panda Photo
page 176 center: Ron Sanford/ Corbis
page 176 bottom: Getty Images
pages 176-177: Getty Images
page 182 top right: Theo Allofs/Corbis
page 182 center left: Catherine Karnow/Corbis
page 182 center right: Gavriel Jecan/Corbis
page 182 bottom: Theo Allofs/Corbis
pages 182-183: Mark Laricchia/Corbis
page 183 left: Martin Harvey/ Corbis
page 183 right: Mitch Reardon/ Lonely Planet Images
pages 184-185: Paul A. Souders/Corbis
page 189: Roberto Rinaldi
page 190 top: Holger Leue/Lonely Planet Images
page 190 center: Getty Images
page 190 bottom left: Getty Images
page 190 bottom right: Jean-Paul Ferrero/Ardea
page 191: D. Parer & E. Parer-Cook/ Ardea
pages 192-193: Roberto Rinaldi
page 193 top right: Doug Perrine/Nature Picture Library/Contrasto
page 193 top left: Vincenzo Paolillo
page 193 center: J. Watt/Panda Photo
page 193 bottom: Jurgen Freund/Nature Picture Library/Contrasto
page 194 top: Tobias Bernhard/Zefa/Corbis
page 194 bottom: Tobias Bernhard/Zefa/Corbis
pages 194-195: J. Watt/Panda Photo
page 195: Getty Images
pages 198-199: Yann Arthus-Bertrand/Corbis
page 199 top right: Holger Leue/Lonely Planet Images
page 199 top left: Yann Arthus-Bertrand/Corbis
page 199 center: Yann Arthus-Bertrand/Corbis
page 199 bottom: David A. Northcott/ Corbis
page 200 top: Remi Benali/Corbis
page 200 bottom: Remi Benali/Corbis
pages 200-201: Jean Du Boisberranger/Hemis.fr
page 204: Antonio Attini/Archivio White Star
page 205: Antonio Attini/Archivio White Star
page 206 top: Antonio Attini/Archivio White Star

page 206 center: Antonio Attini/Archivio White Star
page 206 bottom: Antonio Attini/ Archivio White Star
pages 206-207: Antonio Attini/Archivio White Star
pages 208-209: George H. H. Huey/Corbis
page 209 top left: Getty Images
page 209 top right: Getty Images
page 209 bottom: David Muench/ Corbis
page 214 top: Atlantide Phototravel/ Corbis
page 214 bottom: Getty Images
pages 214-215: Getty Images
page 215: O. Alamany & E. Vicens/ Corbis
page 216 left: Paul Kennedy/Lonely Planet Images
page 216 right: James L. Amos/Corbis
pages 216-217: James L. Amos/Corbis
page 221: Yann Arthus- Bertrand/Corbis
pages 222-223: Yann Arthus- Bertrand/ Corbis
page 223 top: M.Jones/Panda Photo
page 223 bottom: Yann Arthus-Bertrand/Corbis
page 224 top: Pete Oxford/Nature Picture Library/Contrasto
page 224 center: Getty Images
page 224 bottom: Kevin Schafer/Corbis
pages 224-225: Getty Images
pages 226-227: Art Wolfe
page 226: Getty Images
page 227 top: Arthus Morris/Corbis
page 227 bottom left: Nick Garbutt/ Nhpa/Photoshot
page 227 bottom right: M. Jones/ Panda Photo
page 228 top right: Howard Hall/ SeaPics.com
page 228 top left: Pete Oxford/Nature Picture Library/Contrasto
page 228 center: Stuart Westmorland/Corbis
page 228 bottom: Doug Perrine/ Nature Picture Library/Contrasto
page 229: Getty Images
page 232: Jim Wark
page 233: Ron Stroud/Masterfile/Sie
page 234 top: Jim Wark
page 234 center: Ron Stroud/ Masterfile/Sie
page 234 bottom: Tom Bean/Corbis
page 234-235: Jim Wark
page 235: Jim Wark
pages 236-237: Eric Dragesco
page 237 top: Rod Planck/ Nhpa/Photoshot
page 237 center: Jeremy Woodhouse/Masterfile/Sie
page 237 bottom: Jeff Vanuga/Nature Picture Library/Contrasto
page 238 top: Getty Images
page 238 center right: R. Oggioni/Panda Photo
page 238 center left: Rolf Nussbaumer/Nature Picture Library/Contrasto
page 238 bottom: Getty Images
page 239: Getty Images
page 240 top: Alamy Images
page 240 center: Getty Images
page 240 bottom: Joe McDonald/ Corbis
pages 240-241: B&C Alexander/ Nhpa/Photoshot
page 241: Getty Images
pages 244-245: Jim Wark
page 245 top: Heeb/Laif/Contrasto

303

© 2007 White Star S.p.A.
Via Candido Sassone, 22/24
13100 Vercelli, Italy
www.whitestar.it

TRANSLATION: SARAH PONTING

ISBN 978-88-544-0301-7

REPRINTS:
1 2 3 4 5 6   11 10 09 08 07

Printed in China

This book is printed on FSC-certified paper
(Forest Stewardship Council).